How We Work

COUNTERPOINTS

Studies in the Postmodern Theory of Education

Joe L. Kincheloe and Shirley R. Steinberg
General Editors

Vol. 90

PETER LANG
New York • Washington, D.C./Baltimore • Boston • Bern
Frankfurt am Main • Berlin • Brussels • Vienna • Canterbury

How We Work

Edited by
Marla Morris
Mary Aswell Doll
William F. Pinar

PETER LANG
New York • Washington, D.C./Baltimore • Boston • Bern
Frankfurt am Main • Berlin • Brussels • Vienna • Canterbury

Library of Congress Cataloging-in-Publication Data

How we work / edited by Marla Morris,
Mary Aswell Doll, and William F. Pinar.
p. cm. — (Counterpoints; vol. 90)
Includes bibliographical references.
1. Authorship. 2. Creation (Literary, artistic, etc.). I. Morris, Marla.
II. Doll, Mary Aswell. III. Pinar, William. IV. Series:
Counterpoints (New York, N.Y.); vol. 90.
PN137.H69 808'.02—dc21 98-38982
ISBN 0-8204-4102-3
ISSN 1058-1634

Die Deutsche Bibliothek-CIP-Einheitsaufnahme

How we work / ed. by Maria Morris...
–New York; Washington, D.C./Baltimore; Boston; Bern;
Frankfurt am Main; Berlin; Brussels; Vienna; Canterbury: Lang.
(Counterpoints; Vol. 90)
ISBN 0-8204-4102-3

Cover art by Marla Morris
Cover design by James F. Brisson

Table of Contents

Preface

Marla Morris

Mary called the state troopers. She thought I crashed and was in a ditch on the I-10 coming home from Louisiana State University. The troopers refused to look for me. I hadn't been missing long enough. Why, you might ask, was I missing? Because I had a writing crisis. Picture this: a new graduate student in a doctoral program flipped out over writing a paper. Toby Daspit and I were taking Petra Munro's curriculum theory course that semester. Petra said, "Write a paper around one idea." Toby and I flipped out. We spent three hours after class talking in the parking lot about how to write around one idea. Of course, the state troopers didn't know that I was still in the parking lot talking to Toby. I knew I was running late so I kept stopping at gas stations along the I-10 trying to call Mary but the line was busy. Each time I stopped, time kept moving. The clock kept ticking; it was getting later and later and later. It was a nightmare. By the time I got home it was near midnight. By this time Mary had called Petra.

You see, my writing crisis began a major turning point in my life. My undergraduate degree in philosophy and my master's degree in religious studies shaped the way I understood academic writing. I was trained as an exegete. This is what I call doing a line-by-line. The only kinds of papers I wrote were around a person, say, Dewey, and I'd write an explanation, a line-by-line of what Dewey said. Mirroring the text was my job. But that's really all I knew. I felt somehow that I had said nothing at the end of the day, but I thought that's what academics did: they said nothing. They simply repeated the old masters and that was that. My training in exegesis led me to believe that writing was about saying nothing, until I arrived at LSU.

It was at LSU that I began to learn that writing is more than repeating the great ones, the wise masters. Writing means saying something. It was at LSU that I began to ask all of my professors, Bill Pinar, Wendy Kohli, and Petra Munro, how they wrote an academic paper. I owe my new writing life to these wonderful people who have helped me through many difficult moments while working on my Ph.D. in curriculum theory.

The paper I finally wrote for Petra Munro's class was on ludic postmodernism and it was published in JCT (*Journal of Curriculum Theorizing*). I finally said something. I was finally able to develop an idea for twenty pages and really live in my writing.

Writing is living. And writing can be generative if writers understand that they do have something to say. I haven't abandoned my line-by-line exegetical skills, but I have added to them my voice and my own interpretations. I still have times when I feel I cannot possibly write about X. But now I know that these writing traumas pass; and afterwards, new understandings and generative interpretations and ultimately a new me arrive on the scene.

This book is about writing. It is about what people inside and outside academics go through while writing. A most interesting subject to new graduate students, professors, poets, and fiction writers.

Mary just walked into the house and would like to talk to you about her contribution to this book. (If you are ever on the I-10 having a crisis, she will tell you not to bother calling the state troopers.) Here is my beloved Mary.

Foreword

Mary Aswell Doll

When Marla first asked me how it was that I went about my writing, I did not have an answer for her right away. I was unaware of her panic about writing around a single idea, for one reason. For another, I did not know how I worked, never having thought about it. As days passed I found myself tracking my process, since at the time I was working on the last chapter of a book. Did I write from an outline? (No). Did I have things pretty much worked out before I began? (Sort of). Did I have trouble once I got going? (Yes). What gave me trouble? What got me beyond the sticking points? The tracking of these questions began a discussion that has lasted until this book. And as the reader will see from the essays, there are as many variations of producing work as there are instruments in an orchestra. To us, the symphony of responses is extremely entertaining, occasionally cacophonous, always fascinating, ever complex.

It was my idea to include in a primarily curriculum-centered book the additions of writers in other fields. Some of those whom we asked to share their writing processes rejected our invitation outright. Many rejections were gracious, like the ones from Toni Morrison, Seamus Heaney, and David Herbert Donald, among others. Many responded that time commitments interfered. They wished us well and wrote in their own hand. Others responded to our invitation but had what I feel are telling comments about how personal writing reveals the person. One felt he had already written enough or more on the topic. One wrote that it recoiled her to describe the me-me-me of her work habits. Another wrote she never writes essays "to order." Another wrote that he had no desire to reveal any of his work secrets nor did he care about anybody else's. And one, in an obvious dys-salute to our query, sent back an empty postcard with only her return address as comment.

I put in that paragraph to suggest the wide range of attitudes toward a project that asks writers to reveal their habits. There are obviously those who prefer not to disclose, a decision which suggests protection, hiddenness, fear possibly. Webster tells us that "revelation" means something revealed or disclosed, especially a striking disclosure, as of something not before realized. Consider, if you will, ours a book of revelation. I think all of us have learned more about ourselves as we have delved into the writing of how we write. I am grateful that the writers have opened themselves to vulnerable disclosure; they have taught me much. Perhaps, in the pages that follow, readers will take courage that they, too, can write—if only they dare.

Introduction

William F. Pinar

How do we work? Why ask such a question? Who cares?

We ask the question in order to reflect on the conditions in which we read, think, write, and learn, realizing how intertwined—even simultaneous, it sometimes seems—these are. By such reflection and self-report we hope to encourage our readers to become more aware of how they work, what conditions support not just productivity but contemplation: thinking that moves beyond the calculation of means to ends, learning that deepens and widens our understanding of our work, of education, of who we are in this historical moment. We are not only curious but professionally obligated to understand, remembering the subtitle of Nietzsche's *Ecce Homo* "How One Becomes What One Is" (1968, p. 281). This is not narcissism, of course, as, recalling Nietzsche (1966) once more, even "our body is but a social structure" (p. 26). The "self" is social even when solitary.

But our interest is not to engage in tired debates with pseudo-Marxists. Our interest is to study how we work, to shed light on what many—except maybe the famous—tend to keep private. We do not assume that readers are interested in how we work because we are who we are. We think readers might become interested in how we work if such narratives refer them back to themselves, to their own work lives, to their own efforts to move through what for many is a deep resistance to thinking, to learning, or writing. This resistance is often psychological, but it is also partly cultural. Maybe all cultures swirl like eddies, returning always to the center, circulation that goes nowhere, just disappears under the surface. Culture is, of course, profoundly conservative. Our work, however, as intellectuals and often as artists, is dedicated to cultural movement, to cultural progress, however contentious and complicated those concepts are. For Americans, this resistance is also specific; it has to do with the United States, dedicated so completely, it seems, to calculation and accumulation. In America, thinking, learning, and working make sense only when they lead to capital accumulation. In America, contemplation is for kooks.

Not a few Americans consider intellectuals and artists as kooks, or worse. And so our vocations position us in tension with, even in opposition to, many, perhaps most, of our fellow citizens. This is not just an American problem, of course; the intellectual's (and on more than a few occasions the artist's) vocation often pits her against her own (conservative) culture, regardless of where or when. While we cannot be unduly anxious over the response of our fellow Americans, we cannot afford to alienate them either, at least not irrevocably. As teachers we try to keep the bonds that bind alive, in order to be heard, in order to hear, in order to teach and learn. Our interest in our students is partly parental; we wish them, in the deepest sense, well. We want them to succeed, even if our ideas of success differ from theirs. When we fight for cultural progress, we do not seek our own narrow political gain; we fight for what we perceive to be in the public's—in the next generation's—interest.

There is also a resistance to knowing that has to do with the field of education specifically. Because education is construed as a "professional" field, an "applied" discipline, it has tended to reject scholarship not obviously linked to the workings of schools. Theory and scholarship that seek to understand education (which may and sometimes may not attend to schools explicitly) have been contested or ignored. Partly, this comes from a genuine (if distorted) loyalty to the schools, to the children and teachers who inhabit them. But partly this suspicion of theory, of open-ended intellectual exploration, has to do with an anti-intellectualism peculiar to the field of education itself.

That's not possible, you say. How could there be anti-intellectualism in education, of all fields? The simple answer is that most professors of education are former schoolteachers (many states require it, as if the schools weren't already too much with us). That is to say, professors of education are individuals whose first interest was teaching in the schools. It was not to engage in original research; it was not to press back the limits of thought; it was not to participate, however modestly, in the centuries-old "conversation" that could be said to comprise intellectual life in the West. They wanted to teach kids. Sure, if they were secondary teachers, they chose a subject. But that subject was chosen not as a life-long medium of intellectual labor. It was something to teach kids.

This isn't awful, of course. Thank goodness teachers' first obligation is to the children, although school reform (curriculum reform specifically) of the last thirty years has tended to weaken as it complicated this bond, making performance on standardized texts the main thing. Such right-wing, business-minded reform plus profound political, social, and economic changes—not a one of which seems to make coming of age in America any easier let alone sensible—have led to more detached, even cynical, teachers; to more alienated students, to less engaged thinking, teaching, and learning. More than ever—and social engineering has typified American institutional life for at least a century—there is the idea that if only we make the appropriate adjustment (in curriculum, in teaching technique, in how teachers are prepared, in testing, etc.) the school engine will then hum smoothly, and test scores will soar. Ah, America. Then we won't take second seat to Japan and Germany; our scores on math and science tests will be second to none. World-class.

It is a complicated situation that we face, live in, and try to think and learn our way through. Our work lives have embedded within them and express many of these often contradictory and conflicting tendencies. Additionally, there is the semi-colonial relationship we suffer vis-à-vis arts and science professors, vis-à-vis practically everybody else in the university. No one hesitates to tell us what the field of education should be, what its inadequacies are, how profound our responsibility is for those educational failures, i.e. students, to whom our "colleagues" (as we characterize them more hopefully than accurately) try to teach physics or history or mathematics. Education professors are not happy creatures, although many of us appear to be, some by constitution and character, others through determination or denial. Be like arts and science professors! we are told. Be like business professors! Make the schools better! Bring in grants! Teach large classes! Produce scholarship of quality! There is a gendered element to this institutional abuse, as the figure of the education professor tends to be female (vis-à-vis her university colleagues but "male" vis-à-vis his "female" colleagues in the schools).

Despite these powerful problems, there are scholars of education who press ahead with the project of understanding. These often embattled individuals proceed on their own terms, decline to scramble after what bureaucrats, even arts and sciences colleagues, imagine they ought to be doing. This project of understanding education proceeds not at an arrogant distance from those in schools, but in fact inspired by love for and commitment to those children and teachers who are trapped in a huge bureaucratic machine, a machine with, it sometimes seems, no one in charge. There is, in many public schools, a kind of gridlock, a paralysis precipitated and maintained by intersecting, often conflicting, rarely cooperating stakeholders: parents, politicians, business people, the new right, the so-called Christian right, students (not always eager to take advantage of educational opportunities), and teachers (not always intellectuals, as we have noted). Certainly education professors exert a very limited influence over what transpires in American public school classrooms. Perhaps some day we will enjoy more influence, but for now we must move ahead, not wring our hands over lost or imagined influence. We must work to understand what education is and might be. And this means that we must focus on education, not just on schooling.

It is within this larger project that the current volume seeks to make a contribution. We wish to explore how we work in order to contribute to our field's understanding of the dynamics of intellectual labor, including resistance and breakthrough, not to mention the relations among work, society, and life history. We are curious about everything, and so we asked our contributors to report whatever they wished, whatever they could bear to confess: from the work space itself, to those more private habits (including eccentricities), psychological blocks, institutional frustrations, and yes successes. "Tell all," Marla and Mary encouraged those they invited to participate. We are pleased with what we have received.

Our title refers to Dewey's *How We Think* and Bode's *How We Learn*, partly to honor their work by recalling it, partly to show how different is the world we live in from Dewey's world of 1910 (when *How We Think* was published) or Bode's world of 1938 (when *How We Learn* appeared). Dewey writes about thinking and Bode about learning very differently than our historical and disciplinary situation asks us to: most obviously, from the point of view of this book, we decline to abstract it from our daily lives. Dewey tends toward a certain proceduralism, a preoccupation with what is almost a methodology of thinking, a preoccupation that has plagued professional education from its beginnings. Bode risks reducing learning to the philosophy of mind, although at the end of his book world politics sends him leftward. Both men say a number of very smart things, and say them better than we can. And some of what they say is as pertinent today as it was ninety years ago (in Dewey's case) or sixty years ago (in Bode's). I have placed a passage from each book before each essay, but not to try to somehow summarize the writing that follows, and certainly not to suggest that the writing is an illustration of the points Dewey and Bode are making. Rather, by inserting quoted passages from both Dewey and Bode before each essay I seek to create an intertextual reverberation of often very different points of view, often very different intellectual and artistic passions, passions differently experienced, differently characterized. As well, I hope the dispersal of Dewey's and Bode's thinking and learning throughout this work underlines the very different historical moments in which we are working. My point—our point—is to stimulate you to reflect on how you think, how you learn, how you work. Our situation asks us to do no less.

References

Bode, Boyd Henry (1940). *How We Learn.* Boston: Heath.

Dewey, John (1910). *How We Think.* Boston: Heath.

Nietzsche, Friedrich (1966). *Beyond Good and Evil.* (Trans. Walter Kaufman.) New York: Vintage.

Nietzsche, Friedrich (1968). *Ecce Homo.* (Trans. Walter Kaufman.) New York: Vintage.

Chapter 1

The Web and the Work

Mary Aswell Doll

Where there is thought,
things present act
as signs or tokens of things not yet experienced.
(John Dewey, 1910, p. 14)

The self is not a fixed quantity or static thing;
it is not an inherited possession, but an achievement.
It expands in one direction and contracts in another;
it is in the making all the while.
(Boyd Henry Bode, 1940, p. 115)

I have written the first line of this essay a thousand times. One first line was to be: I write the title first, always. (I work on titles for several weeks. This one has undergone at least four birthings.) Another was: this afternoon I witnessed a squirrel fall out of a tree. Another: once, a long long time ago, when I was married, when it was Upon a Time, I observed a spider spinning. Of those, I like the last best. It was also one of the first. I like it because it expresses the metaphor I want to draw out about writing and webbing, about the threads that come from the belly. When I watched that spider, one long ago morning in another chapter of my life, I was amazed at her process of creating out of nothing. She parachuted, suspended from the crook in the ceiling by a thin filament that came out of the middle of her body. She spun as she dropped. In falling she was buoyed by the thread of her web, her support structure literally spinning from her center.

The spider moment must have made an impression on me, for one of my handouts for my students, entitled (pompously) "How to Write," uses the web as a metaphor. "Think of yourself as a spider," I urge my students. "You are spinning out of your centerpoint. You do this before you have the whole web pictured in your mind. You spin in order to make your web." What I express here is part of my own creating process, that arises from stuff within. I work with my gut. Sometimes, as with this essay, I put pet words on scrap paper before I turn on the Apple. My prompt-words all have to do with the webbing of structure—a mere filament before I get to work, knowing before I write that key words help lead ideas out. I work, it seems, spider-fashion, what Emily Dickinson (1960, p. 298) calls "from Nought to Nought" or what Gertrude Stein (1920, p. 64) calls the "inside word" from which nothing can be written until there is need. I call this creating from within "the un-world of the unspoken, un-created unconscious": memories, dreams, hints, hunches, gestures, notions, forgotten pearls.

I did not always write like this.

When the time came to write my dissertation, decades ago, I did not write like this. After months of collecting mounds of notes, after a full week of putting together my bibliography, the time came for me to Begin. In my head I saw myself as needing to be a Scholar. I would write with Authority. I pictured myself as needing a three-piece suit and a stern expression. I would produce long words. Everything would be seamless. After countless delays (Was that the doorbell? I must make this phone call. We need more kitty litter. The meat loaf is burning.), I shut the door to Begin.

My topic was Samuel Beckett. Prior to writing, I had decided to mirror in my journal what Beckett's characters all do: they write about writing. So as I was writing my dissertation on Beckett during the day, every evening I wrote about writing on Beckett. The early pages of my journal recount frustration and despair. I could not write. How I tried. I used buzzwords; my lexicon was Latinate. During the day I would labor to make the words bigger, the sentences more complex, but at night I knew I was failing hopelessly. Then one evening I read "The Answer to Job," Carl Jung's masterpiece, written when he had a temperature of 103, was delirious, and was in his dotage. The piece ripped. It sang. It danced and jigged and jagged. It proclaimed heresy. It didn't care. That night I was released from my false perception of the scholar as a dusky ink mark disguised in a three-piece suit. I woke the next morning to begin to write simple sentences with smaller words. I was on my way. My dissertation, subsequently, was published—a strange saga of coincidence and confusion not relevant to this piece.

Other writings have had a feverishness similar to my dissertation. One was a piece I wrote after my mother died. I wrote it in four days.

The piece was spun out of my grief and gratitude, my history of memory with a mother I hardly knew. Writing was cathartic. No one was looking over my shoulder. I wrote about my mother feeling somehow that my experience was not unique, that I had something, if only I could say it honestly, which would resonate with other women. Another piece that was published in an edition on contemporary British drama arose out of a game I amused myself with. I used to keep a notecard on my desk of titles to unwritten pieces. Titles, as I mentioned earlier, are the way I begin, hooks for future weavings. One title was "Humor in Pinter, Beckett, and Stoppard." Attending an MLA (Modern Language Association) convention, I ran across an acquaintance from the Beckett Society who asked me what I was working on. I lied: "Humor in Pinter, Beckett, and Stoppard," never having read Stoppard and knowing little about Pinter. Immediately my friend replied, "Well, you're just the person I am looking for! I need a Stoppard expert for my book on British contemporary drama!" I was delighted; I was terrified. I believe the hardest assignment I ever completed was that Stoppard piece (1993), since I did not particularly enjoy reading his plays and had a devilish time trying to figure him out.

The figure, of course, is in the web. I figured then, as I figure now, by attending to patterns and ruminating. One pattern I could see emerging in the Stoppard texts was his high-spirited romp with audience expectation. I found Stoppard's insouciance and doublecoding maddening, infernal. For all my work with literature and metaphor, I struggle with my own literalism. But as I doggedly filled out my notecards, seeking ever more patterns, it became evident to me that here was a perfect example of postmodernism. I pitched my piece around the postmodern theme of doubling, only to be told by my conservative Australian editor-friend that "postmodern" was a word unfamiliar to the British. Could I change it? What I did was find a euphemism in Martin Esslin's (1961) phrase "post-absurdism." While I satisfied my editor, I felt that the point of the article had been dented. I would, however, do anything to get published.

Used to be I wrote longhand before I typed. I recall pages of scratched-out sentences, X's through entire paragraphs, suggestive of my terror of the white page. Now I work directly on the computer, trusting the flow from within more than I did earlier. Too, I want the writing to reflect life as I live it while writing. For instance, the other day my neighbor showed me his catahoula puppy. It had webbed feet. A week earlier a peacock crossed my path. Contrasted with its god's-eye tail, all flowy and long and iridescent, were its webbed feet. The web metaphor I wanted to use to describe my way of working seemed to be forcing itself on my attention. Yesterday webs were everywhere. Along the palmetto trail of Jean Lafitte Park webs glistened on palm fronds and swamp maple twigs, reaching out tiny tendrils, until I felt I could become part of one swampwide web (http://sww).

In two days I celebrate my birthday. I am a Gemini. There are two of me. I try to write now from the other me, that Mary, the one I was before they got a hold of me and tamed my wildness. I am reminded of Toni Morrison's multiple speaking voices in *Jazz* (1993). Violet lays claim to her other self, the one capable of violence and surprise, not because she is proud of this other but because it cannot be discarded: "Whenever she thought about that Violet, and what that Violet saw through her own eyes, she knew there was no shame there, no disgust. . . . *That* Violet is not somebody walking round town, up and down the streets wearing my skin and using my eyes shit no *that* Violet is me!" (94, 95–96).

All of Morrison's characters in her novel have at least two me's, one public, one secret. I think this is Morrison's intention: to give a sense of the texture of contradiction so prevalent in African-American experience. Indeed, having been torn from their roots in the country, Morrison's characters must re-create themselves in devious ways: through memory or talking or action—whatever it takes. This idea of the potentially creative force of the split self is Jungian. Carl Jung (1930) insists that twoness is essential to the creating artist. He states that the other self has "primordial experiences" which "rend from top to bottom the curtain upon which is painted the picture of an ordered world" (p. 90). The artist, as opposed the "personal self," for Jung, taps the channel to the primordial world, wresting conflict and suffering into manageable shape.

Jung drew much of his thinking about psychology and art from the medieval alchemists, whom he saw as seekers after the secrets of the soul. They described the physical process of changing lead into gold metaphorically, saying theirs was a work against nature, an *opus contra naturam*, since nature's way tended upward, and theirs downward. Translated into psychological terms, this says that we are the work. We must work on ourselves to mine hidden treasure. Certainly, my thinking about my spider-writing subscribes to this view.

But as I emerge gradually, painfully, from encrusted beliefs and enculturated habits in the attempt to spin my own web, I seek to recover the darker female within so as to let my writing reflect her rhythms and her words. I shift my allegiance away from Jung with his white Swiss male (pro Nazi?) bias and toward feminist theory. Yes, I have two selves. But, yes, I have two lips. Luce Irigaray (1977, p. 103) writes "Woman has sex organs just about everywhere. . . . 'She' is infinitely other in herself." Feminist recovery of embodied knowing is as old as the earliest myths. In the pre-Greek myth of Inanna, the queen of heaven and earth, Inanna goes to a sheepfold, which in Sumer is the center of nature, in order to receive and rejoice in her own natural powers. Diane Wolkstein (1983) comments that the word for sheepfold in Sumerian is the same as the word for vulva or womb. This female myth is not about a hero's quest or conquests; it is about rejoicing in the source and power of female embodiment.

What are the rhythms of the body that can find expression in work? How do bodywork and nightdreams combine in the work process?

How indeed.

I remember being struck by Nel Noddings's remark to me years ago about her work habits. She said she needed to pluck weeds in between paragraphs. I think of her as I take forays away from the computer during the writing of any essay. Working with the hands, the feet, the arms, the torso becomes a necessary counterrhythm to working with the head. That sentence is my reminder that I have been up here in front of my screen for too long. It is time to take a walk with Marla . . .

Our walks are as much a part of the web of work as the writing. We are both industrious workers: up before seven, coffee and newspaper by eight (Marla never reads the paper—too distracting), some fumbling with laundry or the Dust Buster (the meagerest of housekeeping), and (for me) some early morning watering of the plants, then (for me) to work by nine. Marla has already been at her desk for two hours. She works in a beam of light downstairs in her study, shades pulled. I work upstairs, cat in window. My Apple overlooks the branches of the ficus tree near and the banana trees far. My scene is green. On goes the classical music station, on goes the computer, and I am off for three hours, working my web. We break for lunch at about the same time, usually eleven-thirty, when we watch CNN; then back to the workstation until two or three, when we walk. This routine is allowable only in the summer months, when I have all day every day to read or write. Otherwise, when I teach my hundred students, with writing assignments every other week, I have little time and less energy to spin.

The walks are like spaces in the web. They allow breath. We might walk in silence for a short bit, but then the notions come. Marla shares her latest chapter titles for her dissertation, a new notion coming from her reading of Holocaust testimony. I share my notion of where I think this essay is heading. She has been reading Derrida all last semester; Marla shares his words, which become our notions: violence, the gift, the promise, the ear, the trace. I share notions from my fiction reading, the new characters with whom I live as I work: Violet from *Jazz;* the narrator in *Hallucinating Foucault*, whose work is webbed in the life of his subject, a madman novelist, from whom he learns to stand at the edge of the gaming tables so as "to see clearly, both the players and the wheel" (p. 71). I dogear pages as I read so as to remember to tell Marla. Sometimes I take notes in the back of the book, with page numbers. Remembered reading is an act of intimacy during our walking. We make love with these notions all the time.

Notions. I think of this word not as "vague or imperfect conceptions" but rather as "small articles, as buttons, thread, ribbon." I build my web on the thread of these notions, these bits of texture and color. I remember myself as a child weaving through the aisles of the magic place, Murray's, Chappaqua's equivalent of the five and dime. I pause at Notions . . .

A dream a few nights ago had the word "obits" in it. It was an anxiety dream about writing this essay, finding a title so I could begin. At the time my working title was "Bits. Threads. Nests. Webs." My dream was playing with bits and obits, the notion of writing as collecting long-lost "bits" of life, but also of dying to past lives. Writing as dying. Writing as helping me kill the tame Mary so as to become more provocative, more dangerous—more like a spiderwoman. I do not want my writing to impress; I want it to allure. Draw them in. They will say you are disjointed, jumping around too much. No, I will answer. I am not spinning my wheels; I am spinning my web.

How synchronistic, that as I prepare to celebrate my birthday (I am not one to mourn the passing of the years. Bring on the gifts!), I write some obits. People are dropping from my life. I am cutting them out, killing them off. My most recent obit was a letter I mailed, to arrive on my birthday, to the minister of a church I had been attending ever since my divorce. It is the wrong time to be leaving the church, absolutely the wrong time, since the church is losing membership and I am seen as a pillar. They appointed me lay reader and church greeter. For two weeks I was flattered in this role, which lasted five months. In my dream the page numbers of my as-yet-unwritten essay were in the upper left-hand corner, the wrong place. Writing to Craig was "wrong" for him but right, even necessary, for me if I am to cut loose from sectarian trappings. Those are the social entanglements I do not wish to be caught in any more. But to avoid entrapment in psalm and psalter I have to use my pen as knife. Just as my brother did.

My brother had to cut loose from the rope around his neck, the strangulation, of his surname. His name was killing him. It was the umbilical cord that tied him to a father he could not love. Not only did my brother change his name (from Duncan Aswell to Bill Cutler—note the first syllable of the last name) he changed his locale, his occupation, and came into his sexuality. These were all willful acts: he willed a different life. But can one psychically cut loose from the ties that bind? Certainly, symbolic acts are significant and of ritualistic importance. But I could see, in those few years before he died, when Bill Cutler became a wine salesman (not an English professor) and the owner of a home in an all-black middle-class neighborhood (not a tenant on the campus of Wellesley College, later Haverford College), I could see that his writing still could not stay away from his father. In writing he referred to that man he despised as "Daddy." Ever the son, he was; ever the child-son; ever-yearning.

In a visionary novel, Banana Yoshimoto (1993) writes: "We all believe we can choose our own path from among the many alternatives. But perhaps it's more accurate to say that we make the choice unconsciously. . . . With the breaths we take every day, with the expression in our eyes, with the daily actions we do over and over, we decide as though by instinct" (p. 97).

Or, to quote from another author closer to home:

> Was it in such a way, one time as he awoke, and heard below his father's lion-ramp of morning that fury came? He never knew, no more than one could weave the great web of his life back through the brutal chaos of ten thousand furious days, unwind the great vexed pattern of his life to silence, peace, and certitude in the magic land of new beginnings, no return. (Wolfe, 1939, p. 75)

I catch my breath. I selected that passage just now at random. I opened the book in the middle, flipped a few pages, and lighted on that passage. It contains my words. Suddenly I remember that Thomas Wolfe's *The Web and The Rock* was a posthumous manuscript my father edited. Once again the web chooses me. I was not going to write about my parents. That material, however, is part of the stuff that textures my work. And my brother, for all his determination to "kill" his father, selected, ironically, the middle name Evarts in the mistaken belief that it was the name of his hero, W. E. B. DuBois when, in fact, it was the middle name of Thomas Wolfe's first editor, Maxwell Evarts Perkins, my father's nemesis.

We kill as we can, but we cannot escape. So we may as well work with what we must.

I am coming to the end of what I have to say about how I work. This has been an easier essay to write than I thought. It has been incubating for several weeks, possibly a month or more. Only when I wrote the prompt words did it begin to urge expression. Its web has been woven around this list:

web
filament
from the center, gut
webbed feet of peacock
sticky
in corners
bits and pieces (dream)
    obits
    page number on wrong side
making things by hand
Bits and Threads and the Ooze of Text

The last entry is yet another title I wanted to bring in with the word "ooze." Omitted from the title, "ooze" is still the last prompt word I want to make about writing. Writing is messy. I look around the room scattered with books, papers, opened boxes, unpaid bills. I run downstairs to pick up a book for a point; it goes next to the writing table, on the floor already piled with books. Other books for other projects tumble from another table. When the cat comes, he disrupts any sense of order by treading on the piles, sometimes treading on the keyboard, making ;ojs'fkjasua[igj out of my sentences. Clothes are discarded on the sofa, along with shoes, hats, and earrings. (I change clothes as I change the tone of a thought, sometimes donning a dress, sometimes a pair of shorts, sometimes a hat (often a hat), occasionally a set of earrings—always dangling.) The room oozes. It will take me an hour to put everything back in place. But for now, I let it all swirl around me, since I am not yet ready to nose my way up through the ooze (Heyen, 1996). Am I turtle or spider? I am both hard-shelled and filament-soft. That is the writing I like to do. I will run down now and shout with Marla; then perhaps we'll go for a walk.

References

Dickinson, E. (1960). *The Complete Poems of Emily Dickinson.* (Ed. Thomas H. Johnson.) Boston: Little, Brown.

Doll, M. (1988). *Beckett and Myth: An Archetypal Approach.* Syracuse, N.Y.: Syracuse University Press.

Doll, M. (1993). "Stoppard's Theatre of Unknowing." In James Acheson (Ed.), *British and Irish Drama Since 1960.* New York: St. Martin's (pp. 117–129).

Duncker, P. (1996). *Hallucinating Foucault.* Hopewell, N.J.: Ecco.

Esslin, M. (1961).*The Theater of the Absurd.* New York: Doubleday.

Heyen, W. (1996). "The plain awakening." In *Annuli.* (n.d.) New York: William B. Ewert.

Irigaray, L. (1977). *Ce Sexe qui n'en pas un.* Paris: Éditions de Minuit.

Jung, C. G. (1958). "Answer to Job." In *Psychology and Religion: East and West: Collected Works ll.* (Trans. R. F. C. Hull. Ed. Sir Herbert Read et al.) Princeton N.J.: Princeton University Press.

Jung, C. G. (1930). "Psychology and literature." In *Collected Works xv* (1976). (Trans. R. F. C. Hull. Ed. Sir Herbert Read et al.) Princeton N.J.: Princeton University Press (pp. 84–108).

Morrison, T. (1993). *Jazz.* New York: Penguin.

Stein, G. (1920). *Everybody's Autobiography.* New York: Vintage.

Wolfe, T. (1939). "Who has known fury?" *The Face of a Nation: Poetical Passages from the Writings of Thomas Wolfe.* New York: Scribner.

Wolkstein, D. and S. N. Kramer, Eds. (1983). *Inanna: Queen of Heaven and Earth: Her Stories and Hymns from Sumer.* New York: Harper and Row.

Yoshimoto, B. (1993). *Kitchen.* (Trans. Megan Backus.) New York: Washington Square.

Chapter 2

Curriculum as Musical Text

Marla Morris

> Demand for the solution of a perplexity
> is the steadying and guiding factor
> in the entire process of reflection.
> (John Dewey, 1910, p. 11)

> Education, like invention, is primarily concerned,
> not with what is, but with what may be.
> (Boyd Henry Bode, 1940, p. 286)

It's five in the morning. I wake up to the thud of gumby falling off of my dresser. Maxx, my cat, is at work again. Gumby sounds a thud, Maxx laughs. I slink out of bed. That dream again. I try to forget it. Mary is still asleep, dreaming probably of gumby, Maxx, green fields, or that childhood house I hear so much about in upstate New York, a virtual Thomas Wolfe Inn. Who knows? Mary's dreams are always elaborate, interesting, and long. When she begins telling her tales, I know that I might have to pour a few cups of coffee. Mary's really into her dreams. I wish I could be rid of my dream-tales. There's a story here somewhere. We all have stories. Writing stories is writing life. My story begins in the morning when I hear the coffee brewing.

I turn on the coffee, turn on the oh-so-1940s green light in my study. But I don't exactly have a study. My workroom is inhabited by all sorts of gumbies. Mr. Potato Head the pencil sharpener, Mrs. Weekly the dinosaur, Fiorello the pink panther, and Pierre the soccer player are drinking their morning coffee too. They are part of my story. I know what you are saying: Marla must be completely neurotic. Yes. You are correct. But isn't that what it takes to be a good writer? A little craziness helps.

My green lamp showers a green glow over the desk. It's still dark outside. I hear the coffee brewing. An essential for writing. I won't remember that dream, I tell myself. There's a story buried. Buried lives. My eyes feel tired from yesterday's reading of Nietzsche. Nietzsche tires me. My dream glosses over Nietzsche's sentences. "Life goes on, but in two temporal directions, at once, the future unable to escape the grip of a memory laden with grief" (Langer, 1991, p. 34). The grief of my dream. It's 1980. I'm back at CMU (Carnegie-Mellon University). All the faces have turned to gumbies. Everywhere I look I see gumby. The same music pouring out of the practice rooms, pouring out of coffeepots, over and over the same sounds brewing. A sickness here. There is a sickness in these walls. A sickness rises in my gut. My jury is too soon and the music is not yet memorized. I'll sink. Remember it, remember it all. Searching for a practice room. There aren't any. I'll sink. I'm a stranger here. Gumby thumps, Maxx laughs. I wake up to a hurting arm. Nietzsche is ruining my arm. "Anguished memory . . . imprisons the consciousness it should be liberating" (Langer, p. 34). It's not Nietzsche who is ruining me; the real problem is memory.

The ruin was gradual. I picked up a pen and my hand froze. I played the first movement of Prokofiev's Third Piano Concerto and my hand froze. My hand was stuck in mid air. I knew then that I was in trouble, but of course I ignored these freezings. I thought they would just go away. But they didn't; they got worse. I kept playing. The freezing turned to numbness and then finally to pain. I couldn't pick up pen, touch a piece of silk, write. Ruined. Tendinitis is every musician's nightmare. Essentially, it means the end of a career. At the age of twenty-two my music career ended.

There's a story buried in dreams. When I was about five I wanted to play the trumpet. But I changed my mind because it didn't have enough buttons. So I decided, at about six, that I wanted to play the piano. And I did. I outplayed my first teacher. My parents decided to send me to a Juilliard man. That was the beginning. And perhaps it was the beginning of the end. I should have known at the age of eight or ten that it wouldn't work out. But I'm being too hard on myself. There's a story here. A buried life. The Juilliard man had studied with a student of Rachmaninoff's. After the Juilliard man, I studied with a student of Schnabel's, with a teacher of Dichter's, with a second place winner of the Van Cliburn competition, and so on. Who cares? But I was never quite good enough. In the music world you have to be perfect. And you have to be perfect by the age of twenty-five. It's kind of like the Olympics. It you haven't placed first at the Van Cliburn, you can forget it. Concert pianists are a dying breed. I am dead. Dead to that world. I was never good enough anyway. In fact, I got worse. I don't know why but I kept getting worse. And one day I got better. But at the height of my career I fell. In fact, I crashed. It was all over when I turned twenty-two. Those years between twenty- two and thirty are a complete blur to me. I used to feel completely attached to the keyboard, as if it were an extension of my body. Now it's gone. The old world is gone. But not quite. My dreams keep tormenting me. Every time I turn around there is some reminder of my old life. Bergamo, for instance, is being held in Bloomington this year. Bloomington is a killer music school. A teacher of mine studied there. In fact, she wanted me to go to school there. But no, I insisted that I had to go to CMU. At CMU, I met two people who have remained my closest friends. And guess what? They weren't good enough either. The cellist waits tables; the opera singer crunches numbers. We should start a band called Musicians in Exile. You have to be good enough. But at every corner in Manhattan there is a concert pianist, a cellist, or an opera singer who is ten times better than you. And whatever you do, don't get tendinitis. And whatever you do, don't spend too many hours in the practice room or you'll go deaf. I'm half deaf from all those hours in the practice room. I've got one good arm and one good ear. But that's not hard to deal with. The real problem is memory.

I am two: the dead musician, the living curriculum theorist. I am dead and alive. I am two Marlas: a "permanent duality, not exactly a split or a doubling but a parallel existence" (Langer, p. 95). I live a parallel existence. I am two, not one. My unconscious tells me this. My dreams tell me this. Since I cannot play, I write. And I write with two selves. Writing curriculum as musical text is what I do.

Writing curriculum as musical text is not a visual act; it's auditory. I like writing that bites, just as playing needs to be biting. If Prokofiev has no bite, it's no good. Writing=biting. And writing is also breathing. Phrases must breathe. The line of a text must rise and fall like breath. Pauses, silences, rests must be heard between the lines. Interruptions in the text are not easy to hear. Bite and breath sound interruptions. Listening for the whole becomes key, too. Without a sense of the end, the beginning does not sound. Soundings. That is what writing is. Soundings. Round soundings. Sounding silences. Silent soundings. Pauses. Lines.

Writing longhand. I like to feel the notes under my hand. Something about two hands deliberating over notes. I cannot write at the computer. I must move the pen under my hand and shape the letters as notes. Hand over hand, deliberation. I listen to the pen move across the paper. "It has been observed, particularly in birds, that precision of hearing is in direct proportion to the obliqueness of the tympanum. The tympanum squints" (Derrida, 1982, xv). The precision of hearing has much to do with good writing. A poet of curriculum re-sounds Derrida's call. She hears well. Listening to the smallest creatures on the page is key. Writing with the ear of a bird becomes key.

I dreamed in d-flat. Why not c-sharp? The concert was quickly approaching. But before I touched the keyboard the conducter turned to me and said, "Skip the virtuoso section." I dreamed of Bach written on orange manuscript paper. A small hallway, an awful upright piano. I do have a key to the grand pianos, but I don't want to walk through the hallway where all my teachers can see me. I hear him coming. I'm not prepared. My teacher looks grubby, old. I fish around in my bag for Bach, the orange one. But I can't find it. I think this is it. I pull out the manuscript, but it's blue, it's a roadmap. I start walking in the rain and another Mardi Gras parade passes by.

> And so, like the poet, the painter, the musician, the "bodyreader," the researcher of lived experience must live a life that allows the possibility for interpreting the usually invisible and unarticulated relations among things. (Sumara, 1996, p. 10)

I am engaged in a process of interpreting a life lived twice, a split life, a memory that perpetually emerges, haunts writing, living, dreaming. The invisible things, of which Dennis Sumara speaks, are memories. Writing is never done without memories, without invisible things, without hauntings. The writing, in fact, takes on a life of its own. Paul Ricoeur (1995) talks of a letting go when interpreting texts. And so too with writing. A letting go happens only after much listening.

Passages of text resonate, stun, shock, drown, amuse. If not, the interpreter, listener falls asleep. Perchance to dream a text that doesn't put one to sleep. Jumpy, staccato, legato, do lend an ear. Writing comes all at once or not at all as the jumpy, staccato, stunning, funny notes stream on by. Passages. Texts breathe passages into a life, a life that breathes. The writing writes the writer. Chords emerge from texts, patterns arise: the writing sounds a symphony, a cacophony of sounds.

> Sound—in all its multilayered richness, in its capacity for formless confusion, in its necessary proximity. . . . The realm of the sonorous might thus provide

> us with better starting places for developing senses of knowledge, of human interaction, and of personal identity. (Davis, 1996, xxiv)

This multilayeredness of sound is what drives me to write in multilayered ways. Intertextual writing sounds the tympanum. A rich piece of musical text crosses currents, currents crossing. Atonality, tonality, blocks of silence rushing all around at once. If I could just write the silences more loudly. The silences write me. Writing silences me too.

Silence is perhaps, paradoxically, the most powerful sound, non-sound. I wrote an entire paper on silence once. I'm good at silences because I work at them. But that paper I wrote once, the one on silence, found its way into the trash. I threw it out. I often throw out my pieces. As a matter of fact, after I've written a piece I can't hear it anymore. I've grown deaf to my words, my sounds. So I toss them in the trash. All good sounds should have a resting place, a place to rest. A rest. A resting place is a dwelling. Dwelling on sounds is key.

My life in the scholarly community is recent. Thanks to Bill Pinar I've been given a second life. Now I've got a new identity: scholar, writer, curriculum theorist. This is a new world to me. It's different from the old. In fact, the longer I'm in the new, the more I forget the old. But the old is always there, no matter what. It always interrupts my life; it seems to remember me. It chokes and suffocates, memory pains. But I've transferred my classical training in music over to my new life in the scholarly world. I like to think of myself as a classicist. I write highly formal, structured essays, like symphonies. I try to write symphonies. But not everyone likes my pieces. In fact, this week alone I got two rejection letters from journals. These letters tell me that I'm silly and weird. That's nice. What-ever. Mary's book (Doll, 1995) is filled with rejection letters. Mary tells me that Samuel Beckett had some sixty rejections. I don't write as well as Mary and I'm no Beckett. Mary can really write. It's that Thomas Wolfe thing. Mary's a born writer. There are born writers just as there are born musicians. Born with an ear. Musicianship cannot be taught, of that I'm convinced. And there are born teachers too. Mary is a born teacher. I should know; I was her student in English 102, pedestrian writing. Now Mary is my lover. I thought I could write my way to her. I did. Anyway, it's good to know that even the big guns get turned down. Then I don't feel so bad when the rejections start coming in. Not everyone likes my work. I think it is because journal editors have sounds already in mind. Many scholars like pieces that sound like this: one, two, three. But my pieces sound like this: one, six, twenty, one, seven, blue, green, red.

Not that I write without form, for my pieces are highly structured. But within that structure I play. I play again in a new way.

> Memory is not only a spring, flowing from the well of the past, but also a tomb, whose contents cling like withered ivy to the mind. (Langer, p. 69)

Mary and I have been invited to a party. Dread overcomes me because there will be musicians at this party. One is a famous Russian pianist. I tell Mary that it won't bother me when they start singing and playing. I tell Mary that when the questions start, I'll say I have no past, I am not me. I am two. One is dead. Dread. How I dread this party. I thought parties were supposed to be fun. The old me no longer lives. No, the party won't bother me at all. We'll go, and tonight I'll feel that heaviness in my heart and sink. I dread that party. Maybe when we come home I'll stay up late and watch MTV. I was never good enough anyway. I suffered from nerves. Once I got so nervous before a master class that I started seeing blue spots and nearly passed out. The older I got, the worse the nerves got. Not good enough anyway. "Tainted memory . . . is a monument to ruin" (Langer, pp. 195–196). The party is over and so too the dream.

I was always good at improvising. No music. Just playing. Where the notes came from God only knows. I remember my grandfather doing this too. No music, just playing. Reading music for me was very difficult because I am not mathematical. The notes got in the way. Notes can get in the way. Getting beyond notes becomes key. I failed a course in eurythmics because I couldn't count. I also can't dance. Many musicians can't dance. But I can dance through my writing.

It is here that I can really hear. So I think God played a mean trick on me. Writing, for me, is music. I am living again, although memory looms, threatens. Writing also helps me work through memory. And it is memory that I write about. I am interested in writing through pain, about pain. My dissertation, not suprisingly, is about pain, memory, haunting. I am writing on the Holocaust and memory. Curriculum as memory text seems to write me. It is not that I choose this text, but that it chooses me. Memory, music and poetics call me to fall backward into the sounds I hear most loudly.

> To philosophize with a hammer Zarathustra begins by asking himself if he will have to puncture them, batter their ears . . . with the sound of symbols or tympani, the instruments, always, of some Dionysianism. In order to teach them "to hear with their eyes too." (Derrida, 1982, xiii)

Derrida, talking about Nietzsche's Zarathustra, keys into something that haunts me. That haunting concerns sound. It is the sound of Nietzsche that first alerted me to the danger of texts. Dangerous texts are noisy. Perhaps texts should be dangerous, not in a battering way, but in a silent way. It is through silence that one begins to hear. And what one hears might be dangerous. Dangerous listening changes readers. Curriculum as musical text might do this. Listening might become dangerous if it speaks colors, hears smells, touches invisibles. Curriculum as musical text pushes across currents, mixes air-waves, wavers, waves, never wavers. Musical memory pushes the line in cross-currents.

It's nine at night. Beethoven blasts on my machine. I'm a Beethoven junkie. This essay is in its final stages. And I must confess it has been one of the most difficult pieces I've ever written. Writing the self pains. Memory kept me from writing this for a long time. On stage again. Writing is the new stage. I am in a new stage of life. The first essay I wrote for this collection I trashed because it did not sound like me. It sounded like someone else. Maybe gumby was writing. So I started again and put gumby back on my dresser. This time, I hear myself. Writing births. This essay has dredged up the old dead me, the musician me, the Marla who spent eight hours a day in a practice room. But the practice room left me half deaf to my inner psyche. Curriculum theorizing writes me out of the practice room. I write myself back into myself, listening to the me who needs to hear silences. Beethoven blasts on my machine but I don't hear him anymore. I hear myself writing Beethoven.

References

Davis, B. (1996). *Teacing Mathematics: Toward a Sound Alternative.* New York: Garland.

Derrida, J. (1982). *Margins of Philosophy.* (Trans. A. Bass.) Chicaco: University of Chicago Press.

Doll, M. A. (1995). *To the Lighthouse and Back: Writings on Teaching and Living.* New York: Peter Lang.

Langer, L. (1991). *Holocaust Testimonies: The Ruins of Memory.* New Haven, Conn.: Yale University Press.

Ricoeur, P. (1995). *Hermeneutics and the Human Sciences.* (Trans., J. B. Thompson.) New York: Cambridge University Press.

Sumara, D. (1996). *Private Readings in Public: Schooling the Literary Imagination.* New York: Peter Lang.

Chapter 3

The Fire Sermon

Jamake Highwater

Genuine freedom, in short, is intellectual.
(John Dewey, 1910, p. 66).

There is a close connection
between our conception of mind
and the conception of the aim or purpose of education.
(Boyd Henry Bode, 1940, p. 279)

When Jean Cocteau was asked which of his possessions he would save from his burning house, he replied J'emporterais le feu ("*I would take the fire*").[1]

I began writing shortly after I was taken from an orphanage and adopted by a family with a home in the then-rural San Fernando Valley in Southern California. I was perhaps seven or eight years old, and so poorly educated that I was virtually illiterate. Despite my difficulty with language, eventually I encountered two established writers whose ability to put their feelings and thoughts on paper astounded me. One very early influence was Arnold Marquis, a neighbor who was a documentary-drama writer for NBC Radio, in an era before television extinguished the remarkable radio dramas created by people like Norman Corwin, Arch Obler, and Arnold Marquis. Such iconoclastic writers, I should add, were silenced less by television than by the Un-American Activities Committee, whose slander destroyed the careers of almost anyone in the arts and media with a degree of social consciousness.

I also knew Mandy Lawson, the daughter of screenwriter John Howard Lawson, one of the famous "Hollywood Ten," the group of writers who appeared before the Un-American Activities Committee and were subsequently jailed and blacklisted. Childhood visits to Mandy Lawson's home and brief encounters with her rather solemn father as well as my conversations with Arnold Marquis inspired me to overcome my fear of language and somehow find my way into the world of writers.

There were no books in my adoptive family's home, so I grew up with little access to the achievements of authors and poets. I did, however, have a constant exposure to films, because my adoptive family was in the film industry. The impact of that early encounter with the techniques and unique sensibilities of the cinema is very evident in my subsequent writings as an adult.

My first efforts to write were childish "plays," with brief descriptions of characters and settings and an abundance of awkward dialogue. Despite an unmistakable cinematic format—with shifting points of view, cuts and cross-fades, close-ups and long shots—I was not consciously attempting a screenplay. Nor was I trying to write a stage play. I had no idea what I was doing, yet I was compelled to write because of an unbounded enthusiasm, ignited by my very slight acquaintance with two "real writers."

The slight rapport with these writers provided important role models, but it was not until I came under the immense influence of the portentous mentors of my youth that I finally realized the magnitude of literature. Those mentors—a schoolteacher named Alta Black; three neighbors, Virginia and Frederic Dorr and Virginia's sister Frances Grigsby; as well as the author Anaïs Nin—gave me a vision of myself and the world that transformed me from a mute, adolescent outsider into a person with a voice capable of speaking with vividness about the marvels of alienation, about the unique and privileged grasp of things from the vantage of an outsider—like the Hubble telescope that can see a vaster cosmos unencumbered by the atmospheric distractions of our little world.

It was my abundant experience of commercial, historical, and experimental films at a little playhouse in Los Angeles called the Coronet Theater that prepared me for the works of James Joyce, Virginia Woolf, Thomas Mann, William Faulkner, Djuna Barnes, and T. S. Eliot. Unlike so many young people of my generation, I had no difficulty with the remarkable manipulations of time and space found in the greatest art forms of the twentieth century. To the contrary, I reveled in so-called *experiments* and *abstractions*, to such an extent that I relinquished the mainstream realism of bestsellers and the prosaic "literature" produced by "giants" such as Norman Mailer, James Jones, Ernest Hemingway, James T. Farrell, and Philip Roth. I wanted no part of their "laundry list worlds." Realist detail meant nothing to me. Like Kurt Vonnegut, Jr., I didn't want to supply my characters with transportation—opening and closing doors, turning on the ignition in their cars, putting on meticulously described costumes and walking through meticulously described rooms. I wanted nothing of the ordinary world to enter my writing except the part of "reality" that was essential to the spirit of my work.

It was most likely Virginia Woolf's *Mrs. Dalloway*, with its famous carriage episode, and *To the Lighthouse*, with its remarkably fluid "Time Passes" chapter, that unequivocally convinced me that a "cinematic"—or, as it is often called, a "visionary" point of view would be the defining sensibility of my future.

While I was discovering literature I also discovered music, another very strong influence on my approach to writing. From the beginning, even as a child, I wanted my language to *sing*. I didn't want my words to die on the page—mute and motionless and sealed in a paper and ink prison. My experience of music and, coincidentally, my discovery of the lilting works of Federico García Lorca, liberated my language from the death of the printed page. For me, every word had to evoke both image and sound. Every sentence had to have a pulse and a rhythm. Every paragraph had to ring out like a melody, with line and shape and form. The concept of the Wagnerian leitmotif found a correlative in my methods of structuring central metaphors in both my fiction and my nonfiction. The musical techniques of variation and recapitulation had an immense impact on my thinking, helping me define themes and metaphors that have been repeated in countless variations in my work. Today, when I hear fine actors read my novels aloud, there is a sense that my artistic goals have been vindicated. There truly seems to be a song hidden within my written words.

Musically speaking, two composers have always been very important in their relation to my work. I regard their manner, techniques, as well as their "folkloric" influences—even the "sound" of their music—as closely akin to the sensibility of my own work. There are a great many composers whose work I admire, but I most closely identify my own "musical" attitudes with those of Béla Bartók and Leoš Janácek—but only in terms of the music of words. Expressively, there is no doubt that the composer who awakened the *Erdegeist* in me was Alban Berg.

The thrust and the shape of my books are very well formed in my mind before I begin to write, though I leave a great deal of openness for the inevitable discoveries that occur while writing. For me, too much outlining and planning disrupts the possibilities of discovery. The only outlines I use are poetic rather than practical. For instance, I usually start my nonfiction with a table of contents, giving metaphoric names to the various chapters. These titles are ambiguous, but they are also essential guideposts to help me along the way—hinting at the book I'm trying to write. For some reason which I can't explain, I have a strong inclination to plan my nonfiction so the finished book contains exactly ten chapters.

I almost always decide on a title for my work before I begin writing, and that title greatly helps to define my intentions and the scope of a particular project. In fiction, one of the most challenging decisions—and the one that probably makes the realization of a novel possible—is the decision about point of view. Before I could begin writing *Anpao* (1977), it was essential that I fully grasped why that book had to be written in the storyteller's third-person voice. Before I could begin writing *The Sun, He Dies* (1980), it was equally essential that I fully grasped why that book had to be written in the first person, despite its exceptionally challenging historical context. Another major decision for me is whether a single point of view will shift or remain constant throughout a novel. I also must decide whether I will use a single or several different grammatical tenses.

The way words appear on the printed page is very important to me. I have done battle with several copy editors just to retain my very deliberate use of one-word paragraphs or italicized words or lines.

An author must have a unique "voice." But each book must also have its own voice. Finding one's own voice and finding the voice intrinsic to a particular project are, for me, two of the most difficult aspects of writing.

Most writers build their fiction and nonfiction on chronologies—a linear progression in which one thing "logically" follows another. Though, on some level, chronology plays a small part in my work, the real basis for narrative progression is an associative mentality rather than a chronological and linear frame of mind. I attempt to create a "flow"—an inexplicit but lucid mythic sequence. I always try to see *connections*. The tidy flow of events and data from A to Z is pointless in terms of my way of thinking. In fiction, even in nonfiction, my associative approach results in images and actions rather than tidy rows of realistic data. In my work this associative approach impels me *to find correlations, to built on connections and relationships between seemingly disparate elements.*

Some readers and critics see this process in my nonfiction as a demonstration of erudition, since I appear to combine a wide range of data. But, as I see it, the creative process is more complex than the studious manipulation of obscure information. I have the good fortune of possessing an uncommon access to my "memory banks." In other words, I have what appears to be a robust capacity for recall. For this reason, as I write, I awaken a lavish flow of half-conscious references to artistic and life experiences, a wide-ranging and detailed recall of reading experience, and the echoes of debates and conversations I have had. In short, my entire life is somehow accessible to me when I am in the frame of mind I must attain in order to write. But I don't use that capacity for recalling a vast array of experience and information to impress the reader or to assemble laundry lists of endless proofs and rebuttals. Instead, I use my memory capacity *to explore relationships—to see a wide variety of ideas and events in the context of other ideas and events—to make unlikely connections between the seeming disparity of the voluminous data in my memory.*

It was because of my very active associative memory that I made the connection, in *The Mythology of Transgression* (1997), between the American Psychiatric Association's belated removal of homosexuality from its official list of mental disorders in 1972 and, contemporaneously, the pardon of Galileo by Pope John Paul II for his "sin" of 350 years earlier, when Galileo proposed that the sun does not revolve around the earth. In this connection of disparate landmark events, it was my intention to deconstruct the absolute authority of both science and religion. Likewise, when I wished to demonstrate the fragility of another scientific "fact," I made my point by calling from memory the extraordinary Paris meteor shower of the nineteenth century that changed the opinion of the French Academy, which had previously found incredible the idea that rocks (meteors) could randomly fall from God's heaven.

This associative process is not intentional or studied. It is an intrinsic part of how my mind works. Without it, I would have no means of going from page one to page two, insofar as the mere linear story or history of a person or an idea means very little to me. I am not interested in how or why B follows A. I'm interested in the space that exists between A and B. I'm interested in the relationship between A and Q. Or, more irrationally, I'm interested in the relationship between totally disparate things that seem to have no connection. In other words, I'm very curious about the relationships that are taken for granted and the relationships that are rarely considered in our particular brand of western reality.

I'm not an "inspired writer." After destroying perhaps a half dozen novels and countless short stories written in childhood, I apprenticed in journalism under the guidance of some of America's toughest and foremost editors at *The Chicago Tribune*, *Vogue*, *Esquire*, *The New York Times*, and several other major publications. I had to be able instantaneously to call on inspiration and not sit idle waiting for it. Such discipline has given me the opportunity to be both prolific and deliberate in my career.

I am a night person. I usually work from about nine in the evening until about three or four in the morning. After work, I listen to music for a couple of hours before I go to bed at six in the morning. I awaken at about two in the afternoon.

When I'm working on a project, I decide approximately how many pages will constitute the finished work. Then I calculate how many pages I must write per day in order to keep a self-imposed deadline—which may have little to do with the deadline indicated in the publisher's contract. If during each week I manage to complete the prescribed number of pages, then I take off a day or two. If I fail to fulfill the schedule, then I work straight through until I catch up. I am pitiless about my regimen, often finishing a book long before it is supposed to be delivered to the publisher.

When I begin a book, I may work for only a brief time, perhaps half an hour each day. As the momentum of the book increases, I begin to work for three or four hours. Toward the end of a project, I may spend as much as ten to fifteen hours writing.

I have no explanation for why I work at night. The fact that it's quiet because the phone doesn't ring fails to explain my night life. Most friends know they can reach me late at night. So isolation from the world isn't a factor in my nocturnal personality. My biological clock has always made me a night person. The daytime is perfect for routine things—paying bills and writing business letters, but the mental twilight necessary for me to write doesn't begin until about nine in the evening. My energy level rises into a quick and steady flow, like a river on which I am somehow able to sail away on a current of words.

For someone who is doubtless opinionated, it's strange to realize that I don't truly know what I think about things until I talk or write about them. I am not a "contemplative" person. I'm a reactive person. I am a person whose grasp of reality results from action and interaction. Many writers use a frontal attack when they recreate the world. They search for words with which to describe events and persons precisely. I favor a sneak attack. So I look for persons and events that cannot easily be described with words. The existence of such elusive persons and events can only be described with allusion—with a twining chains of metaphors.

Long ago I realized that I can only say precisely what I mean if I manage to say what I mean as imprecisely as possible—as allusion, as metaphors that arouse images and idea and an unlimited flow of connections in the reader's mind.

When I write, especially when I am writing fiction, I experience what many writers experience—a sense of being consumed by the process. A big part of me vanishes. I think the part that vanishes is the commonsensical part that fortifies clichés, limits imagination, and restrains the daring it takes to plunge into the creative process.

I don't simply shut down my computer when I come to the end of a session of writing. When my workday (night) ends, I seem to awaken from a special kind of consciousness. But I do not for a moment believe that the creative process is a so-called "out of body" experience. To the contrary, I think the creative process is very much an *in body* experience—reminiscent of the mesmerizing bodily intensity of eating when extremely hungry, or taking part in an ecstatic sex act, or participating in the most gripping experiences of professional sport and dance. Yeats's line "How can we know the dancer from the dance?" is a familiar and powerful metaphor. At least in part, I think it perfectly describes my state of mind when I'm working.

There are writers who remain fully conscious while they write. There are writers who write for a particular audience. I find no satisfaction in such approaches to writing. Yeats's metaphor fails when a dancer consciously calculates the impact of the dance. In such situations, we can easily tell the dancer from the dance. The performer who "plays" to an audience is simply wearing a dance like a costume. But great dancers who give themselves over entirely to movement, who are absorbed and entranced by dancing, give us an entirely different experience of their performances. That experience is what I mean by an "in body" occurrence. If you haven't had such an encounter with your body—of living entirely *within* your body—then I doubt that you can know what I'm saying here, and you may also have difficulty approaching my books.

I don't have any particular audience in mind when I write. My most successful book for young adults (*Anpao*) was not written for young adults. My novel *The Sun, He Dies* was published as an adult novel, but it won the ALA "Best Books for Young Adults" award. What guides my sensibility is not the hope of pleasing a specific audience, but an effort to know when I have succeeded or when I have failed to envision and to convey what I wish to convey, when I have done something extraordinary or when, sadly, I have done something rather ordinary.

World events have an impact on my writing, but the impetus to write a new work almost always grows out of the experience of writing a prior book. In other words, one book leads to the next. Sometimes one book will lead to two or three other books, having only an indirect relationship to social issues that may be consuming the attention of the world. I am an activist about several social issues, but I keep a clear distinction between my political life and my creative life. I disagree fundamentally with people who believe that art is supposed to be in the service of political agendas. Such social concepts of the arts were proposed and enforced by Hitler, Stalin, and Senator Helms; and in every instance they resulted in nothing but defiant artists and censorship of their works or in conformist artists who produced mediocre art.

Except as a child, I have never written my books in longhand. My hand-brain relationship is hindered by the fact that my hand can't keep up with my brain. I started typing when I was in junior high school, so almost all my work was produced on a typewriter. I was one of the first writers to use word processing, and I recall that some writers were very critical of my use of a computer because they believed that the creative process was decimated by technology. It was, however, when I began to use a computer that I realized how flawed the relationship between the brain and the hand had been during all the years I spent writing books on a typewriter. There's no doubt in my mind that the computer is an instrument capable of *connecting* with the body, facilitating the ability of the body to be the direct and vital transmitter of imagination and revelation.

Because we are inclined to marvel at the literary skills of people who use computers with great facility, and who compose letters, memos, and diaries and produce unbounded amounts of E-mail, we are apt to confuse writing with Writing. I fervently believe that writing is not an elaborate display of egotism facilitated by literacy. Writing is something much larger than the self. For this reason, it seems to me that writers have got to figure out how to get out of their own way. How to stop confusing writing with Writing. The kind of writing that authors do is different from the mechanical ability to put words on a computer screen or on paper. The novel is not simply a very long letter; it is a form fundamentally different from the most exceptional of letters. When I am sometimes recognized because of media exposure during a book tour, many people tell me that they plan one day to write a novel. I often ask them why they don't compose a symphony instead. My response is not polite, but it underscores the neglected realization that knowing how to write a letter or a term paper is entirely different from knowing how to create literature. One form of writing is not necessarily better than the other, but each is essentially different, requiring an entirely different technique, sensibility, and gift.

I always write in sequence. I rarely write a scene or a chapter out of order. A book must maturate like a fetus. I can't skip around from one part of the creative process to another without losing the organic nature of the process and the metaphoric mentality that moves the book along from page to page.

I have a very clear sense of the shape and content of a book long before I start work on it. Most of my creative work goes on in my brain before I sit down at my computer. If research is involved (and it usually is involved in both fiction and nonfiction), it usually takes up about three or four months. That research, along with most of what I have read and studied in my lifetime, remains very vivid in my mind. Though my process of writing is wide open to improvisation and surprises, by the time I sit down at my computer the structure of a project is so clearly defined in my mind that it usually takes me only about six to ten weeks to write a book.

I am two different writers working in harmony. There is the one who dreams up his books as he writes them, and there is the one who is an exacting editor, thanks to a decade of learning from some of the best newspaper and magazine editors in the world. I tend to spend a session each week editing what I have written during prior work sessions. As a result, a book is scrupulously edited and revised by the time I finish the last page. There are rarely second and third drafts. In most cases, my work requires very little editing by my publisher. Often my manuscripts go directly from my editor to a copy editor who deals with matters of syntax, punctuation, etc.

Like Alban Berg, a composer whom I greatly admire and with whom I strongly identified as an adolescent, I hope to create works impelled by "an almost demented intoxication of the dramatic gesture, a hysteria in declamation swelled out to unbearable proportions" (1990, p. 3).

The modern novelist's psychological approach to characters has never been of great interest to me. Almost all the psychological workings of my characters are expressed with dramatic descriptions of the natural world. I discovered a parallel of my own approach to emotion in the Russian novel. For instance, anger is not a burning Freudian clot in the mind of a character. Instead, it is a bolt of lightning, a whirlwind, a sudden gloom that falls over the land. In my work the "hidden" domain of the psyche is released onto the landscapes of the world, where it assumes the form of all the spectacular events of nature. "The old man working in iron" appalls Anna Karenina at both the beginning and the end of Tolstoy's novel. The entire drama of my mind is played out, like the works of so many American painters, in the extraordinary power, ugliness, and beauty of nature. Even the most abstract images, even the most elaborate string of words, finally refers to that "nature" in which we are intrinsically and inextricably involved.

I slowly learned how to find the "sounds and rhythms" of the immensity of nature by listening to the music of Alban Berg and Béla Bartók, Harry Partch, and Edgard Varèse. I learned reading the writings of Federico Garciá Lorca and Virginia Woolf, William Faulkner and T. S. Eliot, Arthur Rimbaud and Miguel Angel Asturias, where time and space collide, where Garciá Lorca (1992) fell asleep "in the moonlit plaza of your forehead," (p. 87) where Woolf (1927/1955) told us about "experiences, again experiences, such as change a face in two years from a pink innocent oval to a face lean, contracted, hostile" (p. 207), and Faulkner (1987) caught the scent of a woman who "smelled like trees." (p. 17), Eliot (1952) discovered a river that "sweats oil and tar." (p. 45), Rimbaud (1968) sailed away on his "drunken boat" (p. 9), and Asturias (1968) saw "a torrent of lost memories falling like yellow rain" (p. 83).

In these artistic experiences I found the world in which I truly live and in which I hoped to find the skill of evoking extraordinary images and ideas.

I never have "writer's block." I do, however, live two distinctly different lives. When I am writing I am a very different person from the person I am when I am not writing. I suffer a nagging sense of loss when I finish a book and have difficultly making the transition from the isolation of writing back into the world where I am a rather extroverted person. I have an even more difficult time giving up the world when it's time to confine myself to my work. But I am entranced by an empty computer screen. As soon as I type any group of words, I am immediately impelled to change them, move them around, extend them. In short, when I confront a sentence I must begin to change it by writing. And so, I am off once again, sailing away into that separate and isolated world of words.

In my fiction I constantly orchestrate various leitmotifs that are important to me, though I am incapable of expressing their specific meanings in words. The recapitulation of these leitmotifs is not simply a matter of copying myself. Instead, by constantly quoting myself and others, by creating variations on themes, I am intentionally making connections between the events, characters, and ideas of one novel with the events, characters, and ideas of another novel. The most obvious example of this interplay is the fact that the love scene involving Sitko and Eric in *Kill Hole* (1992) is a paraphrase of the love scene involving Sitko's grandmother and grandfather, Amana and Jean-Pierre, in *Legend Days* (1984). But this overt "social" statement is far more direct than many other connective motifs in my novels. The motif of the moon is paraphrased countless times from book to book. The motif of the swimmer emerging from the depths is another image that often recurs in my fiction. The embodiment of death and disease in a horrific but placid character is carefully repeated in novel after novel, with each repetition adding something increasingly horrible to all the other repetitions.

Unquestionably, the theme of abandonment plays a major role in my novels.

Not only are motifs from my own work recapitulated, but I also orchestrate many images from the works of other authors: Melville, Kafka, Garciá Lorca, Woolf, Camus, and Hoffmannsthal. In *Kill Hole* the hospital nightmare sequence ("Can someone perish while he is still alive? Like a handkerchief devoured by moths?") is drawn from Hoffmannsthal's monologue for the character called Clytemnestra in Richard Strauss's opera *Elektra*. In *I Wear the Morning Star* (1986) the reunion of Sitko and his brother Reno ("Look at this signet ring that was our father's! Then tell me if I am lying!") recapitulates the dramatically and ideologically complex recognition scene between Electra and her brother Orestes in the drama of Sophocles.

I am fascinated by the process of extending mythic images by combining them into an orchestral expressiveness. I am also interested in merging mythic motifs with scientific concepts—like the description of the beginning of the cosmos in *Anpao,* which reiterates a central Blackfeet Indian creation story at the same time that it merges with the astrophysical concept of the Big Bang. There is also the sorrowful farewell to Washi spoken by his guardian, the Monkey King, in *Dark Legend* (1994) that addresses humankind's abandonment of its Darwinian animal kinship—"Look into my eyes," whispered the Monkey King. "Though you have torn yourself out of the core of my life, still you can see yourself in me. I was your father. But now I will become your captive. One day you will even forget that I am your family. You will look at me and despise what you see. Tormented by a reflection of yourself that you do not wish to know. No longer will you speak to me in the language of the animals. No longer will you see the light of the blue world in my eyes. Sorrow. Sorrow. Sorrow" (pp. 128–129).

It doesn't concern me that readers do or do not recognize these leitmotifs. The power of the motifs is found in the fact that they make connections that drive my mind and my work. They are the footprints faintly left by my imagination among the pages of my books.

In the unexpected and in the unknown we are able to imagine ourselves. What this seems to mean is that *impersonation* is the means by which we find out who we are. Culture is a living process; it is not simply a self-contained abstraction, an immovable monument that withstands all the assaults of time. Culture lives and dies. It changes and grows. It is the act of both individuals and groups of people imagining themselves, because cultural and individual identity is not innate but created and invented out of mind and spirit and emotional sensibility. And though there are a great many people who play at the arts, there are also a great many people who succeed in discovering themselves in mirrors that reflect the unexpected, the unknown, the otherness of ourselves.

Jean Cocteau told us: "The artist is a mirror. When you look into an artist you are likely to find out more about yourself than you will about him or his art."

Cocteau also said: "I am a lie that tells the truth." I want my work to be such a lie. And if people happen to catch a glimpse of the truth about themselves in my books, then I will have succeeded in making a ripple in the artist's mirror.

Note

1. This and all other references to Cocteau are from the Cocteau-Highwater correspondence. The Highwater papers. Archives Department of the New York Public Library and Archives Department of the Library of the Performing Arts at Lincoln Center.

References

Asturias, M. A. (1968). *Strong Wind.* (Trans. Gregory Bateson.) New York: Dell.

Berg, A. (1990). *Wozzeck* (Opera Guide No. 42). New York: Riverrun.

Eliot, T. S. (1952). "The Fire Sermon," in "The Waste Land." *In The Complete Poems and Plays 1909–1950.* New York: Harcourt, Brace (p. 45, lines 266–267).

Faulkner, W. (1987). *As I Lay Dying.* New York: Vintage.

García Lorca, Federico (1992). *Selected Poems* (Trans. Merryn Williams.) Glasgow, Scotland: Bell and Bain.

Highwater, J. (1977). *Anpao: An American Indian Odyssey.* New York: HarperCollins.

Highwater, J. (1980). *The Sun, He Dies: A Novel about the End of the Aztec World.* New York: Lippincott and Crowell.

Highwater, J. (1984). *Legend Days.* New York: Harper and Row.

Highwater, J. (1986). *I Wear the Morning Star.* New York: Harper and Row.

Highwater, J. (1992). *Kill Hole.* New York: Grove.

Highwater, J. (1994). *Dark Legend: A Novel.* New York: Grove.

Highwater, J. (1997). *The Mythology of Transgression: Homosexuality as Metaphor.* New York: Oxford University Press.

Rimbaud, A. (1961). *A Season in Hell and the Drunken Boat.* (Trans. Louise Verese.) New York: New Directions.

Tolstoy, L. (1978). *Anna Karenina.* Indianapolis Ind.: Bobbs-Merrill.

Woolf, V. (1927/1955). *To the Lighthouse.* New York: Harcourt Brace Jovanovich.

Yeats, W. B. (1959). "Among School Children." In *The Collected Poems of W. B. Yeats.* New York: Macmillan (pp. 212–214).

Chapter 4

The Real Work Is What We Really Do

David W. Jardine

Concentration does not mean fixity, nor a cramped arrest
or paralysis of the flow of suggestion. It means variety
and change of ideas combined into a single steady trend
moving toward a unified conclusion.
(John Dewey, 1910, p. 40)

Our present civilization is full of conflicts which imperil its future.
(Boyd Henry Bode, 1940, p. 297)

I

The whole leap depends on the slow pace at the beginning.
Anything you want to move has to start where it is,
in its stuckness. That involves erudition—
probably too much erudition. One wants to get stuck
in the history, material, the knowledge, even relish it.
I gobble everything up and it gives me appetite to go on.
Now that's the same thing I do when I write.
Deliberately spending time in the old place.
Then suddenly seeing through the old place.
(James Hillman, 1983, p. 154)

Poring over the dust of barely illuminated manuscripts—pages and pages and pages and pages. Repetitions. Thudding the dulling work of words, of passages, of dead throat corridors, of referentialities, of detailed, meticulous notitia.

I still spend time writing out the words of others by hand: guilty pleasures of too much erudition. Exacting citations. Penning underlines. A different color each time through until it gets to the point of eyeburned images of open pages and knowing by bloody heart that certain words are near the top, on the left, near the end of the chapter, redstroked like little fleshscars underwriting the writing.

How I work: working over the words of others. Guilty pleasures of reading and its plunderings. Making margin notes. Considering minutia. A hidden scholarliness. Years of ibidem and op. cits. Committing things to memory, sometimes 'til the point that I can recite every single hum of bolded passages. Like sacrificial chants, sacrificial enchantments, dying to know. Drawn into spellbound breathwork.

Sometimes all this time spent in the old place, poring over details, comes to nothing more than whirls of words that go nowhere. Sometimes, in all of this scholarly work, it is hard to hear the howls of the ancestors.

And then again, sometimes it is hard to get them to stop. Sometimes I can't read more than one sentence, hear more than one whiffy phrase caught by accident in the hallway, before the whole of things starts to "waver and tremble" (Caputo, 1987, p. 7).

A slow pace at the beginning, and then, perhaps, the leap. Some sort of bodily heat works in the work of writing: alchemical transformations of leads into golds, of dead spellings on the page into living, unexpected voices, of linear lines of texts into multifaceted bloodline splatters.

II

Transforming according to circumstances,
meet all beings as your ancestors.
Hongzhi Zhengjue (1091–1157)

The bloodlines of writing are not at all limited to human ancestries. Human ancestries are by no means the sole old places.

Here is part of the tough work of interpretive writing. Learning to meet all beings as your ancestors (Jardine, 1997b). So that each topography, each place, each thing, each corkscrew yellowy fall aspen leaf bears in its meaty heart an old place with a wisdom of its own.

So each can be the happenstance occasion of "seeing through."

Part of the hard work of interpretive writing is to find the wisdom of a place that it holds as its own; that it hides away from interlopers and their constructions; that it shares only with those who will wait, who will walk the place and learn its ways, who will show some dedication beyond the pales of reward, who will learn what (*if anything*!) this place needs from these ebullient, ever-ready words, who will give up the odd little dream of authorship for just one blessed moment.

The writing I do requires becoming caught in the grips of familiars.

Deliberately spending time in the old place and waiting for wee arrivals. Befriending the little hidden bare-teethed animal spirits that haunt a place, a topography, a topic, and liven it, speak it in little whispers, in little slow fleshpuncture pleasures in the skin.

Letting myself get written by a place. Bodily scars as the agelines in the droopy skin on the backs of my hands betray. Legibilities of having, once again, lived-through.

Sitting squat. Spending time. Waiting. Reserve. Quiet. Composure. Patience. Letting the boredom arrive. Wasting time. Doing nothing with great deliberateness. Collecting dry bones. Boredom: this is one great little demon we have banished from the discourse of authorship and expression and self-annunciation. Deliberately spending time in the old place, feeling through moist weaknesses:

> Perception of opportunities requires a sensitivity given through one's own wounds. Here, weakness provides the kind of hermetic, secret perception critical for adaptation to situations. The weak place serves to open us to what is in the air. We feel through our pores which way the wind blows. We turn with the wind; trimmers. An opportunity requires . . . a sense . . . which reveals the daimon of a situation. The daimon of a place in antiquity supposedly revealed what the place was good for, its special qualities and dangers. The daimon was thought to be a *familiaris* of the place. To know a situation, one needs to sense what lurks in it. (Hillman, 1987, p. 161)

Deliberately!

And then, perhaps, the leap. Interpretive writing crests an animate world come alive, the fearsome spittle nightflutters that belief in a single God has banished. Something deeper and more giddy and more sensuous and more pleasurable than "wanting and doing" (Gadamer, 1989, p. xxviii).

III

The sole work of La Loba is the collecting of bones.
She is known to collect and preserve especially that which
is in danger of being lost to the world. Her speciality is
said to be wolves. She creeps and crawls and sifts
through the *montanas*, mountains, and *arroyos*,
dry riverbeds, looking for wolf bones, and when
she has assembled an entire skeleton, when the last bone
is in place and the beautiful white sculpture of the creature
is laid out before her, she sits by the fire and thinks
about what song she will sing. And when she is sure,

> she stands over the *criatura*, raises her arms over it,
> and sings out. That is when the rib bones and leg bones
> of the wolf begin to flesh out and the creature becomes furred.
> La Loba sings some more, and more of the creature
> comes into being; its tail curls upward, shaggy and strong.
> And La Loba sings more and the wolf creature begins to breathe.
> And still La Loba sings so deeply that the floor of the desert shakes,
> and as she sings, the wolf opens its eyes, leaps up,
> and runs away down the canyon.
> (Pinkola Estés, 1992, pp. 27–28)

Ever since being asked to write this paper, I have been carrying it around with me—carrying the idea itself, bearing it, caring for it, and keeping it on hand as a witness to my life, my experiences, the words I hear and read, the voices that fill the air.

It has slowly become a form of noticing, a call to attention, a clarion, a lightning rod, readied and steadied in the flow of experience, causing brief currents, eddies, and flows.

The arduous gathering of bones. Placing them. Filing them away in soft folders. Little notes. Sketches of possible relations. Flashes of insight followed by disappointments. Too soon! The giddiness has fled. Waiting, again. Finding little life-breaths.

Singing, soft coos.

How I work: slowly a little familiar started sitting on my shoulder, whispering breathy of its own accord deep into the dark bloodwarm bends of outer ear cartilages.

Slowly. Not at first. It took its own sweet time peering silently into those waxy depths. It ate it up despite my impatiences. It hid when I wanted to work. It howled when I wanted to rest.

This is how I work in the most literal of senses. Right in the middle of the comfortable stuckness of too much erudition there is a moment of arrival, where something claims, something strikes, something addresses, something calls. I'm not sure what this is, but it has the feeling of a demonology. It has the feeling of a gift from an animate world.

This intimacy is contradictory: without the waiting, the gathering, the boredom, the patience, it would not arrive. But the waiting, the gathering, the boredom, the patience do not *make* it arrive. The arrival is not *produced* through "erudition." I can only cultivate my readiness for such arrivals. I can only cultivate my own composure.

Example. I've been teaching a course on interpretive inquiry and hearing the demands Ph.D. students in educational psychology are under regarding "validity" in their research. Now I might, with some

Herculean effort, be able to reconstruct exactly who said what and how and when and in what real-world, literal order, but what has actually happened—how I actually work—is that I have re-imagined this series of conversations over and over again, hallucinated, added new voices, changed partners, thieved, re-decorated, re-designed. Even with the aid of La Loba, I could not quite tell you any more the difference between the found-bones and the life that arrived afterwards. Even if I had transcribed every word of every happenstance, videoed every curvy move, the leaping up and running away outruns such work. Seeing through the old place makes it impossible to imagine any longer the "real" old place somehow "without" the seeing through.

OK. In giving up the ghost of who exactly said what, interpretive writing "testifies to the openness of the imagination" (Snyder, 1997, p. 116)—an openness that it depends upon, provokes, creates, cultivates, seeks . . . *all of these*, as contradictory as they are when brought together like this. Interpretive writing gives up all purification-ritual dreams of uncontaminated data, all the witchy stake-burnings that despise the messy, swelling life of things (Jardine, 1997a).

It fingers the contaminated wound. It festers. It is a body function.

Contradiction: Interpretive writing forgoes the belief that the life is in the bones while at the very same time it condones (in fact, requires) the collection of bones as a necessary moment in its own work. But the life leaps out past the bones. (And it often hides all the boring work of their collection: danger!) Exact citations will not save your life. You must save such citations by singing over them. (But as an aside, some interpretive work seems to sing too soon, seems to forgo the boredoms and becomes, dare I say it, a song only about the singer with no wolf leaping beyond the author's wanting and doing. Sometimes interpretive writing becomes only wound-display.)

So, thus: talk of "validity" and "invalidity" in this Graduate Class: nursevoice. "In our work we can't let ourselves be so afraid of the invalid." BANG. Sudden coalescing point. Sudden howl. The old bones of "qualitative-research-methodology-issues-of-validity-in-interpretive-work" (each hyphen little more than a dry tendon at first) suddenly leap up into life and run off of their own accord in unanticipated directions.

(An old joke I often use when Hermes starts flying like this: "I feel a paper coming on!")

All these bones I never even knew I was collecting. Hanging unawares from pierced ears and pierced lips and pierced eyelids. And then, suddenly, something rips through all that has gone on in this class, all the dry old places, tears across deadened terrains.

Now there is a new little familiar, shouldersitting, earlicking, with its own name: "Learning to Love the Invalid." (Great title, eh? I've always been good at titles.)

Another thing about how I work: at the right moment, giving proper names, giving titles. So, at some point, sketching a title page with my name and affiliation beneath becomes a vital moment in how I work. It fixes, but what it fixes is important. I don't know, as of yet, what is going to arrive under this title of "Learning to Love the Invalid," but its titular inscription, along with the inscription of my own name under it, names my commitment to carry on, to persist, to remain, to suffer the boredoms required, to find the breath and the song that these still-dry-bones desire from me.

Yes, there is still boredom required. The flash arrival of animating spirit does not mean that the work is done. Now, the work of taming, disciplining the wild just long enough for a bit of a glimpse. Interpretive writing "is a tool, a net or trap to catch and present; a sharp edge; a medicine, or a little awl that unties knots" (Gary Snyder, cited in Berry, 1983, p. 28).

And, oh, yes, by the way, the pain of watching it dying in your arms! This has just happened! The life of that "Invalidity" paper just drained away to a bony pallor, and I've laid it to rest for now, and done all the grieving I can stand, both of us weakened, exhausted, hoping that reading Bronwen Wallace's "Cancer Poems" will help in its and my revival.

"All obligations have proper names" (Caputo, 1993). But, of course, the name must be proper, it must be fitting, it must be *becoming*. This paper has had three names thus far; the first two were not right, would not do. And, well, this here thing is another little familiar I'm working: "Meditations on the pedagogies of the name" (Great title, eh?)

IV

> Learn to walk around in memory and imagination,
> smelling and hearing things.
> (Snyder, 1997, p. 109)

And then, this is how I work: literally carrying what I've written with me, printed out on paper that is handleable, foldable, inscribable, on hand. Physical presence, physical nearness, is necessary to how I work. I can stand these blue screens for just so long, and then I need something to hold, to cradle, to protect, to work, to cultivate, to pray over, a sacred object, thingness. The odd comfort of just knowing it is there, torn from the virtualities of computer pecks and physically stored in a world that is far more intractable and resistant and insistent, naggy little reminders of words made flesh.

This is how I work in the most literal of senses. A flat of folders—strange (im)plications—stuffed with bones gathered around titles and entitlements. Quotes, ideas, citations, hints, allegations, hopes, outlines, rough and ready sketches. Leaps. Only with such materialities can I then sit down with this writing, leaning back on the couch, Sunday Morning, 5 a.m., lefthanded pen, coffee, fire lit, late November, Big Chinook Arching.

Re-wording. Again. A new boredom.

Praying that I can soon set this thing free. Praying that I can soon set myself free of it.

Praying for it to run away beyond the editorialities, beyond overdone attentions, too much damn care, smotherloving.

Hating the fact that it finishes itself when it is damn well ready.

Enough!

But there is a lie here. I might as well admit it. I have often thought of keeping each version of a particular paper I am writing, so that perhaps, in the small edits and editions and drafts, in the little gaps and differences, perhaps something could be glimpsed about how I work that final versions cover over. Some hope that underlying the work of leaping wolves, some "direct" evidence of the bones and their assemblages might be somehow revelatory.

It never seems to turn out that way. Because here we are. This piece on how I work has been, well, worked. It therefore harbors its own falsities and deceptions. It protects its own young and refuses the outing desired.

"The real work is what we really do" (Snyder, 1990). But the real work was already done before the talk of real work began, here, in this work of "capture and present."

But then again, that's how I work.

References

Berry, W. (1977). *The Unsettling of America*. San Francisco: Sierra Club.

Berry, W. (1983). *Standing by Words*. San Francisco: North Point.

Caputo, J. (1987). *Radical Hermeneutics*. Bloomington: Indiana University Press.

Caputo, J. (1993). *Against Ethics*. Bloomington: Indiana University Press.

Gadamer, H. (1989). *Truth and Method*. New York: Continuum.

Hillman, J. (1983). *Inter views*. Dallas: Spring.

Hillman, J. (1987). *Puer Papers*. Dallas: Spring.

Hongzhi. Z. (1991). *Cultivating the Empty Field: The Silent Illumination of Zen Master Hongzhi*. San Francisco: North Point.

Jardine, D. (1997a). "Their Bodies Swelling with Messy Secrets." *Action Research as a Living Practice*. (Eds. T. Carson and D. Sumara.) New York: Peter Lang (pp. 161–166).

Jardine, D. (1997b) "All Beings Are Your Ancestors": A Bear Sutra on Ecology, Buddhism and pedagogy." *The Trumpeter: A Journal of Ecosophy*. vol. 14, no. 3 (pp. 122–123).

Pinkola Estés, C. (1992). *Women Who Run with the Wolves*. New York: Ballantine.

Snyder, G. (1990). *The Real Work*. New York: New Directions.

Snyder, G. (1997). "Gary Snyder: The Art of Poetry LXXIV." *Paris Review*, vol. 141 (pp. 89–118).

Chapter 5

On Writing My Love Child

Denise Taliaferro

Interest in knowledge for the sake of knowledge,
in thinking for the sake of the free play of thought,
is necessary then to emancipation of practical life
—to make it rich and progressive.
(John Dewey, 1910, p. 138)

Education, therefore, must devote itself to the task
of revealing the inequity, the needlessness,
the brutality of existing conditions.
(Boyd Henry Bode, 1940, p. 294)

My Love Child

Recently, I put aside my writing to take a trip up north. While I was away I acted like any proud but weary mother. I talked a lot about my precious little one—about the amazement and frustration that comes with the birth of a little one. I even pulled out snapshots, as parents usually do, to share with old strangers and new acquaintances the awkward beauty of my four-month-old. And of course, I waited and looked intently for their reactions as I talked up my pride and joy while always contemplating the possibility that my onlookers might not see the same beauty in my baby. You know, you cannot always go by what they say—"Oh what a gorgeous baby!"—because they may very well be thinking—"What an uuugly thang that is."

On my return trip, an older lady sitting in the seat next to me asked if I was glad to be going home. I responded excitedly, "Yes, I miss my baby." She flashed a big smile and said, "Oh, so you have a little one?" I smiled back, realizing the impression I had given her, and said, "Well, why, yes I do. I am actually writing my dissertation." It dawned on me then that although my baby's snapshots were not the usual 5 by 7 but 8 ½ by 11 and she's weighed in pages, not pounds, I still have a very strong motherly love for her and a commitment to her.

At this time in my life, when many of my friends are getting married and raising children, I find myself raising/writing a dissertation. Sometimes when I am flipping through pictures with them, listening to funny baby stories or helping them plan their special day, I feel a little sad inside, wishing I could be filled with that kind of excitement and glow. The other day, I shared this bit of sadness with a close friend, who said to me with an envious look, "Denise, anyone who knows you knows that your passion, your excitement, your glow is evident when you talk about your work, your writing, your teaching." She's absolutely right. I do feel an intense passion for and excitement about my work. "But that's different, I'm sure, from the feelings that are evoked by motherhood and being a wife," I quickly surmised. "Maybe, maybe not," she said, "it's all in the way you look at it." She's absolutely right, again. So here, I have decided to look differently at my work, my writing. I have opted to release my imagination and envision what, in this world, has often been impossible for Black women to confess or profess—I love my work, my writing, as I imagine I would love my child. While I have often heard people talk about being "married" to their work, I am less inclined to think of my writing that way. Rather, my relationship to my writing is less like my love for a man and more like the love I imagine I would have for my child, my daughter child.

In an article entitled "Black Women Intellectuals," bell hooks (1996) discusses how representations of Black womanhood through stereotypical mammy images have perpetuated a cultural thinking that imposes on sisters a caretaker role which suggests that we are "innately more capable of caring for others." As she goes on to point out, we even feel a responsibility to be the "all nurturing breast." hooks recognizes that:

> This thinking is often reinforced in Black communities by religious teaching emphasizing the necessity of selfless service as the highest expression of Christian charity. Collectively, many Black women internalize the idea that they should serve, that they should always be available to meet the need of someone else whether they want to or not. (p. 363)

In her analysis, hooks proposes that such thinking not only tends to de-emphasize the intellectual pursuits of Black women but also inhibits many Black women from engaging in intellectual work. I would be remiss if I did not admit that I have internalized the "all-nurturing breast," which has inevitably caused me to question my love for the intellectual work I do, the most important of which is, at this moment, writing my dissertation. However, this piece of writing on writing my dissertation is an attempt to reconsider the relationship of the mammy image to intellectual work. I do this not by shedding my caretaker role but by claiming it as the ontological perspective from which I write—birthing, raising, and loving my work, my love child.

In *Bitter Milk*, Madeleine Grumet (1988) looks back on the origins of theory and notes that:

> Theory was the perception and expression of the order that bonded society to nature, for once the natural laws of the heavens were observed and understood through theory, they would be replicated in the development and comportment of the individual and in the order and harmony of the polis. (p. 184)

From a feminist perspective, Grumet contends that we need to reclaim ourselves from this entrapment in the natural order of things by thinking back through our mothers: "When women think back through our mothers we look past the natural order expressed in physics, astronomy, biology, our second nature, to the first nature that male identity and male science have repressed" (p. 184). In this paper, I intend to share my writing as a process of thinking back through my mothers, who symbolize, for me, a particular ontology. Their being has signified not only a gendered knowing but a particular raced and cultured knowing which together implicate the mammy image. So I look back not only for that which has been repressed by male identity but also for that which has been repressed by the normativity (the natural order) of whiteness.

It is important to me that I express to you that writing my dissertation is not even mostly about putting words on the page, getting the punctuation right, or following a rational format. It is, for me, like a child, a project that comes from within: one that is shaped and nurtured by the past in the present moment; one in which I hope to see, to impart, the best of myself and those before me. It is an ever-peaking culmination, not in spite of but because of its constant contradictions—you know the way you want your child to "fit in" but at the same time you claim her as "special." As an African-American, a woman, and an educator, I write from within and against a tradition of women who have been "innate caretakers" not in spite of but because of who they are. While the mammy myth may, at times, make me feel as though I need to put aside my writing, my intellectual pursuit, my theoretical musings for the practical benefit of my people, so to speak, there are the other times when I am acutely able to recognize the mammy at work in my writing, nurturing not only myself but those about whom, for whom, and with whom I write.

In contemplating the work of African-American women, I have imagined four ontological aspects that reflect our being and thus influence our epistemology and our methodology of expression. First, we are outsiders within. Being both Black and female, we experience being both a part of and simultaneously not a part of raced and gendered groups. Second, because we have been marginalized as women and as Black and perhaps even as poor, where we have been, by the status quo, ignored or shut out, we have had to cultivate the wild or the "inner will to rebel." Third, in society in general and in the academy in particular, both our womanness and our blackness have been abused; we have had to express, to affirm a be-loving of ourselves and our people. Fourth, somewhere between gaining access and acceptance in society and at the same time resisting its imposition, we make do. My writing—process and product—is an expression of these ontological aspects; it is my thinking back through my mothers in an effort to raise (write) my daughter (my dissertation, my love child).

Writing the Outsider Within

For Black women, I think it is appropriate to say that there is a doubling of DuBois's double-consciousness, subversions between black and white, male and female. Our blackness and our femaleness have sometimes been recognized as a "double jeopardy" (Higginbotham, 1990) or a "peculiar burden" (Guy-Sheftall, 1990); essentially, we suffer for both our race and our gender. However, this double jeopardy, so to speak, not only burdens us but also allows us a predisposition for articulating alternative ways of being and making connections between marginal and seemingly oppositional positionalities. Although we have often been criticized for choosing between racial solidarity and feminist solidarity (Guy-Sheftall, 1990), from another perspective, it is impossible to choose, so we navigate the in-between as necessary. We are, as Patricia Collins (1990) theorizes, outsiders within. Collins explains how the historical place of the Black woman domestic worker in the white family represents this peculiar marginality:

> As outsiders within, Black women have a distinct view of the contradictions between the dominant group's actions and ideologies . . . African-American women question the contradictions between ideologies of womanhood and Black women's devalued status. If women are allegedly passive and fragile, then why are Black women treated as "mules" and assigned heavy cleaning chores? With no compelling explanations offered by a viable culture of resistance, the angle of vision created by being a devalued worker could easily be turned inward, leading to internalized oppression. But the presence and legacy of struggle suggests that African American culture generally and Black women's culture in particular provide alternative interpretations. (p. 12)

While Collins suggests that our consciousness is shaped by this experience of being both a part of and simultaneously not a part of a group, Boyce-Davies (1994) explains how such a position allows us only to "go a piece of the way" with the theories conceptualized outside of our own realities. In other words, we engage in a tradition of "critical relationality," which means "negotiating, articulating, and interrogating simultaneously a variety of resistant discourses relationally and depending on context, historical and political circumstances" (p. 47).

My dissertation is a theoretical reflection on the practical performances of African-American identity and its relationship to education. In topic, content, and style, I write as an outsider within. As a Black academic in a majority White institution, I am an outsider within. As a woman in a male-defined institution—the academy—I am an outsider within. As a Black person in academia, I am also sometimes an outsider within many Black communities. Intellectual pursuits for a Black person, as Cornel West (1994) notes, marginalize that person in and to the Black community. As a Black researcher looking at Black identity as cultural performance, I am still an outsider within. In looking at others perform their identity around the idea of blackness, in some sense, I become a stranger to my culture. All of these outsiders within me frame my work in a layering of the autobiographical double-consciousness (Deck, 1990)—myself Black and not, woman and not, academic and not, researcher and not. While this is, on many days, a wonderful, wonderful way to be inside out and outside in, navigating the spaces inbetween, it is difficult to avoid contradictions. I often find myself waking in a cold sweat of confusion in the middle of the night, asking, "Do I really know what in hell I am talking about?" I find myself crumbling between the double-bind (Edgerton, 1996): I am this but don't call me that. I said this but it doesn't mean that. I can calm down again only when I think back to my own momma saying: "Denise, just be yourself and everything will be okay." Of course that calm is only temporary until I realize that I, unavoidably, am and my child will be the outsider within.

Writing Wild

In the essay "Revolutionary Black Women," bell hooks (1992) talks about cultivating the wild, which is, as she states, "the metaphoric expression of the inner will to rebel, to move against the grain, to be out of one's place. It is the expression of radical black female subjectivity." By virtue of the fact that Black women have typically been marginal to both Black history and women's history, for our own survival literally and representationally we have had to be out of our place, to challenge the status quo. Our voices and experiences are the ruptures in seamless sameness. Petra Munro (1998) notes that history as we know it limits contradiction, multiplicity, and difference. As the embodiment of contradiction, multiplicity, and difference in white male-dominated discourses of rationality, the Black woman is chaos; she is wild. And though "wild" may invoke images of the vicious, untamed, and unruly, it is actually incredibly nurturing. It is the way we say, "I am a Black woman" and "We are Black people," or, in the words of young street poets, "You better recognize." To be wild is to look beyond the evidence, to make possible what has been impossible. To be wild, in some sense, is not rational. Historically, rationality has been based on theories of objectivity, binary oppositions, absolutes, and authority, all of which have excluded and consequently named the irrational, the wild. Alice Walker's Shug Avery, Toni Morrison's Sula, and Ntozaki Shange's colored girls are all representations of writing wild, against the grain, out of place.

I want very much for my love child to be wild. The rationality of content and structure is the second knowing that can too often repress the first—the spirit of imagination and creativity. I imagine and create the content of my child's character to agitate hegemony. My writing is meant to disrupt, to challenge that which is taken-for-granted as rational, traditional, the way things are "suppose" to be or have always been. My starting point, for instance, is not the voice of authority—white, male, academic authority. In writing about African-American identity as an African-American scholar, I seek the original voice in the I/We of Black perspectives. The I/We of Black voices speaks against and within the grain of the dominant European intellectual tradition. It reflects ontologically the importance of the individual/group dialectic in Black discourses, which is of course out of step with the lone-centered self of western philosophy. My child rests not on validation by the other but on the significance of self actualization, awareness, and critique. I write against the grain of a tradition that has "othered" these voices (Bell, 1997; Gordon, 1994; Outlaw, 1983; Stanfield, 1995). The African-American theorist Beverly Gordon (1994) recognizes that the Black voice has epitomized "otherness" a fringe dweller not quite believable or adequate—and she insists on the importance of viewing the Black voice as "the voice" rather than the "other voice" of its own experience:

> African-American scholars have illuminated and analyzed from an African-American perspective the internal structure of the black community, the effects on African-Americans within their subordinate position in the larger society, and various forms of resistance which African-Americans have developed in order to survive—and advance—in the capitalist and racist society in which they find themselves. It is this kind of self-knowledge that emancipates people. African-Americans must learn their own seldom-explored history, because their own history makes the dominant society's "commonsense" interpretive knowledge problematic. Exploring their own history also provides the opportunity for African-Americans to critique the dominant culture's world view, and to formulate their own cultural and epistemological statements. Furthermore, we can trace in the evolution of black scholarship the evolution of a uniquely African-American cultural mode of rationality. (1993, p. 267)

My writing, in this vein, is a constant effort at centering Black voices, and a difficult task it is. Always a bit panicky about my own "miseducation" (Woodson, 1933) or historical discontinuity (Cruse, 1967), I am forever searching for Black sources and forever contemplating how to place them strategically at the center of my work. And for sure, difficult decisions arise—those that point not only to the grammatical considerations of dissertation writing but to the political ones as well. So sometimes I must choose, for instance, to cite the less well-known Black intellectual Amilcar Cabral as my original voice on culture and liberation rather than the better known philosophy of, say, Paulo Freire. At other times I must say, "Like bell hooks, Peter McLaren agrees," rather than the opposite. I read and re-read, I write and re-write, wildly, I might add until I have centered the I/We of Black perspectives.

But do you know what's really wild about my child, or should I say, "wile 'bout mah chile?" Her black voice is represented not only in content, but in style as well. She's about talkin' back, as bell hooks (1989) would say, or testifyin', as Geneva Smitherman (1977) would say, or soul speaking, as I like to say. I raise her in narrative rhythms and refine her in theoretical reflections. My wild child switches codes—moving among storytelling, soul speaking, and academic theoretical rhetoric. I assert my radical subjectivity by moving, writing, being against the grain, problematizing the capacity of the standards of dissertation writing—i.e., proper English and rational (objective) argumentation—to speak fully the experiences of blackness. When I disrupt the standard, I think of how June Jordan describes our (Black) language. Because our culture has been threatened by annihilation and blurred by assimilation, Jordan asserts that:

> our language is a system constructed by people constantly needing to insist that we exist, that we are present. Our language devolves from a culture that abhors all abstraction, or anything tending to obscure or delete the act of the human being who is here and now/the truth of the person who is speaking and listening. (p. 129)

Of course this creative navigation—code switching—makes both Adrienne Rich's dilemma (It is the oppressors' language yet I must use it to talk to you) and Audre Lorde's affirmation (We cannot use the master's tools to bring down the master's house) central and consistent considerations in my writing process. There certainly is always tension between wanting to raise a wild child and also wanting that child to be accepted and understood on some level. Another wake-up call—cold sweat during midnight proofreading—is my child too wild? Momma says, "Denise, stand up for what you believe in." And I do until the next proofreading panic.

Writing in Love

What has love got to do with it? Well, I suppose that depends on how one may theorize love. There are of course all kinds of love, but again the love I feel and express for my work is the love I imagine a mother would have for a child. When I think about the love I have for my work, my child, I reflect on how my mothers—my birth one, my ancestral ones, my intellectual ones—loved and still love me and what they have both sacrificed and gained in the process. Unquestionably, their love is not confined to the emotional; it is, in its most powerful form, action. Their love, I think, is best captured in Susan Huddleston Edgerton's discussion of love in the margins:

> I write about a problem that has no solution other than love—and that is no solution because it resists the framework that anything called a "solution" requires. Not being "rational," love is well suited for dealing with the call to abandon the privileging of certain rationalist discourses. (1996, p. 63)

In an intellectual context, then, my mothers nurture me, take care of me, love me through the work that they do to disrupt, to rebel against the discourses that invisible-ize us and make me impossible. It is the mother tongue—the love words and ideas of Anna J. Cooper, Mary Church Terrell, Ida B. Wells, Assta Sharkur, Angela Davis, bell hooks, Michelle Wallace, June Jordan, Nikki Giovanni, Sonia Sanchez, Toni Morrison, and so many more—that forges, that creates the spaces of my existence by challenging the paradigms that have either made me invisible or confined me to degrading constructions.

Edgerton speaks of love not only as a process of deconstruction, but also as a process that requires listening: "This love I speak of is also listening—listening on many perceptual levels. Listening, as a part of language, is itself marginalized by so much philosophical writing that privileges the saying aspects of language" (p. 63). My mothers have listened to me. They have heard my cry for respect and recognition for who I am, just as I am. It is through their work that I know they have listened and heard. Momma hooks (1992) says, "Being intellectual is a radical and revolutionary feat for you." Momma Sanchez (1971) says, "Be who you be." Momma Davis (1975) says, "Liberation not only requires political action but intellectual pursuit as well." Now I must respond—what do my mothers expect of me?

What has love got to do with it? Everything! I could not imagine taking on such a monumental task as writing a dissertation without having love for the process of writing, which necessitates concentrated and continuous thinking, theorizing, organizing, creating, questioning, and problematizing, and cycles of redoing everything. Thus, when I say I love my work as I would love my child, I do not mean, for the most part, the mushy feelings of warm fuzzy love. When I say love, I am referring to the sum total of all the feelings—excitement, frustration, fear, disappointment, wonder, satisfaction, confusion, anger—and all the actions such as writing, rewriting, sharing, thinking, rethinking, organizing, reorganizing, reading, and proofreading, that define my relationship to my work, my love child. Although very important, this is only part of the love I have for my work. The other part of my love makes the process part possible—the love I have for my subject.

As I mentioned previously, I am writing about African-American identity and its relationship to the concept of education as a path toward liberation. In this endeavor, I use Black scholarship for my theoretical foundations, but I also include the theorizing of the African-American students, teachers, and other scholars whom I encounter on a daily basis—I listen to what they believe, perceive, conceive about who they are in the context of "we" and how that affects their ideas about education for liberation. This project, for several reasons, is an act of love, love in the margins. First, it is an act of self-love. My writing is a journey to self-understanding through the context of my culture, which affects both how I write and what I write. Second, it is an act of love for African-American people in general and the young in particular. In this way it affirms and nurtures the peculiarities and nuances of blackness and what that means in the I/We context. Third, it is an act of love in the sense that I hope to create even more possibilities for others to listen, to understand the complexity of blackness in representation (image) and presentation (performance). I turn again to the theorizing of bell hooks (1992), who confirms the importance of loving blackness as political resistance:

> Collectively, black people and our allies in struggle are empowered when we practice self-love as a revolutionary intervention that undermines practices of domination. Loving blackness as political resistance transforms our ways of looking and being, and thus creates the conditions necessary for us to move against the forces of domination and death and reclaim black life. (p. 20)

Ultimately, writing in love is the alpha and the omega in my process. I literally love writing it because I have such great love for what and whom I am writing about and the people for whom I write. And this love, like that of a mother for her child, is a great cyclone of emotions spun into action, respun into more intense emotions, and so on. And of course this love leaves me, at times, confused and frustrated, but that is all a part of the nurturing and growing of ideas. Just as I suspect my child will at times, my work, my dissertation, gets on my last nerve. I retreat and let my baby sit for a while. Then I go at it again.

Making Do in a Room of One's Own

When Virginia Woolf recommended a room of one's own as a necessary requirement for women writing, she was speaking, I presume, both literally and metaphorically. Literally, we need space and time alone to read, write, and think. Metaphorically, we need to write in ways that validate our process and product without remaining, in Grumet's image, trapped by the natural order of things. However, when we intersect these gender analyses with the specificities of race and culture, I wonder what Virginia would require and recommend if she were Black—culturally and racially?

What may a room of one's own mean to a Black woman writing? In Alice Walker's *In Search of Our Mothers' Gardens,* Walker highlights the work of Buchi Emecheta (1975), an African author who writes because of, not in spite of, her children. The protagonist in Emecheta's *Second-Class Citizen* is an Ibo woman named Adah who integrates her profession as writer into her role as mother/worker, and thus requires that her room be filled with the chatter of her children—for whom she lives and writes. Reading this essay made me think of the cultural situatedness of having a room of one's own. Growing up, I never really had a room of my own; I had a sister and two brothers and plenty of cousins, but I nevertheless successfully did homework and wrote poetry, plays, and short stories. My mother, also a wonderful poet, wrote with our noise and our noisy requests for any little thing to get her attention. I thought about this again when I watched Nikki Giovanni and Sonia Sanchez on Black Entertainment Television. Both talked about the relationship between their writing and their children. Alice Walker and June Jordan have also written essays that discuss the importance to their writing of their role as mother. Repeatedly, I heard these women put their roles as caretakers, as mothers, at the center of their work, naming it as a special kind of inspiration. Another common and significant aspect of the work of these particular women is that it is written in the love of and for the love of Black people. So, in this sense, they not only mother their own children but mother a people. I imagine, then, that a room of one's own for these women might not always mean solitude—not literally or metaphorically. They hear the voices of many generations of oppressed people—men and women and children—calling them to write, committing them to write wild, and making them responsible for the nurturing of a people. For these Black women, self-actualization happens through their relationships with family and community. Perhaps having a room of one's own is about being, as Dara Abubakari (1972) once said, liberated in our own minds, making do in the context of our own lives. And many times we see that liberation as a process of self-seeking through self-giving, mother-loving.

I finally do have a room of my own, but I do not associate it with solitude, at least not for the purposes of my writing. I have furnished it with plenty of love for my work, my child, which is only an extension of my love for myself and Black people in general. I have pictures and music—R&B, Jazz, and Hip Hop—to help me write. I have my love words and ideas all over the walls. I have books and tapes, but most importantly I have the idea that I am never writing alone, whether I turn to the words of a Black scholar or to the words of my mother speaking ever so clearly in my head or to the rancor of debate among my students and colleagues playing and replaying in my head. Just as I don't associate it with solitude in a literal sense, nor do I in a metaphorical sense. For me as a Black woman, my own room is truly about being liberated in my own mind. And my idea of liberation does not begin or end with me; it simply passes through me by virtue of a great many Black people—sisters and brothers. Then, I pass it on through my child, in my work.

References

Abubakari, D. (1972). "The Black Woman is Liberated in Her Own Mind." In *Black Women in White America.* (Ed. G. Lerner.) New York: Vintage (pp. 585–587).

Bell, D. (1997). "Racism Remains the Primary Obstacle Facing African Americans." In *African Americans, Opposing viewpoints*, (Ed. W. Dudley.) San Diego, Calif.: Greenhaven (pp. 269–278).

Boyce-Davies, C. (1994). *Black Women Writing and Identity: Migrations of the Subject.* New York: Routledge.

Collins, P. (1990). *Black Feminist Thought: Knowledge, Consciousness, and the Politics of Empowerment.* New York: Routledge.

Cruse, H. (1967). *The Crisis of the Negro Intellectual.* New York: Morrow.

Davis, A. (1975). *Angela Davis: An Autobiography.* New York: Bantam.

Deck, A. (1990). "Autoethnography: Zora Neale Hurston, Noni Jabavu, and Cross-Disciplinary Discourse." *Black America Literature Forum, vol. 24,* (pp. 237–256).

Edgerton, S. H. (1996). *Translating the Curriculum: Multiculturalism into Cultural Studies.* New York: Routledge.

Emecheta, B. (1975). *Second-Class Citizen.* New York: Braziller.

Gordon, B. (1993). "Toward emancipation in citizenship education: The case for African American cultural knowledge." In *Understanding Curriculum as Racial Text.* (Ed. L. Castenell and W. Pinar). Albany: State University of New York Press (pp. 263–284).

Gordon, B. (1994). "African-American Cultural Knowledge and Liberatory Education: Dilemmas, Problems, and Potentials in Postmodern American Society." In *Too Much Schooling, Too Little Education: A Paradox of Black Life in White Societies.* (Ed. M. Shujaa). Trenton, N.J.: Africa World Press (pp. 57–80).

Grumet, M. (1988). *Bitter Milk: Women and Teaching.* Amherst: University of Massachusetts Press.

Guy-Sheftall, B. (1990). *Daughters of Sorrow.* New York: Carlson.

Higginbotham, E. (1990). "Beyond the Sound of Silence: Afro-American Women in History." In *Black Women's History: Theory and Practice,* (Ed. D. Clark.) New York: Carlson (pp. 175–192).

hooks, b. (1989). *Talking Back: Thinking Feminist, Thinking Black*. Boston, Mass.: South End.

hooks, b. (1992). "Revolutionary Black Women." In *Black Looks: Race and Representation*. (Ed. b. hooks.) Boston, Mass.: South End (pp. 41–60).

hooks, b. (1996). "Black Women Intellectuals." In *Racial and Ethnic Diversity in Higher Education*, (Eds. C. Sotello, V. Turner, M. Garciá, A. Nora, L. Rendon). Needham Heights, Mass.: Simon and Schuster (pp. 263–294).

Jordan, J. (1985). *On Call*. Boston, Mass: South End.

Munro, P. (1998). "Engendering Curriculum History." In *Curriculum: Toward New Identities*, (Ed. W. Pinar.) New York: Garland (pp. 263–294).

Outlaw, L. (1983). "Philosophy, Hermeneutics, Social-Political Theory: Critical Thought in the Interest of African-Americans." In *Philosophy Born of Struggle*. (Ed. L. Harris.) Dubuque, Iowa: Kendall/Hunt (pp. 60–88).

Sanchez, S. (1971). *A Sun Woman for All Seasons Reads Her Poetry*. New York: Folkways Records.

Smitherman, G. (1977). *Talkin' and Testifyin': The Language of Black America*. Boston: Houghton Mifflin.

Stanfield, J. (1995). "Ethnic Modeling in Qualitative Research." In *Handbook of Research on Multicultural Education*. (Eds. J. Banks and C. Banks). New York: Macmillan (pp. 175–188).

Walker, A. (1984). *In Search of Our Mothers' Gardens*. Orlando, Fla: Harcourt Brace Jovanovich.

West, C. (1994). "Dilemmas of a Black intellectual." *Journal of Blacks in Higher Education* (pp. 59–67). vol. 2.

Woodson, C. (1933/1996). *The Mis-Education of the Negro*. New York: Africa World Press.

Woolf, V. (1986). *The Essays of Virginia Woolf*. London: Hogarth.

Chapter 6

Inventing a More Interesting Subject

Dennis J. Sumara and Brent Davis

> The aim of education is precisely to develop intelligence of this independent and effective type—a disciplined mind.
> (John Dewey, 1910, p. 63)

> Education gives a person a new world to live in.
> (Boyd Henry Bode, 1940, p. 146)

For us, the search for knowledge is a search for identity.

Of course, this is hardly news. Literary workers have always known this. In the latter part of her life, for example, Margaret Laurence suggested that her novels were necessary interpretations of her lived experiences (see King, 1997). While she did not claim to write autobiographically, the writing out of characters in imagined situations could not, for Laurence, be considered apart from her involvement in her own psyche.

As Shoshana Felman (in Felman and Laub, 1992) has explained, because all writing is a form of testimony, the marking of personal experience with writing creates experience that can be witnessed by others besides the writer. And, significantly, because the act of writing in itself contributes to the making of identity, what is witnessed by the writer is the creation of a situation and a character that are known and invented only through the writing. The work of writing, then, is always the work of bearing witness.

Other literary workers, namely critics and reviewers, have suggested that their involvement with literary forms is also an event of autobiographical interpretation. In her memoir *Vertigo*, for example, Louise De Salvo (1996) explains how literary engagement provided her with a needed imaginary and interpretive structure. For her, literary engagement became a place to invent an identity that escaped the experience of living with a family that was not of her making. Later, as a Virginia Woolf scholar, literary and biographical work continued to assist her with the process of complicating her identity. As De Salvo suggests: "It has been easier for me to understand my own life by first trying to understand someone else's" (p. 43).

Mary Aswell Doll (1995) has commented similarly about years of reading and teaching Virginia Woolf's (1955) *To the Lighthouse*: "The reason I will never not teach this book . . . is that I never understand it enough" (p. 15). If involvement with a literary text, with writing, and with students are all considered interrelational, then acts of interpretation are always personal. Reading a text, writing one, studying one (alone or with others) is a kind of traveling—a traveling where the destination is oftentimes unexpected. Never being able to understand the text enough may be interpreted as never understanding oneself enough. And if identity is considered an ongoing process rather than an achievement, interpretive work is necessary to the making of the subject.

In recent years, curriculum theorists have come to understand this. Linking autobiographical interpretation to studies of curriculum, William Pinar and Madeleine Grumet (1976) have shown how the acts of remembering, representing, and interpreting personal experience function to help the writer gain awareness of her or his own situation, history, and possibilities. Marking these acts of autobiographical exegesis and interpretation as a form of theorizing, Pinar (1994) and Grumet (1988) further showed that, because identity is a complex relation, autobiographical representation is always the study of culture. As well, they and other curriculum theorists, such as Janet Miller (1990) and Paula Salvio (1990), have suggested that the study of *any* phenomenon is always already a study of one's involvement in that phenomenon.

Paying attention to the way in which literary and other cultural works create aesthetic objects—in literature (Sumara, 1996a), in mathematics (Davis, 1996), in curriculum theory (Sumara and Davis, 1997)—has, for us, been an ongoing area of study and interest. Because we believe that what one is able to know and accomplish depends largely on how one learns to perceive, our studies of curriculum and cognition have been supported by a study of our own habits of mind and habits of learning. Rather than studying human cognition as an activity that is applied to curriculum and culture making, we have endeavored to develop an "enactivist" theory of cognition that understands the inextricability of the biological, the phenomenological, and the ecological (Davis and Sumara, 1997). For us, then, the study of cognition has, in large part, included the study of studying, specifically framed by the questions: How do humans learn? What are the conditions of our learning? What are the practices? What theories guide thinking and our practices of thinking?

For the remainder of this essay we will attempt, briefly, to accomplish two tasks. First, we will provide some autobiographical description and interpretation of each of our formative years, suggesting that particular childhood conditions, in part, created the possibility to accomplish creative work as adults. Second, we will specifically outline the ways in which the production of curriculum theory and the conditions of its production are cospecified for us, focusing particularly on the present conditions of our work.

Learning Estrangement

> I really am an aberration. I was always a lonely child
> —(boo hoo—poor me) but I see suddenly that
> I *am* very strange & odd. How can one live for 60 years
> & feel fairly normal when one *isn't*?
> (Margaret Laurence, quoted in King, 1997, p. 382)

While differing in particulars, the biographical and autobiographical studies of persons known for the production of creative work are unanimous on one count: school was not a place where one learned to do this work. In fact, because schools are overly concerned with the production of what is known rather than what might be known, they are likely to squash the possibility of invention. It is, perhaps, only the interstices of schooling, those spaces not noticed by adults but significant to children, that become locations for the creation of insight. As John Willinsky (1997) suggests, it was these unacknowledged spaces that, in part, shaped his capacity for thinking otherwise. Explaining his habit of playing with a paper clip that happened to be on his desk during a tedious afternoon of school, Willinsky reveals how imagining the possibilities for this object—as a bridge across an inkwell, or as a stick figure, for example—was part of the creation of a structure of thinking that has become useful in his current intellectual work:

> What even the most acute of my teachers failed to recognize was that I was actually, I can see now, in training for work that now stands me in good stead;

> I was apprenticing methodologically in a form of critical inquiry. I was getting the knack of playing with a term or label, getting a feel for how it sat and how it aligned itself, and worked against itself. (p. 329)

We recall similar experiences—prolonged engagement with fantasy, and imagining; and, particularly, aloneness and isolation. Because, as Felman and Laub (1992) suggest, identity must be represented in order to be known, children who spend time in isolation learn to accomplish this task outside the known structures used by adults. Further, because solitary time requires interpretation, children learn to bear witness to their own experience, thus becoming, in some ways, estranged from it enough to make it more interesting to itself. Here are snippets of what we remember of our early years:

Dennis: *Because I was a fat child, schooling was something to be endured. Any learning that mattered to me, for the most part, occurred through my involvement with fiction—armloads of books borrowed from the public library. It was through these literary relations that habits of mind, which continue to serve me well, were developed: I could fall in love with a literary character. I could, neatly, abandon my love affair. I could imagine the possibility of living, say, in New York City instead of Lethbridge, Alberta. I could notice the internal lives of characters. Specifically, I could bring my reading life into other (usually less satisfactory) lived experiences and learn that these strange juxtapositions could yield insight, direction, possibility.*

But, of course, involvement with text is not a sufficient condition for transformation: identification and interpretation are required. In many instances, the life of the child, suffused as it is with adult structures, does not present conditions for this needed work to be accomplished. When visiting elementary schools, in my role as professor of teacher education, I notice, for example, that every moment of a child's life is planned and structured by adults. "Where can children go to be alone?" I ask. "Must they be involved in activities of the teacher's making at all times?" I wonder. "Might daydreaming and thinking count as events of learning?" I suggest. Of course, because I have some authority, I do receive answers, but none that strike me as satisfactory. For it seems to me that what I found necessary in my early years—time alone, freedom to invent things to do and to think about, places to go where I might not be under adult surveillance—are not generally available for most children.

Because my parents were immigrants who raised a child during a time when Canada's social service net did not include money for child care, I spent many hours alone, before and after school, while my parents worked. It was during these hours that I learned how to have a relationship with a thought, how to live with a book, how to imagine a life without adults. And, because I was, indeed, a very fat child, one who, of course, lived with daily abuse from other children and from adults, I learned that to be alone could be a lovely time to think about revenge. I created elaborate plots for the painful and final destruction of my enemies, including plans that could be fulfilled only when I had become a fully achieved and influential adult.

My childhood world was, for hours each day, lived outside the "real" world imposed by adult teachers and caregivers. While many might consider my childhood experiences damaging, they were, I believe, productive: benign neglect gave me time to structure my own thinking and to develop a complex subjectivity that departed from those of my parents' and teachers' making. In learning to form, for example, enduring relationships with literary characters, I included in my repertoire of memory and identification traits that were unknown to adults I knew. Like Margaret Laurence, I spent considerable time alone, yet I do not recall feeling lonely.

***Brent:** I grew up in a small community in the heart of a sparsely populated area of northern Alberta. My parents and their siblings were all born within a few miles of my place of birth. And my grandparents, if they weren't born there, came as young children with their parents, almost all of whom arrived as homesteaders around the turn of the century.*

My parents were both raised on farms. In their adult lives, and to the disdain of their siblings and parents, they moved to the "city"—Grande Prairie, population near 8,000. Having forsaken farming, my mother went to normal school to become a teacher and, later, a school administrator. My father was employed in the lumber and pulp mills, the mainstays of the local economy. Ours was a happy, normal home: with loving parents, financially secure, comfortable—a Leave It to Beaver sort of childhood, as it were. Life matched up well with the TV sitcoms we were permitted to watch, with the Hardy Boys books my oldest brother devoured, with the imagined happenings in the surrounding three-bedroom bungalows. It was a picture of social stability, of normality.

I, however, never felt "normal." Unlike my very social siblings, with their constant streams of friends at the door, their unending phone calls, their calendars filled with plans, I don't recall having many visitors or conversations or engagements. I loved to walk alone, to play by myself, to do "nothing" for hours—and I knew that, under the surveillance of my parents, my aunts and uncles, and the neighbors, I was thought odd for doing so. In spite of the fact that I come from a large family and that my youth was lived out in a thoroughly modern suburban-esque setting, my memories of my childhood are of empty expanses, quiet places, solitudes. I recall spending a great deal of time alone, obsessively and fastidiously working out the details of the next thing I wanted to create. Steam engines, dynamos, clocks, phonographs, adding machines, musical instruments, an alphabet. I loved to study how such artifacts worked and to imagine how I could duplicate their functioning. Secret plans and secret codes were stashed deep in drawers, concealed from my brothers, who, I feared, would ridicule me and my imaginings.

Apart from the encyclopedias in the basement, I never read much. I hated reading, and still find myself resisting unfamiliar texts. Far from offering a sanctuary or an escape, my reading of works of literature was labored and uncomfortable. The predictable plotlines of science fiction and "children's literature" were all right—although I found them boring and often avoided them—but I didn't like the novels on my mother's bookshelf or those the teacher read aloud. Mathematics, on the other hand, was one of my safe places. Imagined to be predictable, consistent, stable, and universal, mathematics was, for me, real knowledge.

I could have been, I think, the poster child for "the thoroughly modern man"—caught up in my own subjectivity, striving for solitude and independence, making a fetish of mathematics and logical thought, trusting in a world that could be known completely, socialized into a concept of white, masculine, conservative, middle class, heteronormativity. In an earlier decade, I'm certain a person like me would have become a mathematician. But, in fact, it was mathematics that actually deflected my wanderings away from such a course.

At it turned out, branches of mathematics like catastrophe theory and chaos dynamics were just beginning to open up in the 1970s, at the time I was making the move from elementary to junior high.

I would arrive at school early in the morning with my brother, and while he went to play one-on-one basketball in the gym, I would go to the library to scour the latest magazines and books for any reference to such topics. Building an understanding of these emerging topics on the basis of single paragraphs, low-resolution images, and cryptic captions, I recall feeling that this was something big, that we were, collectively, on the edge of knowing a very different universe.

Reading as an Interpretive Activity

In her acceptance speech for the National Book Foundation medal for Distinguished Contribution to American Letters, Toni Morrison (1996) tells the story of a young man who, despite years of the best schooling, learned an important lesson only while studying for his Ph.D.:

> In all those years of schooling he had never learned to sit in a room by himself and read for four hours and have those four hours followed by another four hours and have those four hours followed by another four without any companionship but his own mind. He said it was the hardest thing he ever had to do, but he taught himself, forced himself to be alone with a book he was not assigned to read, a book on which there was not test. (p. 10)

Western practices of education do not encourage the risk and discipline necessary to free oneself from the shackles of normativity. As the historians of curriculum theory have taught us (see Kridel, 1990; Pinar, Reynolds, Slattery and Taubman, 1995; Schubert, 1986), and as the cognitive theorists Maturana and Varela (1987) have suggested, *we can see only what we can see*. Learning to perceive differently requires, as Grumet (1991) has suggested, that experience become re-organized. This is unlikely to occur when one insists on being surrounded with the overly-familiar. Practices of invention require, as Maxine Greene (1995) has consistently reminded us, practices of estrangement, practices that place us in an unfamiliar set of relations; practices that ask us to think in a new language.

While it is certainly true that the acquisition of already-existing and already-represented knowledge is best apprehended by the learner when there are opportunities for personal application and interpretation, we have come to understand, in our own work, that these practices are limiting and do not produce sites for the *production* of knowledge. In order to learn to understand differently, we have found that we must create specific conditions for this learning to occur, and that we must follow particular practices of invention. Creating these conditions and participating in these practices, we have found, requires quite deliberate planning of our working situation.

Following lessons learned in childhood, we have come to understand that we must, to a large extent, extract ourselves from familiar sociality for significant periods of time. This has not necessarily meant living in isolation. Although we currently live on a rural property northwest of the city of Toronto, our experience living in downtown Vancouver provided similar conditions, since one can remain isolated even in the most densely populated locations. Removing ourselves from familiar sociality, for us, means creating (and insisting upon) a great deal of time for relations that are not directly connected with our university or with the obligations of friendship. This does not mean that we do not have social relations; it means, rather, that ours are configured differently. In recent years, for example, we have taken to developing primary relationships with our two cats and five dogs. An enormous amount of time is spent engaging in relations of caretaking, of play, of shared activity (like long walks) that do not involve the usual human tendencies to argue, to reason, to justify, to ameliorate. These intimate relations, developed in and around different communicative forms, mean that, while our animals require our time and energy, they do not require our thoughts. These remain for ourselves. And, while doing the domestic labor associated with keeping our animal companions healthy and comfortable, we are free to think—a prerequisite, it seems, to interpretive writing.

Other nonhuman intimate relations are with books and with ideas announced by books. Because our practices of representation are textual practices (that is, we write), our practices of learning, to a large extent, are also textual (we read). While this is not such an unusual pronouncement (most academics read), we have learned that in order to foster invention, we must continue to challenge ourselves to develop relations with texts that are unfamiliar to us. And so, while we continue to maintain relations with books that have become influential to our thinking, we continually interrupt this familiarity by reading some that are strange.

This has meant, of course, that our book selection practices have needed to accommodate this reading practice. Rather than collecting books that are obviously related to our interests, we troll through bookstores to select books that are and are not. It is significant that it is *bookstores* we visit and not libraries. Because libraries always organize books according to subject, we seldom find what we need, since it would be too challenging to search through the entire building, across disciplines, for interesting texts. Bookstores, however, usually have tables with "new releases" (both fiction and nonfiction) and, because their interest is in marketing books, bookstores will often locate one title in several places. Also, bookstores are much smaller than libraries, contain more current selections, and are more interested in popular culture. We do rely somewhat upon friends/colleagues for suggestions, but, interestingly, we have found that the only ones who seem to be challenging and helpful are those who, like us, hunt for disruptive influences in bookstores.

Significantly, as well, we like to own the books we read. While this has meant that a significant amount of our income is used for these purchases, we consider these to be an investment in our thinking. Important to note, as well, we do not always immediately read the books we buy. Any given book-buying jaunt, for example, usually yields a catch of four to six books, only two or three of which are immediately interesting. Others are stacked on a shelf to be used later—often months later—during some project of thinking and writing. In preparing to write this essay, for example, we scanned our shelves, selecting books that we had already read and several books that we had not, but which we suspected might help us to organize our thinking in interesting ways.

Owning books also means that we are free to mark them, leaving a trace of our thinking in them. Because we frequently re-read books, the trace of a previous reading is also, for us, an interesting trace of former relations of reading and our former identities as readers. And, because we read these books independently of one another, it is interesting for each of us to notice what the other has noticed, and, to juxtapose our markings next to each other's. The book, then, begins to function as an archive of individual and collective thinking, providing beginning places for future conversations and, most particularly, for future written representations of thinking.

Selecting, collecting, reading, and marking books, have become an important way for us to organize our thinking and learning. While it might seem as though our thinking is located *within* each of these texts, we have come to understand that it is our *relations with* this ever-evolving personal library that organize what we call "commonplace locations" for thinking and learning (Sumara, 1996b). As cultural artifacts that bear complex traces of writerly and readerly relations with words and ideas, the books dot the landscape of our relationship to our own thinking and, in interesting ways, our relationship to one another. And so, while each of us does produce inventive work that is considered "single authored," we are never able, of course, to decide where one person's thinking becomes demarcated from the other's. Nor are we able to separate what might be called our "domestic" labor from our "intellectual/academic" labor. A conversation about a book, or about an idea, generally happens in the middle of washing the dishes, preparing a meal, feeding the dogs and cats, responding to movies we watch.

Writing as a Focal Practice

It is important for us to plan some organizational structures for representing our thinking. While we do not always have a writing project in process—since we believe that there need to be significant periods of reading, thinking, and teaching in between representations of reading, thinking, and teaching—when we do write we create conditions that support our writing.

These conditions are similar to what Albert Borgmann (1992) has called "focal reality"—a term which, he suggests, becomes "a placeholder for the encounters each of us has with things that of themselves have engaged mind and body and centered our lives" (p. 119). Although Borgmann was referring to activities such as gardening and caring for animals, we believe that writing must also be understood as a focal practice. As with literary workers such as De Salvo, Doll, and Laurence (in King, 1997), writing practices, for us, become centering and collecting places for interpretation. Writing is not merely a representational practice; it is a generative practice.

It is not, however, a practice that is necessarily comfortable or immediately comforting. Like many writers about whom we read, we resist writing. What is resisted, however, is not so much the labor associated with the work of writing but, rather, the labor associated with what we must eventually do when the writing produces new thoughts—ones that interrupt the familiar landscape of our thinking. And so, we can develop a relationship with pending writing only when we become committed to a thought, make time to represent it, and are prepared to accept the anxiety and worry that occur when what we thought becomes transformed into what we had not expected to think.

These practices of invention and representation are, for us, not unlike meditation in that they require not only *time* but also a contemplative attitude, and a deep belief that interesting writing must always be allowed to emerge in ways that surprise the writer. Practices of writing are, for us, best depicted by Jeanette Winterson (1995), who suggests:

> The act of writing, itself, is an evolution; from the Latin *Volvere, volvi, volutum*, to roll. The unrolling of the secret scroll, the thing suspected but not realized until present. (p. 160)

Because we understand identity as a relation, not an object, we know that becoming surprised by new insight means becoming surprised by the transformation of subjectivity. When the practice of writing yields a new and interesting thought, at the same time it yields a new subject of that thinking. So what are these practices? While there are collective practices that we share, a great deal of our writing emerges from personal habits of production that need to be outlined.

Dennis: *As I already mentioned, my writing practices are supported by interpretive reading practices. As I read books, I use a pencil to circle/underline words or phrases of interest, to write in the margins, and to write "connections" or "ideas" in the back of the book. For example, as I read Louise De Salvo's (1997)* Breathless*—a book that chronicles and interprets her learning to live with asthma—it occurred to me that there was a close connection between her theorizing the body as a site responsive to trauma and Maurice Merleau-Ponty's notion of "double embodiment" which he develops in his* Phenomenology of Perception *(1962). In the back of the book I wrote the note: "Like M-P's biological/phenomenological relation." I also stick small yellow Post-It notes in the margins of books to mark passages (usually also underlined) that I wish to hang on to. These become typed into a set of notes that I call "booknotes" stored in a file on my computer desktop, with hard copies kept in a binder. In addition to typing in quotes from books I like, I type, in between the quotes (usually in italics), interpretations I have of the concept being developed, with connections I am making to other books/authors/concepts. The concept of "double-embodiment," for example, is one that Brent and I have relied upon to develop our "enactivist" theory of learning. Through De Salvo's use of the idea, we came to understand that the body's response to remembered traumatic stimuli from the past is not unlike the complex structuring of the human cognitive system.*

Alongside these interpretive booknotes, I often keep a running journal of my thinking. Usually the journal surfaces during times when I am preparing to work on a new thinking/writing project, especially one that is very unfamiliar to me. Last year, for example, in preparing to write a chapter for William Pinar's collection, Queer Theory in Education *(1998), it was necessary for me to begin a journal that brought together my thinking from my reading of new material in queer theory with work that Brent and I had been doing with a group of teachers. This "thinking journal" became a way for me to fool around with new ideas and to try strange juxtapositions of concepts, outside the constraints of anything that I imagined to be a publishable academic article. And so, while entire paragraphs were indeed lifted from the journal and worked into the chapter that Brent and I eventually wrote, most of the writing was playful and exploratory.*

It is at the intersection of reading, making booknotes, and working in my thinking journal that new ideas begin to present themselves—ideas that I could never achieve by trying to just "think them into presence." As I worked on this chapter, for example, it was in my playful writing, emerging from my reading of literary workers, that it occurred to me that most of them, through their writing, were deliberately crafting a new identity for themselves. Moreover, these literary wordsmiths were trying to create more interesting identities for themselves, by inventing characters. Thinking about my own experiencse as a child, I found myself typing the phrase "inventing a subject," followed by "creating an interesting subject" and, finally, "inventing a more interesting subject." Once this phrase was coined an interesting commonplace location had been announced for thinking about the relationship between Brent's and my work, our living circumstances, and our reading and writing practices.

I began by typing in the title and then, for three hours one morning, I worked from my booknotes and my journal notes to piece together the introduction that this title seemed to announce. Because this writing is/was meant to represent our shared writing practices, I continually passed newly typed paragraphs and pages to Brent, who would read them and write in his own thinking that was sponsored by this beginning structure. Usually on the same day, while making or eating a meal, or going for a walk, we would have a discussion of the piece of thinking/writing that was emerging.

Brent: *I'm still not what you'd call an avid reader. But I do read a great deal, mostly through force of will. Early in the 1990s, as the start of my doctoral program, I began a book-per-week regimen—and, except when grading papers or writing proposals, I have managed to maintain this practice.*

I have two preferred areas of reading: popularized accounts of events in mathematics and recent discussions of cognitive theory. These texts I read with a certain amount of pleasure. Other books—in particular, works of literature—require much more effort and take considerably more time. For the most part, the novels I read are on Dennis's recommendation (and occasional insistence). Even though our academic interests and our thinking about thinking have a great deal in common, our preferences for literary forms and our choices in scholarly writings differ dramatically.

I read a book from start to finish, rarely giving up on a text once begun. Current readings always have a pencil and a pad of Post-Its stuck inside. When done, depending on the sorts of thoughts it has prompted, a book is either "put away" on a bookshelf or placed in a pile on my desk for reference as I work through current projects. For those readings that have really prompted my thinking, I summarize and resymbolize the central themes and pivotal arguments, jotting these thoughts on loose-leaf paper and, rather randomly, tucking these pages into some logical-at-the-time place: a drawer, a pocket, a backpack, a file. Many of these notes end up being inserted, almost unrevised, into emerging papers. (When I finally sat down to compose my doctoral dissertation, in fact, I found that it was more than half-written on scraps and stickies and book flaps.)

In many ways, I write the way I read. I start a paper and work through to the end, usually at a particular self-imposed pace (of four or five double-spaced longhand pages per day). I have to be sure to line up several diversions before sitting down to write—shoveling snow, doing the morning crossword, playing with the dogs, going for a walk. At best, I seem to be able to write for a half hour at a time without taking some sort of a break. I haven't figured out why this is the case.

I rarely use any references in a first draft. It is a collection of ideas, a montage. The sentences are convoluted, the paragraphs are short. The second stage in the project is thus a matter of elaborating and smoothing, usually re-thinking ideas in discussions with Dennis (who, invariably, seems to be working on very similar no-

tions in another context) and re-writing passages with more explicit reference to current readings and to the books on my desk. Post-Its are rearranged, new notes are scrawled in the margins.

I've never had the experience of actually producing the paper that I thought I was going to write: at the end of a first draft, it's always something very different, and usually something that's taught me a great deal about what I do and do not know. By the end of the final draft, especially with pieces that have been traded back-and-forth with Dennis, it's often something even more unexpected.

At times, I write several drafts by hand. I've found that I can't do much original composition at a computer. When I get to the stage of typing a paper, I try to do it all at once. Usually it's the first time I'm able to consider a paper in its entirety, to trace the lines of thinking, the diversions, and the inconsistencies. Typing the paper is thus more than entering data or refining prose; it is, rather, another critical step in an endlessly recursive process. The first version that appears on-screen is always something different from what was on the notepad. Parts get re-arranged, elaborated, deleted. It is usually in this stage that I find Dennis's voice speaking, realizing that somehow his sentences have been transcribed into my writing (or, in a parallel way, that he has somehow written my thinking into his own writing, which he insists on reading aloud). While the joint, collective character of our thinking continuously asserts itself, it is always most obvious to me as a paper nears the final draft stage. In this way, whether we state it explicitly or not, every text that bears either of our names is co-authored.

Inventing New Subjects

These practices of interpretation and resymbolization, fully integrated into our shared domestic relations, continue until there is something that seems to represent the intentions of our writing. At the same time, because we do not write outlines or make decisions about how the writing will evolve, or what the conclusions will be, we are usually surprised at where these writing/thinking practices have taken us. As Jeanette Winterson suggests, the act of writing is an act of discovery and invention. What is invented, though, is never merely a new essay. Invented, as well, is a new writer.

Our challenge is to make them both interesting.

References

Borgmann, Albert (1992). *Crossing the Postmodern Divide.* Chicago: University of Chicago Press.

Davis, Brent (1996).*Teaching Mathematics: Toward a Sound Alternative.* New York: Garland.

Davis, Brent and Dennis Sumara (1997). "Cognition, Complexity, and Teacher Education." *Harvard Educational Review, vol. 67, 1* (pp. 105–125).

De Salvo, Louise (1989). *Virginia Woolf: The Impact of Childhood Sexual Abuse on Her Life and Work.* New York: Ballantine.

De Salvo, Louise (1996). *Vertigo.* New York: Dutton.

De Salvo, Louise (1997). *Breathless: An Asthma Journal.* Boston: Beacon.

Doll, Mary Aswell (1995). *To the Lighthouse and Back: Writings on Teaching and Living.* New York: Peter Lang.

Felman, Shoshana (1987). *Jacques Lacan and the Adventure of Insight: Psychoanalysis inContemporary Culture.* Cambridge, Mass: Cambridge University Press.

Felman, Shoshana and Dori Laub (1992). *Testimony: Crises of Witnessing in Literature, Psychoanalysis, and History.* New York: Routledge.

Greene, Maxine (1995). *Releasing the Imagination: Essays on Education, the Arts, and Social Change.* San Francisco: Jossey-Bass.

Grumet, Madeleine (1988). *Bitter Milk: Women and Teaching.* Amherst: University of Massachusetts Press.

Grumet, Madeleine (1991). "Curriculum and the art of daily life." In *Reflections from the Heart of Educational Inquiry: Understanding Curriculum and Teaching through the Arts.* (Eds. George Willis and William Schubert.) Albany: State University of New York Press.

King, James (1997). *The Life of Margaret Laurence.* Toronto: Knopf.

Kridel, Craig (1990). "Teaching Curriculum through an Historical-Biographical Perspective." In *Teaching and Thinking about Curriculum.* (Eds. James Sears and Donald Marshall.) New York: Teachers College Press.

Maturana, Humberto and Francisco Varela (1987) *The Tree of Knowledge: The Biological Roots of Human Understanding.* Boston: Shambhala.

Merleau-Ponty, Maurice (1962). *Phenomenology of Perception.* London: Routledge.

Miller, Janet (1990). *Creating Spaces and Finding Voices: Teachers Collaborating for Empowerment.* Albany: State University of New York Press.

Morrison, Toni (1996). *The Dancing Mind*. New York: Knopf.

Pinar, William F. Ed. (1998). *Queer Theory in Education*. Mahwah, New Jersey: Erlbaum.

Pinar, William F. (1994). *Autobiography, Politics and Sexuality*. New York: Peter Lang

Pinar, William F. and Madeleine R. Grumet (1976). *Toward a Poor Curriculum*. Dubuque, Iowa: Kendall/Hunt.

Pinar, William F., William M. Reynolds, Patrick Slattery, and Peter Taubman, Eds. (1995). *Understanding Curriculum*. New York: Peter Lang.

S[illegible]o, Paula (1990). "Transgressive daughters: Student Autobiography and the Project of Self-Creation." *Cambridge Journal of Education*, vol 20, 3 (pp. 283–290).

Schubert, William (1986). *Curriculum: Perspective, Paradigm, and Possibility*. New York: Macmillan.

Sumara, Dennis (1996a). *Private Readings in Public: Schooling the Literary Imagination*. New York: Peter Lang.

Sumara, Dennis (1996b) "Using commonplace books in curriculum studies." *Journal of Curriculum Theorizing*, vol. 12, 1 (pp. 55–58).

Sumara, Dennis and Brent Davis (1996b). "The work of interpretation." *Journal of Curriculum Theorizing*, vol. 13, 1 (pp. 2–5).

Willinsky, John (1997). "Accountability in action." In *Action Research as a Living Practice*. (Eds. Terrance Carson and Dennis Sumara.) New York: Peter Lang.

Winterson, Jeanette (1995). *Art Objects: Essays in Ecstasy and Effrontery*. Toronto: Knopf.

Woolf, Virginia (1995). *To the Lighthouse*. New York: Harcourt Brace Jovanovich.

Chapter 7

"Nothing's Died; It Just Got Buried": Theory as Exhumation, as Duty Dance

(for Thomas Wayne Daspit and Mandy Jo Delcambre)

Toby Daspit

To be playful and serious at the same time is possible,
and it defines the ideal mental condition.
(John Dewey, 1910, p. 218)

Most of our seeing is done behind the eye.
(Boyd Henry Bode, 1940, p. 144)

No art is possible without a dance with death.
(Kurt Vonnegut,1968, p. 21, paraphrasing Louis-Ferdinand Celíne)

this is an essay about the realm Bob Dylan (1991) identifies where "everything stays down . . . wounded."

there is a bitterness now, as i begin looking, begin revising words that i first set to paper nearly two years ago—a bitterness as i begin re-thinking the world of "magic and loss" (Reed 1991) and how it relates to my thinking, my theorizing, my living.

in November of 1996 we buried my godmother after she battled cancer for over two years. outside of my parents' house and school, hers was the place i spent the most time in growing up. on Xmas eve, 1997, we buried an uncle unexpectedly. within the past three years, two of my best friends have lost mothers, women i had adopted as surrogate mothers in the town where i taught high school for six years.

with the Rolling Stones' Sticky Fingers *(1971) in the background, i begin again this walk with the wounded.*

midnight chess . . .

this is where this rambling (for there are no stories, no tales . . . there are no structures we can impose that weave the disparate fragments of our lives, our thoughts, into a unified tapestry . . . though we continue to display, to promenade, to exhibit . . . to watch, to listen . . . to wait)

midnight chess, once again, is where this (my) spasmodic excursion begins, ends, resuscitates.

"all art is a duty dance with death"—this is how i imagined and recited the above Vonnegut/Céline quote when i told Jasmine, my "spouse," earlier this evening over Chinese food, that i planned on using it (once again) as an epigraph for this exploration of my requirements for free intellectual play, for envisioning that which is not, but may be, for theorizing, for working . . . i knew exactly where to find the quote for citation purposes (near the beginning of *Slaughterhouse-Five*) . . . i asked Jasmine exactly what a "duty dance" is (she is a dancer, after all), seeking additional corroboration for my idea—she asked in response, "doesn't it have to do with cards, and parties, and being forced to dance with the person whose card you are dealt?"—sounded good to me, and it certainly fulfilled the definition i needed . . . until later in the evening, just a few minutes ago, when i checked the source to confirm, and discovered that it read instead, "No art is possible without a dance with death."

no "duty," and so no party, no cards.

midnight chess. which i only remember now, which i only relate to you now. "—Hypocrite reader, you—my double!" Baudelaire (1857/1989, p. 2) says of this relationship, this bizarre, artificial, collapsible schism between audience/performer, voyeur/exhibitionist, reader/author, you/me) . . . again, i only remember midnight chess now, only related it to you now, because of death.

and because of "Ulalume" (Poe, 1980).

i am returning to the scene.

tricky, "impure memory," Borges calls it. and we are moving toward it, toward, he continues, "the abuse of literature/and at the border, death, beyond surmise" (1996, p. 37).

i wanted "duty" even when it wasn't there. even with Vonnegut/Céline's absolute, "No art is possible without a dance with death"—i wanted to make sure that we wouldn't lose focus of the forced nature of this "dance." this card game. this party trick. Céline's own words are not enough: "The truth is death. I've fought nicely against it . . .

danced with it, festooned it, waltzed around it . . . decorated it with streamers, titillated it" (in Vonnegut , p. 21).

i wanted "duty."

so this is my "duty dance."

i am returning to the tomb . . .

to Ulalume's "vault."

i think i first encountered Edgar Allan Poe's "Ulalume: A Ballad" (1980) through Stanley Kubrick's film version (1961) of Nabokov's *Lolita*. i can hear the luscious voice of James Mason, portraying the perverted Humbert Humbert, with the young Dolores Haze perched on his knee, envelop Poe's words, drawing out "immemorial" and "Ulalume" like molasses, in attempts to impress the precocious nymphet.

the poem's narrator, the poet, begins by wandering in a sinister, mysterious place—a zombie, unaware of his surroundings, surroundings which are familiar, albeit unknowingly at first.

the male narrator, the conscious poet, walks side by side with his female Psyche, his soul, his unconscious—they walk in an area they have traveled before, but both are oblivious to its significance.

i am returning to the tomb.

i am returning to the scene.

i am returning to the Rolling Stones—and "Sister Morphine"—and "Dead Flowers"—

and beer runs. and hazy midnight chess.

but mostly i wander, a zombie.

Poe's narrator is tempted out of his daze by a crescent moon, which he prefers to view as the fiery, erotic Astarte, Phoenician fertility goddess, rather than the chaste, Roman, Diana. the speaker, the logos, the voice of reason, of sanity perhaps, seeks the refreshing soothing waters of Lethe—the only genuine panacea, because it induces forgetfulness, it erases memory. but his soul, his eros, his psyche, his artistic core, his she is alarmed

but the logos ignores this inner voice, this different mode of relating to the world. he presses on, with the chicanery of reason, with the deceit of rhetoric and persuasion, with the promise of aesthetic bliss.

and it works. the divided self dissolves into a sexual union of artistic voice and inner wisdom. but it is not a balanced self.

i am returning to the tomb, to midnight chess, to "Wild Horses" (Rolling Stones, 1971) and alcohol fire.

the narrator is unified, transfixed on a future, myopic. he has "conquered" his Psyche, his artistic soul—the region where impulse and desire dwell.

the true marriage of logos and eros, of exterior voice and interior dialogue, occurs at the end of the journey, which is of course also the beginning.

the narrator, the logos/eros, is startled into the realization that he has returned to the very site where he buried his young lover who died exactly one year ago (in undisclosed circumstances). despite attempts to eradicate his grief, the narrator knows there is no "balm in Gilead" (Poe, p. 476)—no forgetting—no escaping. that art is melancholy, life is death. a "duty" dance . . .

i have my Ulalume, as i suspect you have yours. i have my buried memories, my buried people, that repeatedly surface . . . my paths that inevitably lead to the inescapable.

what tempts me now, tempts me repeatedly, to midnight chess, to the Rolling Stones' *Sticky Fingers*, to the beer and hazy conversation that i can never replicate.

my oldest brother died fifteen years ago in a car accident. the last night i remember with him was one of chess at midnight (and after), beer (lots of beer), and loud, omnipresent music (Rolling Stones, Doors, etc.). he left a wife and two daughters. and two parents . . . and three brothers . . . and one sister.

once, while writing with my students in a poetry exercise based on Stanley Kunitz's (in Gorrell, 1990, p. 27) "The Portrait," in which a young boy is slapped by his mother for finding a picture of the father he never knew, the father who committed suicide while his mother was pregnant with him—(the concluding lines read, "In my sixty-fourth year/I can feel my cheek/still burning"—the exercise asked us to use the power and simplicity of a recurring image)—i wrote the following excerpts from a "poem" i refuse to revise:

i never forgave myself
for that night . . .

i was a wandering adolescent
like all boys wanting to be men but not wanting to grow up
and i was sleeping over at my favorite cousin's house
and after a night of rebellious wallowing in teenage angst
and mixing the jack daniels and the beer and the cutty sark
a habit i have never abandoned
never will

i assumed when i heard my uncle tell my aunt in
the haze of the Sunday morning
"we'll talk to him together"
that he was referring to the trips during the night to
spill my guts
a habit I've never abandoned
never will
but when they opened the door
as my mind raced for excuses
god my parents can't find out
i saw their faces
pallid
sunken
and my younger brother trailing behind
tears streaming down his atypically ghastly face

how i wish they were coming to tell me
what i worried they were coming to tell me . . .

i was sixteen years old. is it any wonder that most of my health problems originate in my stomach?

ulcers. fear and trembling. nausea.

you see, theory for me is about survival. it's about freedom. it's about moving beyond capital "T" Theory, which often involves, as the poet Ruth Forman (1993) puts it, "Styrofoam words" (p. 47). it's about finding a reason for getting out of bed. it's about finding a reason not to anesthetize myself to the point of oblivion. it's about struggle.

it's about finding a reason to step into the classroom, or sit at this keyboard in spite of the fact that after my first year of teaching, a beautiful fourteen year-old student of mine, one of only five i taught in the whole school, rode her bicycle accidentally into the path of an oncoming car and died the next day. she told me of her future plans—Columbia or Stanford. imagine that. someone from the tiny shrimping town of Delcambre, Louisiana at Columbia or Stanford.

another "poem" i wrote with students, modeled on Edgar Lee Masters's "Spoon River Anthology," (1915/1992) where characters speak from the grave, explains:

I only wanted for them
A better life than I had
And to help them climb the rugged ascent
Of knowledge to Truth.
That is why I became a teacher
And that is why we read the

Miserable lives of Richard Cory and Miniver Cheevy
And Albert Schirding and Jonas Keene —
So that my students might envision a better life.
And then one summer day
A student of mine
A week from fifteen
Rode her bicycle into an oncoming car.
Wondering why we bother to
Read tales of misery
With so much of it in front of our eyes
Started my demise.

i know it is overly sentimental, but i want a classroom, a curriculum, a world, where everything i do, everything i did with this student, this child, for instance, or with my brother, makes some sense—when my brother slipped from consciousness what did he think of?

midnight chess?

it's what i'm left with. my brother died the summer before my senior year in high school.

the previous year i had read William Cullen Bryant's "Thanatopsis" (1980) in American literature. i remembered that Bryant had composed a draft when he was only sixteen. that's what i wanted to do. write a poem that would immortalize my brother, immortalize me, and offer some immortal solace to future children coping with death.

i never wrote the poem that i envisioned. but i did turn to poetry, to language. i still turn to what my brother helped teach me—alcohol trances and rock and roll.

and solitude. something about weekends with my brother taught me the value of being apart from people. sometimes i feel like Henry in Charles Bukowski's *Barfly* (1987) when asked if he hates people: "No, but I seem to feel better when they're not around" (p. 47). it's where I'm comfortable thinking, seeing.

i've come to understand that our lives are poems, that we are poetry.

Dylan Thomas (1957) is right, of course: "After the first death, there is no other" (p. 112).

and Baudelaire (1869/1970) is also right when he speaks of various modes of intoxication:

> One should always be drunk That's the great thing; the only question. Not to feel the horrible burden of Time weighing on your shoulders and bowing you to the earth, you should be drunk without respite.
>
> Drunk with what? With wine, with poetry, or with virtue, as you please. But get drunk.

> And if sometimes you should happen to awake, on the stairs of a palace, on the green grass of a ditch, in the dreary solitude of your own room, and find that your drunkenness is ebbing or has vanished, ask the wind and the wave, ask star, bird, or clock, ask everything that speaks, ask them the time; and the wind, the wave, the star, the bird and the clock will all reply: "It is Time to get drunk! If you are not to be the martyred slaves of Time, be perpetually drunk! With wine, with poetry, or with virtue, as you please." (p. 74)

and i would like to join Jim Morrison (1989) in his incantation, first brought to my attention by a student: "I want to hear the last Poem/of the last Poet" (p. 119).

this is why i must return to the tomb, to midnight chess.

to reinvent a theory for dying, a theory for living.

i had a short Xmas list last year. all i really wanted was a copy of Greil Marcus's (1997) Invisible Republic: Bob Dylan's Basement Tapes. *i had read a review in* Rolling Stone *that said reading this book was like visiting Greil Marcus while listening to* The Basement Tapes *(Dylan and the Band, 1975) and while each song plays, Marcus jumps up and says something akin to, "You've also got to see/read/hear this," alternately grabbing books/videos/albums." it immediately struck me—this is how i work—bouncing from keyboard to turntable to refrigerator to keyboard to bookshelf to CD player to VCR to keyboard . . .*

my only copy of The Basement Tapes, *the album that first turned me on to Bob Dylan, is a tattered old promotional vinyl copy that belonged to my late brother. it's on the turntable now.*

References

Baudelaire, C. (1970). *Paris Spleen.* (Trans. L. Varèse.). New York: New Directions. (Originally published 1869.)

Baudelaire, C. (1989). *Flowers of Evil.* (Trans. S. Kunitz). New York: New Directions. (Originally published 1857.)

Borges, J. L. (1996). *J.M.* (Trans. R. Mezey and R. Barnes.) *The American Poetry Review*, vol. *25*, 2 (p. 37).

Bryant, W. C. (1980). "*Thanatopsis.*" In *The Norton Anthology of American literature: Shorter edition.* (Eds. R. Gottesman et al.) New York: Norton (p. 81).

Bukowski, C. (1987). *The Movie: "Barfly."* Santa Rosa, Calif: Black Sparrow.

Dylan, B. (1991). Series of Dreams. On *The Bootleg Series, vol. 3.* New York: Columbia.

Dylan, B. and the Band. (1975). *The basement tapes.* New York: Columbia.

Forman, R. (1993). *We Are the Young Magicians.* Boston: Beacon.

Gorrell, N. (1990). "Taking off the Mask: Teaching the Recurring Image in Poetry Writing." *English Journal* (pp. 27–29).

Kubrick, S., Director (1961). *Lolita.* MGM/UA Home Video.

Marcus, G. (1997). *Invisible Republic: Bob Dylan's Basement Tapes.* New York: Holt.

Masters, E.L. (1915/1992). *Spoon River Anthology.* New York: Dover.

Morrison, J. (1989). *Wilderness.* New York: Vintage.

Poe, E. A. (1980). "The raven" and " Ulalume." In *The Norton Anthology of American Literature: Shorter Edition.* (Eds. R. Gottesman et al.) New York: Norton (pp. 474–479).

Reed, L. (1991). *Magic and Loss.* New York: Sire.

Rolling Stones (1971). *Sticky Fingers.* New York: Rolling Stones.

Thomas, D. (1957). *The Collected Poems of Dylan Thomas 1934–1952.* New York: New Directions.

Vonnegut, K. (1968). *Slaughterhouse-Five.* New York: Dell.

Chapter 8

Why I Write

Bill Davis

In order, then, that playfulness may not terminate in arbitrary fancifulness and in building up an imaginary world alongside the world of actual things, it is necessary that the play attitude should gradually pass into a work attitude.
(John Dewey, 1910, p. 162)

A selfhood is built up, and it is built up in terms of a social content.
(Boyd Henry Bode, 1940, p. 262)

I started writing songs when I was seven years old. I think the main catalyst for my musical jump-start was a television show called The Monkees. Those guys were having so much zany fun, getting into lots of trouble and (very enviably) running from girls. So I took pen in one hand, and ukelele in the other and wrote "The Things Are Gonna Get Ya"—my first musical composition. From there, it wasn't until my high school years that the music bug chomped again. At the time, girls were still a priority for any budding rock star. But more important, I was hanging out with a group of pot-smoking guitar/drum bangers (this was before slackers were invented), and we prodded each other into better songs and cooler riffs. It wasn't so much the women's attention for which we were rockin'—it was just as important to write meaningful, if not profound, rock lyrics. I mean, this was 1975, and the 1960s weren't too distant a memory. Bob Dylan and John Lennon were still fresh in our pot-addled noggins. I left high school with degrees in the Beatles and Pink Floyd.

In college, the punk era was in full snarl and I slam-dived into the pit with abandon. Punk lyrics had no guidelines except that they needed to be clever and anti-bourgeoisie. Why be normal? Fuck the World.

The most obnoxious ideas that sprang from all night beer and speed parties ended up in the set list. My band was called "The Noise" and later "The Human Rayz" (we each had a "ray" name, such as Ray Gene Bull, E. Ray Sorehead). In the Rayz one could sing about almost anything. We had a song about a refrigerator (at the time it was our most valued appliance—it held the beer); a song about a Baptist Minister who abused his cat, wife, and kids and then died (to no one's concern or notice); and our hit "Chemical Kids," about mutants growing up on Three Mile Island. We even invented a dance called "The Body," during which the audience would lie on the floor like a carpet of cadavers.

The whole acid-driven experience might now seem a little silly, but it helped mold my love for all things Dada and the prolific world of drug-fueled creativity. The pop art accelerator was always pushed to the floor; every waking hour was spent dreaming up the most ridiculous and incredible songs. Most would pale and wither after a few days' study (whereupon we would sober up and pee out all the chemicals), but some stood the test of levelheaded examination, and those are the songs I most cherish from the whole period.

While at school in Baton Rouge, I was introduced to the romance and depravity that flow through most southern literature. I embraced the psychotic cruelty of Flannery O'Connor's antiheroes, the flowery prose of Mark Twain's adolescents, and the brilliant eloquence of Thomas Wolfe's white trash coming-of-age sagas. Also, studying British/American poets, I became interested in the ramblings of T.S. Eliot and even more enamored of two Imagistes—Ezra Pound and Hilda Doolittle. I loved the idea of taking the smallest observation, the tiniest glimpse of nature, and turning it into a multi-tiered blast of neurotic rambling. I was trying to figure out how I could use these poetic themes and structures in the punk rock music my bands were playing. At the same time I was reading my way from the Rio Grande to the Rappahannock, there were a few popular southern rock bands who were beginning to explore the use of southern lit. tricks in their songs—bands such as REM, Guadacanal Diary, and Love Tractor. They were singing about kudzu, barn rape, putting favorite horses down, and murderous grandparents. These bands were reading the same books I was, and they were melding the romantic age-old beauty of deep southern thought with springy pop/rock music. This was exactly the synthesis I had been struggling to create. So I joined the fray.

One of the first songs in which I tried the use of poetic imagery is "Marsupial." The song was written after a long, arduous LSD trip that spanned two days, two cities, an ex-wife, and three bottles of rum. While a tad under the influence, I was walking with my best friend, my ex-wife, and a few other friends. A possum had been hit by a car and was standing in the middle of the road in a daze. I tried to help the critter, but he hissed and snapped at me. We left the poor guy standing defiantly in the street, knowing that when we returned he'd be road kill. Sure 'nuff—a few hours passed and we walked back out to our car and the possum was now a black heap in the road. The whole episode was traumatic enough, but with the help of mind-altering chemicals it became a murderous travesty and short story all rolled into one. After the trip, we returned to Baton Rouge and I considered the possum occurrence with a poet's eye. I figured the possum was a sick metaphor for my ex-wife's dying love. And, even more unbalanced, I took the marsupial and turned it into the protective womb of a woman—that loving pouch most men like to climb up into and hide from the hardships of existence. Hence:

> Start my car, no reason to drive. I forgot the things I wanted you to remember.
> Marsupial—you're a pouch that I climb into.
> Think of me and sing until you have a song.
> Live and breathe the thoughts you keep around
> Last I heard, your kiss was cold. Lying flat dead on the gray Houston road.
> ("Marsupial," Dash Rip Music, BMI)

The song was a college radio hit. It was even a favorite of Elvis Costello, who heard the song in England on the radio and called for a copy of the record. He admired the chord structures and the obscure lyrics. "Marsupial" helped my band get a record deal and we began touring the United States. We were accepted as a bona fide entry in the New Southern Rock Intellect sweepstakes, and we began hanging out and touring with the very bands I had been admiring a few years earlier. But most important, I was on my way as a serious songwriter.

So now I was fully inspired to pen the next great southern rock poem. I looked to Mark Twain, Eudora Welty, William Faulkner, and the diseased lot to guide my pen and ear for the next few songs. Also, I remembered the old tales and scary stories my parents and grandparents used to relate when we were kids. There were stories about Great, Great Granpa and his adventures in the Civil War. Nightmares about when old man Williams cut his neck and fell down a flight of stairs—his ghost left to inhabit a broke-down mansion nestled up in the St. Helena woods. My family history, as told by my ancient relatives, seemed to mirror the old southern folklore spun in the weirdest great books. I began to draw from these familiar themes, and a whole bait of songs danced out of this experiment. I was paying tribute to the souls of my past relatives. From the poor red dirt of the most backwoods Louisiana-sprung songs and poems heralding the obscure, the nameless, and the forgotten. When you read most southern literature, the characters are amalgams of many typical beasts—the cruel father, the doting mother, the criminal wayfarer, and the tortured poet. How many contemporary popular songs explore this world so often exposed by southern writers and novelists? That was the question I asked when I set out to create new songs for an album. Who else is doing this? The answer was hardly anyone.

On the first Dash Rip Rock album the songs "Old Bridge," "Buried Treasure," and "Big Daddy Liked the Whiskey" were written from a historical, familial perspective. The lyrics were intricate and fit in well over the driving rock base. The songs became crowd favorites and journalist/critics were impressed by the complexity of the themes. What? This set to rock music? It was almost too bizarre an experiment. The most important factor in the existence of these songs was that they worked; they clicked—for the band and for the audience. It wasn't like some fool idiot overstepping the boundaries of good taste and breaking the rules of "rock lyric writing." It was a pleasant mixture of deep south history and new eclectic art rock—which, in the big picture, was completely changing the way fans looked at rock and roll. From Chuck Berry to Bob Dylan, rock music was slowly taking a more intellectual bend. Southern college rock bands of the 1980s routed that bend into their region and localized their song themes. It was a sense of historical pride and preservation that led me to jump on this wagon. The beauty and deep romance of the south should always ring in words and songs.

This sums up the start of my writing career. Throughout the years I have tried to explore themes never touched in popular music. It is my love for unique creativity that keeps me from taking the low road (the quest for popular hit songs). Sappy, repetitive music and lyrics may have won some gold records, but I feel that the songs I create will stand the test of repeated listening. And like the south itself, they'll survive, I hope, the ravages of history.

Reference

Davis, B. (1984). *Marsupial*. Dash Rip Music, BMI.

Chapter 9

How I Work

Peter Alson

The most vital and significant factor . . . is . . . curiosity.
(John Dewey, 1910, p. 30)

In terms of the development of selfhood
it means that no one can escape from the necessity
of integrating or harmonizing his various interests.
(Boyd Henry Bode, 1940, p. 259)

I read *The Sun Also Rises* on a train ride to Yugoslavia in the summer of my seventeenth year. It was the first time I felt that I knew what I wanted to do with my life. I was in love with an American girl who had warned me not to go see her, but I was going anyway, Jake Barnes hopelessly in love with my Lady Brett.

A year later, as a college freshman, I attempted to turn that heartache into a novel. I got about thirty or forty pages into the writing, then lost steam. There was nothing I wanted more in the world than to write a novel, but I was too self-critical for my own good. The burst of energy with which I began the book imploded from the negative force of my own expectations.

This was to happen to me again and again over the years, with such neurotic and depressing regularity that by the time I was thirty-seven I had sworn off writing entirely and fallen into a life as a bookie. Therein, of course, lies a story, and even before the night the cops raided our office and I was arrested, I was beginning to make notes, with the telling of that story in mind.

My eventual night and a half in the Brooklyn House of Detention persuaded me to retire from bookmaking. It also persuaded me to give book writing one more shot.

I knew two things, going in. The first was that I would die if I failed again; the second was that if I did what I had always done up until then, I would almost certainly fail.

What I had always done up until then was this: at some point in the writing process, I would start to question the story and go back to the beginning to see where I had gone wrong. Then I would begin fixing things. There was something circular in this compulsion, a snake eating its own tail. But I couldn't stop myself. I spent six years of my life on one novel, wrote and rewrote hundreds of pages, and never got to the end. I was approaching middle age with narrowed options. I had worked as a waiter, proofreader, repo man, and bookie. My degree in English from Harvard qualified me for nothing. If I began another book and repeated the old pattern—well, it wasn't a prospect I wanted to consider.

So I made a deal with myself. I would start writing and I would never look back. No matter what happened, how bad I felt, how lonely, how afraid, I would keep going forward. My finances were sufficient to last me for a little while; I had managed to stash eight thousand dollars away while booking bets, all in cash.

One definition of insanity is that someone keeps doing the same thing over and over, each time expecting a different result.

Was I insane? There was only one way to find out.

When I began the book, I was living in the apartment I still live in, a tiny one-bedroom on a tree-lined street in Brooklyn Heights. Each morning, I would wake at nine, go through my ablutions, then walk around the corner to the Muslim-run variety store for the morning paper, usually the *Post* or the *News*, rarely the bulkier, more time-consuming *Times*. I am not a coffee drinker or a breakfast person, so I would sit at my desk, read the sports pages, and by 10:30 or 11 a.m. take a deep breath, put the paper down, and open my laptop.

At first, my process was to consult my notes to see what they inspired. I had about thirty legal pad pages worth of notes, plus assorted random thoughts and snatches of dialogue written on old betting slips. The notes were a comfort; they made me feel less naked in front of the blank blue computer screen. I can remember that on one scrap of paper I had jotted down: "Dapper Dan would leave in the middle of a poker game to get more money, but instead of going to a cash machine he would go out and stick up a Seven-Eleven. Then he would return to the game. One night he didn't come back. We discovered that the cops had nailed him." Though I didn't wind up using that particular bit in the book, it was typical of the kind of stuff I had recorded.

Each morning when I opened the laptop and turned it on, I allowed myself to read one paragraph back, that was all, no matter how I felt, how much I thought it might benefit me to read back a bit further. To make temptation more difficult, I wrote short chapters and saved each chapter in a separate computer file.

The narrative of the book, I realize now, was not simple; there were a number of different plot strands that I was weaving together. But because the story was told in the first person and in chronological sequence, I fooled myself into believing that it was simple. This was a necessary self-deception. I was a head case and knew it, and like the coach of a talented but schizo ball player, I was using every cheap psychological trick I could think of to prevent the player (who happened to be me) from a meltdown.

My work habits were nonetheless atrocious. I am not one of those people with free flow; I am a bleeder, squeezing each word out with difficulty, and I could not sit at my desk for more than fifteen minutes without having to get up. I needed relief too badly. So I made trips to the bathroom, the refrigerator, the phone, the dictionary, and the mailbox downstairs, not to speak of the supermarket, the drugstore, the library, and the post office. I could use the cop-out that I am a child of television, conditioned by commercial breaks, but who really knows? For a while, I tried tying myself to my chair with the terrycloth belt of my bathrobe. Finally I stopped fighting it. The only truly important thing was that I keep going forward.

Three and a half months into the writing, I had my first real crisis. By then I had somehow accumulated a hundred pages. I had also exhausted my notes, and I was having to face the empty screen alone each day, without props. Also money was running out. I can't remember what prompted the episode; maybe I just woke up flat on that particular day and sat down feeling low and vulnerable. Maybe the lack of feedback, the isolation had finally caught up with me. But for the first time, in a profound way, I doubted what I was doing. The compulsion to go back and look at what I'd written, to see if it was worth anything, was overpowering. In such a mood, I was capable of tearing things down, of doing terrible destruction.

I began to think of how I'd begun the book and I suddenly knew what it was missing, what I could do to improve it. The old thought processes started up like a cold engine, coughing a few times, then rumbling fully back to life. If I didn't go back and fix the beginning now, I'd never be able to. The pull was just like the pull of an addiction. I almost gave in. Instead, my heart beating, I got up from the desk, went outside and took a long walk on the Brooklyn Heights promenade. Across the East River, Manhattan was hazy in the summer heat. "You made yourself a promise," I said aloud. "You have to keep that promise no matter what. You have to." People on the benches facing the river looked at me as I continued to mumble out loud my words of self-encouragement—another crazy soul who was not locked up (or at least hadn't been for several months).

I went back to my computer. It didn't matter whether the book was any good, I told myself; what mattered was that I finish it. Anything that needed to be fixed I could fix later. That day I began jotting down in a notebook the thoughts I had about what changes I might want to make after I'd finished the first draft. But the crucial point was: after.

The money problem was another matter. I didn't want to get a job, didn't want to break my work routine. I asked Eddie, one of my former business associates, for a loan, but he turned me down. The bookie office had opened up again after the bust, and he asked me to come back. But I told him I couldn't go. I said, "Instead of a loan, how about staking me in the no-limit poker game at the Mayfair Club?" The Mayfair was a poker club in Manhattan in the east 20s. I had played there a number of times, and I thought I could make money in the big game if I had a stake. Eddie said he'd have to watch me play first.

So he went with me one night and we both played on his money. At the end of the night, he had lost a thousand, but I had won $2,800. He said, "Ok, that's your stake. We'll leave the money on account here. Whatever you win, I get half."

After that, I began playing at the Mayfair three or four times a week. I would go in at eight or nine at night, play until they closed at four in the morning, then cab home to Brooklyn and sleep in until eleven or noon.

My writing routine remained the same, if on a slightly different clock. I usually got down to work after lunch, which, now that I was again flush with cash, I ate out at a local diner. At one-thirty or two, I would go back to the apartment, and I would keep writing in my usual fits and starts until I left for the club or for an occasional evening out on the town. (New York is a great place when you have a pocketful of hundred-dollar bills.) My writing pace slowed, but I was enjoying myself. I felt that I had discovered a viable way to live. In three months, I wrote another seventy-five pages and made fifteen thousand dollars playing poker, of which I kept half.

Then I hit a bad streak.

I lost six thousand dollars in two weeks. Sitting at my desk, I found myself thinking about poker hands I'd played the night before. At the poker table, I was worrying about whether I'd be able to finish the book. The perfect balance I'd maintained for months was gone. I needed to come up with another plan.

A good friend of mine, who happened to head up the east coast development office of a big Hollywood producer, said that maybe I would like to let her take a look at what I had written so far. The notion made me very nervous. Then she found out that I had not even printed out the pages I had written up until then.

"Are you crazy?" she said. "Haven't you heard that computers crash? What kind of self-destructive idiot are you?"

It was a rhetorical question. She'd known me for years. I tried to justify myself anyway. "If I print it out, I'll be tempted to read it."

"Print it," she said. "And mail it to me. I'll keep it for you."

Grateful to have someone concerned and telling me what to do, I followed her orders.

Of course, as I knew would happen, when she received the 175 pages in the mail, she asked me if she could read it. I was dying for some feedback but said I didn't think it would be a good idea.

"Look," she said, "I have a confession to make. I already started reading it. I thought you'd say yes and—" the pause between "and" and what followed was maybe a millisecond, but it felt the way I imagine it feels after you hear the word "Fire" and you're standing blindfolded in front of a firing squad.

"And it's good," she said. "Really good."

I tried to let that sink in. "You liked it?"

"I like it a lot."

"Really?" I felt my head get hot with tears. "How far—how much have you read?"

She cleared her throat, laughed, and said, "I actually stayed up until four in the morning. I read everything."

I forgave her immediately. How could I not? She had liked it! I wanted to hear more, but at the same time I didn't want her to say anything that would take away from what she'd already said.

The next morning she called me again. Would it be all right, she asked, if she showed it to her boss?

Looking back on all this, I suppose that bringing other people in while the book was still in progress was dangerous, even foolhardy of me. I might have been setting myself up, just differently from what I had done in the past. But after months and months of working in the dark, a certain dementia sets in, the way it does if you do anything alone for too long: it becomes difficult to trust your own judgment, and you lose your place in the world—at least I do. In this case, however, I was lucky.

A week after my friend gave the 175 pages to her boss, he said he wanted to meet me, and at the meeting he told me that he wanted to option my book for a movie. Again, I suppose this could have gone either way. Expectation might have crippled me. But for some reason it didn't. In fact, the opposite occurred. I wrote the next 150 pages in a month and a half. I was energized in a way I never had been before, eager to finish, barely able to sleep at night.

After all these years, I have come to understand a few things about myself. But my writing process is still essentially a mystery to me, as mysterious as love. I know that faith is a big part of the picture, a necessary component for making something difficult work. Sometimes I think of writing a book, metaphorically, as being dropped into the middle of the ocean with no land in sight. There's only one real strategy, though it remains difficult for me to follow: pick a direction, start swimming, and never turn back.

Chapter 10

Acts of Love and Discovery

Jane Futcher

In short, our conceptions attain a maximum of definite individuality
and of generality (or applicability) in the degree to which
they show how things depend upon one another or influence one another,
instead of expressing the qualities that objects possess statically.
(John Dewey, 1910, p. 134)

This process of reconstruction goes on inevitably;
the school does not invent it,
but undertakes rather to speed it up and to give it direction.
(Boyd Henry Bode, 1940, p. 254)

When I was ten years old, I had a recurring nightmare. I would wake up in terror, convinced that my world was coming to an end because I had to write a 100-word composition and no words would come.

"I had the dream again," I'd say, climbing the steps to my parents' room and slipping under the covers next to my mother.

"The fox chasing you?" she'd ask slowly, rising from her dreams.

"The 100-word composition," I'd cry, feeling a black, unforgiving mountain of words looming over me, demanding that I scale them. And I couldn't. Couldn't think of a single word, didn't know where to begin. The constriction in my throat relaxed as my mother stroked my forehead and began the ritual that had become so familiar.

"You know it's a dream?" she'd ask gently.

"Yes." Her satin nightgown would brush my cheek as her warm hand reached for mine. "And you know that although a hundred words sound like a lot, it really isn't that many." I would listen skeptically, heart still pounding. "If you write ten sentences, with ten words in each sentence, " she'd continue, "that equals about a hundred words. A ten-sentence composition equals about two paragraphs. You've written that much before, haven't you? Lots of times."

My father, unburying his head from the pillow he wrapped around his ears would open his eyes.

"It's the nightmare, Dad," I'd say miserably. "The terrible hundred-word one."

"So sorry," he'd say. "Is Mum helping you?"

"It feels as though they'll strangle me," I would whimper. "I'm walking across this A-bomb site of no words and word-mountains that are going to kill me."

"Poor baby." My mother's sympathy and the light of her logic would dissolve enough of my fear to guide me back downstairs to my room, staying close to the wall so the dangerous, unattainable words could not find me.

I'm not sure when that nightmare first started, but I have a feeling it was around the time my fourth-grade teacher was trying to get her students to use more metaphors and sensory description. I remember a particularly daunting series of in-class assignments in which we were told to describe inanimate objects vividly. Dread froze me as I sought to describe a bowl of Campbell's tomato soup. No metaphors, no dandy turns of phrase popped into my brain like the ones that seemed to ripple like water from Ginger Morton's pen. Writing was a torture designed to make me feel stupid, lost, and alone in the world.

In the winter of seventh grade, I learned that Mr. Hinckle was dying. Mr. Hinckle was a New Hampshire lobsterman whom I had watched every summer for as long I could remember rowing his gray Swampscott dory in the cove at Little Boar's Head, twenty miles south of Portsmouth. I could see his yellow oilskin move as he reached for his red and white buoys, inspected his pots, and returned, stroking the oars with the rhythm of the waves, allowing their momentum to carry his dory onto the beach, where he pushed it up to the high rocks on wooden rollers. Mr. Hinckle sold his lobsters in a brown-shingled fish house on the embankment above the beach, next to the weathered shack where my father's friend William Fowler kept the dory we used each summer to go fishing.

Mr. Hinckle couldn't die. I wanted him to be there next August when we came to stare into his huge bubbling tanks, where dark green lobsters swam, eyes bulging, menacing as primordial sea monsters. A treasured piece of my universe was going out with the tide, and there was nothing I could do to stop it. Grief and disbelief took me to the little mahogany desk in my room and a white ruled pad of my father's, and I began to write about the man and the rocky cove where I had spent so many happy hours each summer.

I remember that as I wrote, as I tried to describe what that man and that place meant to me, I felt alive and engaged, taken away from my life in a row house in Baltimore and the pages of homework that were due in the morning and my mother's insistence that ballroom dancing classes and piano lessons and Girl Scout meetings and confirmation classes at church were crucial to my development. As I wrote, I felt connected to a ruddy-faced New England fisherman in a yellow slicker and high black boots, who spoke in a strange New England drawl and lived by the sea.

For the first time that I can remember, I felt a power and pleasure in writing, and the words came. Not easily, not lightly. But they came, and as they did I found myself crying, and then, even more surprising, eager to edit and rewrite to ensure that I had said it well. I remember my pride and amazement when my story was published in the school literary magazine alongside essays by glamorous eighteen-year-old seniors who dated boys and flew to Bermuda for spring vacation and knew their way in the world.

Writing became a release, a place, like the treehouse I built in our backyard maple tree in Baltimore, where I could breathe and look around and bring things I loved closer to me, through words.

And I was good at it. Not all the time. Not, unfortunately, in class or for school; but when I wanted to write, needed to sort things out, I could.

Soon something pushed me even harder toward the words that had once been so terrifying. I was beginning to develop crushes on girls and teachers at school. Frightened and exhilarated by the intensity of my feelings, I wrote oblique poems to my beloveds, made notes on conversations with them, tried to describe the longing and desire that drew me toward classmates in a way that I had learned was considered inappropriate and perverted. Still, in my little brown spiral, I wrote of my longing to lie on a raft in Chesapeake Bay with Betsy McDavid, my older sister's petite friend who was "stacked'' and knew how to bop and could sing the lyrics to every song on the Hit Parade. Writing didn't take away my guilt and confusion, but it helped, even as I went underground, writing in code, avoiding the pronoun "she" in my poems and usually visiting only the tortured side of love.

As profoundly as I had once feared the 100-word composition, I now feared my lesbianism, wondering how to change the girl I was to someone more like Betsy McDavid, whose love for boys seemed as natural and spontaneous as mine for girls. I knew nothing good could come of being queer. Look at what happened to Shirley MacLaine in

The Children's Hour or the gay man in James Baldwin's *Another Country*, living alone on the margins of society. Pansies, dykes, fairies were sideshow freaks, not nice girls from Baltimore whose families had high expectations.

In high school, a favorite English teacher was the first to recognize in me the glimmer of a writer. We corresponded during the summers, and each letter from her became an event that made my heart pound and my breath quicken. I wrote back to her, of course, and once she chided me for my misspellings and poor penmanship. I loved her for caring, hated her for reminding me, as so many adults seemed to, that form is essential to good writing. When I stumbled across an ancient edition of Emily Post's rules of etiquette at a summer yard sale in New Hampshire, I sent it to her, highlighting the most absurd, quaint, or outdated rules of decorum. I could not tell her, because I don't think I knew, that my messy style was one of my most powerful defenses against the adults in my life who told me what to do, whom to love, how to stand, where to go, and how to get there. Advice on grammar seemed perfectly reasonable to an English teacher, but for me, it was a cattle prod from yet another adult with expectations. Perhaps she sensed in me that abysmally low self-esteem that seemed to crumple my papers for me, misspell my words, leave my sentences unfinished. What I loved was her encouragement, her insistence that despite my embarrassed, flawed presentations, my words had meaning and value. That loving encouragement kept me going for years.

Up until the time I came out as a lesbian at twenty-six, my writing blocks were, I think, closely related to my shame and fear of my homosexuality. To write fiction well, I would have to expose myself, wanted to expose myself; but to expose myself was to admit that I longed to do something unnatural, wanted to hold my sister's best friend's hand and undress the math teacher in her skintight ski pants.

All that changed when I moved to New York City, determined to stop hiding, and fell in love with a woman who loved me back. At last I began to feel free enough to write about my life and the women I loved. The process of coming out, of expressing my sexual desires and acknowledging them to others, made my writing easier and more spontaneous. On weekends, I would take the F train eagerly to my office at a midtown Manhattan book publisher, turn on my enormous green electric IBM, and write love poems to my curly-haired, Mick-Jagger-look-alike lover from Arkansas, in her jeans, vests, silk scarves and Frye boots. Writing about her, I felt the connection and elation I had felt as a child working on my story about Mr. Hinckle.

I wrote, and still write, to remember, to honor, to name the colors and pleasures of love. And the pain of losing it.

For most of my life, I could write only in a quiet room with the door closed. The presence of another, even someone I loved, interfered with the silence and sense of privacy that allowed me to relax and go deeper. Writing for me was and still is about letting go, being free of my desire to please, my need to perform, my constant efforts to second-guess what someone wants or expects from me.

As I became more comfortable with my sexuality and won some recognition for the writing I was paid to do—freelance arts reviews and educational slides, tapes and filmstrip programs—my poem fragments no longer seemed like the right creative outlet. I wanted to write stories about the lives of the women I knew in Greenwich Village, my circle of lesbian and gay artists and professionals who were succeeding in the world—buying a theater company, editing and designing books, studying law and medicine, and still being true to themselves, and the world, as women and as lesbians.

Writing fiction, I found, was very different from writing love poems, in which I rode a wave of passion and desire until the poem was done. A short story or novel required more deliberate, sustained, conscious effort, not to mention plot, character, and invention. There often were times when I felt the tyranny of the 100-word composition lurking in my brain, but I continued down the rockier and, in the long run, for me, more satisfying road of fiction.

In 1977, my lover and I moved from New York to San Francisco the day before my thirtieth birthday. I had severance pay from the publishing house where I'd worked, and I qualified for unemployment, so I had money to support myself while I began my first novel, called *CRUSH*, about a passionate attraction I'd felt for a girl in high school. It was part invention, part autobiography: the feelings I described were true, but most of the events were fabricated. I wrote, as I often write now, to understand a painful and emotionally tumultuous time in my life that continued to haunt my thoughts and affect my behavior. I wanted to exorcise the demons of secrecy and shame that were making it difficult for me to sustain intimate relationships in adulthood.

Because my lover worked at an office in San Francisco, I was alone a lot, something I found hard, after the rich, busy life we had led in Greenwich Village. The few friends we had were my lover's colleagues from work. Through one of them, I joined a fiction writing group of six women, all much older than I, all married or divorced, all straight.

That writing group, which met once a month, all day, for potluck meals at members' houses, helped me survive the loneliness and uncertainty of writing a novel. At first I was so insecure about my lesbianism that I feared the group's criticism of my novel might be motivated by homophobia, by disgust at and disapproval of my characters' homosexuality. If they said my dialogue was stiff, I wondered if they really meant they didn't approve of the feelings my characters were trying to express. If they said the pace was slow, I thought perhaps they were uncomfortable with a scene itself, like the one in which the girls finally kiss. Eventually, though I came to trust the group, took enormous comfort from their support, and learned a lot from the war stories they shared about the publishing world—crazy agents, myopic editors, greedy publishers. The usual.

Twenty years later, I am still in a writing group, this time with four lesbian novelists, and we still vent regularly about the perils and pitfalls of publishing. All of us have struggled to gain acceptance from mainstream publishers and still wonder from time to time if this or that rejection slip had something to do with our sexual orientation. We talk about the frustration of juggling schedules, finances, and relationships so that we have time to do what we love. We celebrate, sometimes with a degree of envy, when a member sells a manuscript, and we commiserate, sometimes with unspoken relief, when a member's book has come back with a nasty rejection letter.

Writing groups do more than offer feedback on manuscripts. They provide emotional support for the creative process, for the often lonely and financially challenging job of writing fiction. Most of my writing blocks have their source in a loss of confidence that comes when I feel hopeless and helpless, alone and frustrated, paralyzed by self-doubt and the fear that no matter how hard I try, the story I am writing may not sell. Sharing the challenges of the creative and publishing processes helps me laugh, reminds me that I am not alone, and sends me back to my keyboard prepared to lunge again at the windmill.

Occasionally, I have felt so vulnerable that any criticism of my work sets me back, turns me away from a project that I thought, or hoped, was going well. But more often, the group's careful response to my writing spurs me on. There is nothing like praise to keep me writing. That encouragement makes it easier the next time I'm gazing at the dark monitor and wondering if my words have described how my heart aches when I watch the muscles in my lover's forearms contract as she lifts a bale of hay or slices onions for a casserole.

Most of us don't create, can't sustain the creative process consistently, without support and a modicum of praise. Writers like to show off, to display their talent, to be admired, seen, heard. Without that sense of an audience, however small, the creative and economic uncertainties of a writing career are often intolerable.

Today, I work full-time writing editorials for a daily newspaper in northern California. Often, when I come home after a long day of deadlines and stiff shoulders, the last thing I want to do is to sit down at my computer to the novel or story I'm writing. On weekends, I would rather hike to the ocean with my lover and our dogs than sit in my room hoping words will come. Usually, my lover and I compromise. One day of the weekend is for us to do something together; one day is for me to write. There never seems to be enough time.

Working in a newsroom with sixty journalists has taught me to write without privacy, without a closed door, with phones ringing and the TV on. My muse knows that she'll survive the interruptions of office birthday parties and CNN special bulletins on the latest Clinton sex scandal. Still, different tasks are required of me when I write fiction, and regrettably, what I've learned about newswriting does not translate into better fiction.

Fiction involves an expansion of the facts, a widening of the lens. Journalism often compresses the writing. What this means is that at end of my workweek, when I am at home at last and working on a piece of fiction, the ten editorials I have written at work do not aid the process of remembering, imagining, feeling, and inventing. With fiction, I must loosen my grip, encourage my internal editor to disappear, take a nap, go for a hike, so that I can write without inhibitions.

My fiction is always about love—falling in love, losing love. To be open to that intensity of feeling, to the colors of love and longing, I still prefer a quiet room, a closed door, and, more recently, music. Music without words. Electronic music by Kitaro or Brian Eno or the piano improvisations of Keith Jarrett, sounds that relax me and lull into silence my ruthless internal editor, who rips sentences apart before they're finished and questions my abilities at every turn.

When I stall, passion is what brings me back. Falling in love brings the joy of words back from the 100-word mountain. Today I am in love with an old friend from elementary school whom I saw for the first time in twenty years at a school reunion at a dude ranch last summer in Wyoming. I am also in love with a young lesbian reporter at work who leans beguilingly against my desk as she tells me what her therapist said or dishes the copy editor who has just changed her lead. Today I am in love with places, too—the long breakers at Kehoe Beach on the Point Reyes peninsula, the coral reefs on Cozumel, the "painted ladies" of San Francisco, the city's multicolored Victorians. Sometimes passion blooms as I write, so that to write about someone or something is to fall in love with it.

I have not dreamed of the 100-composition in four decades, but I still fear failure. I know now that I can write 100 words, but I don't know if they'll be any good. I wonder if they will be original, wise, surprising. Will anyone see the grace I've tried to describe as an old man in a gray wooden dory glides out past a reef into the New Hampshire dawn? Can readers empathize with a scene in which a woman learns from her lover, whom she had planned to be with for a lifetime, that she is having an affair, that the relationship is over? Have I communicated the awesome dignity of my closest friend as she struggles to accept that the tumors in her brain are taking her away from everything that matters to her? Do you feel the lush beauty of the California hills in winter, when the streams, dry all year, roar with rain, and green feather ferns kiss the rocks?

Each word is a burden and a treasure. How can I describe my southern mother, tall and loud, leaving the Mississippi delta town in Arkansas where she grew up, to live on 98th Street and East End Avenue in New York? Do you know that in that rural Arkansas town, the remnants of slavery still haunt each dusty, unpaved alley, each unemployment line, each maid slipping in through the back door of a white woman's house? Can you see my sister who has refused for ten years to see me, tall, white-haired, lurching toward my lover and me, slapping at our hands as she tries to push us down the stairs?

As I tell you what I see, I begin to know what I am seeing, and the story that comes can entertain and change us both. It doesn't always happen. But sometimes it does. And it is always about love—having it, losing it. Without love, I cannot write. For it is love that inspires me to honor, remember, describe, and transform the people and places I have known. And it is love that pushes me to read or watch or listen to the creative expression of others.

Without love, we shrivel, as people, as artists. We turn away from the pleasures of engagement. The creative process is essentially a spiritual experience, an opening to the unknown, a prayer to the universe, a willingness to see and express something that is very personal and, one hopes, universal.

How many words are enough? One hundred? One hundred thousand? If love is there, and commitment and intention, something happens, and that something connects readers and writers, lovers and ex-lovers, parents and children, estranged siblings and dying friends.

Sometimes 100 words are far too few. Sometimes they are more than enough.

Chapter 11

"Johnny's in the Basement, Mixing Up the Medicine," or I'll Trade You Two Metaphors for a Metonymy

Alan A. Block

To maintain the state of doubt and to carry on systematic and protracted inquiry—these are essentials of thinking.
(John Dewey, 1910, p. 13)

[T]eachers must make common cause with the laboring class in order to hasten the coming of a humane industrial organization as an enduring basis for democratic living.
(Boyd Henry Bode, 1940, p. 294)

Consider the paradox. I've been asked to write an essay on how I work while I work on the work. That is, to elaborate on the creative process while I am, in fact, steeped in the midst of it. That is, to talk about the process of bringing a semblance of seeming order out of apparent chaos while immersed in the chaos. And to produce a piece that appears seamless and polished and has flaws only you, the reader, will be able to see. This could be quite a dangerous undertaking—like trying to breathe evenly while focusing on breathing, or trying to tie my shoes while minutely describing the process of tying my shoes. Frankly, I'd rather go barefoot. I already know that writing is almost always maddening; when I work I descend into the swirling whirl of the deep waters of the unconscious. Some call this space the imagination, but that is too romantic a notion for me; it smacks too much of inspiration, and I work alone. I am too often afraid. I fear lostness. I fear dissolution. I eat a lot of chocolate chip cookies. I think often about Poe's "A Descent into the Maelstrom" (1967). The story's narrator, risking life and limb to fish in the choicest and yet most dangerous waters, details how he and his brothers are caught in the horrors of a great storm and are threatened by the ensnarement and dissolution of their vessel and themselves in a huge maelstrom. Sucked into the dangerous turbulence "in dizzying swings and jerks, that sent us sometimes only a few hundred yards—sometimes nearly the complete circuit of the whirl" (p. 351), the unnamed narrator considers "how magnificent a thing it was to die in such a manner" (p. 349). I, too, when I write—as I write even this—am not unconcerned about my safety, though it is impossible to consider *not* descending into the maelstrom, to anticipate *not* writing.[1] I recall that Poe's narrator gets to the surface, he discovers that in the experience "My hair, which had been raven black the day before, was as white as you see it now. They say too that the whole expression of my countenance had changed" (p. 353). The ascent will change me in ways I cannot now know.

The narrator of Poe's tale then proceeds to tell the townspeople his story, but he avows that "they did not believe it. [And so] I now tell it to you—and I can scarcely expect you to put more faith in it than did the merry fishermen of Lofoden." When I ultimately arrive at the surface, I am certain it, too, will be an auspicious event, though I can scarcely expect you to put much faith in the tale. The process is, of course, all mine, and its description can only sound fantastical because it is produced by and produces me and not you; you will see only the carefully wrought surface and not the turbulent maelstrom into which *I* descend. But I am relieved by the awareness that my willing descent into the maelstrom is prevented from final tragedy by the willing recounting of the tale of the willing descent into babel; the narrator of this tale is saved, as it were, in the process of narration. In the Jewish folktale retold by Phoebe Gilman as *Something for Nothing* (1992), Joseph, too, is able to transform and thereby save his experience by writing a story about the loss of his precious cloth. Narration possesses the power to transform loss into substance. The experience, however, irrevocably alters the narrator's existence. So now I begin a narration of how I work, though I can scarcely expect you to put more faith in it than did the merry fishermen of Lofoden. I intend to make this descent into the maelstrom, that is, to write this chapter about the process of writing this chapter while writing this chapter; and so that I might save myself and surface again, I will make my ascent possible by strapping myself to the water casks—my metaphors—and observing and reflecting upon the details which swirl maddenly about me. I think this is going to be fun.

I work in the basement of a two-story house in rural Wisconsin. In order to engage in the work I must literally descend into the basement. There, I have built an office space and surrounded myself with the accouterments of my profession—books, desks, papers, pencils, pens, bulletin boards, computers—oh, you know the scene. On the walls are familiar icons—posters and pictures that remember me to my life. They stare mutely at me as I descend. One is a picture of Dorothy Gale: "Toto, I have a feeling we're not in Kansas anymore." Around me are my books—they comfort me. It is quiet down here in the basement in the early mornings except for the padded steps of four felines who await my arrival with incredible patience, and who then with incredible impatience try to force their way onto my lap or atop the computer. My family—Beth, my wife; and Emma and Anna Rose, our two daughters, continue their dreams upstairs even as I abandon the safety of sleep to engage in the work. I close the doors to their rooms as I pass them—it is a noisy business to which I am heading. I awake—always before first light—and I stumble down the stairs of our home, passing the idoled (pun intended) coffee machine on my way. I have readied it the evening before, and I have only to weakly brush the switch as I make the first pass by it and wait three minutes to have fresh (relatively) coffee.[2] While it brews, I open the basement door and descend to perform my morning ablutions. I also feed the cats and check the litter boxes. I clean when necessary. I return upstairs for the coffee and re-descend, caffeine in tow. I sit at the computer and stare blankly at the screen. It is immensely quiet here despite the sound of the furnace blowing on behind me. Upstairs all are asleep and the cats know now to stay away. I ingest the first sips of the coffee as I move my fingers toward the computer—it is between 5:30 a.m. and 6:00 a.m. I search for the requisite piece—and, sipping more—descend.

I write because it cures me; I write because it comforts me; I write because it produces me. Writing has become a way of life. Writing is the dialogue in which I engage with myself so that I might produce some interesting ideas that will get me through the days. I want to think about my life and the world and my world and the life. Writing down here in the basement is where that activity takes place. That is, down here in the basement I mix up the medicines so that I can finally ascend out of here and engage in a relatively healthy manner in the life that I build. Writing down here in the basement facilitates my activity in the world. Down here is where I produce and, therefore, prepare for the world up there. Regardless of the particular content in any particular act of writing, the process itself irrevocably alters my life. It will probably be good for me. I have descended to the basement and when I ascend I will know different things; I will have produced new thoughts; I will be inevitably different. It is not just the thoughts that lead to this metamorphosis—it is the very process itself that merits the responsibility: there will be some notable perspectives taken along the way. The work begins when a challenge appears in my life—an assignment ("Would you write about this and that and such and such") or an issue (the teacher's authority or the school as text) about which I would like to think—and this encounter is the not unpleasant irritant that only can be relieved by the production of writing.

Metaphor One

I spent a number of years attending concerts of the Grateful Dead; I recall these years fondly as times of freedom and good cheer, challenge and growth, youthful abandon,[3] and serious movement. I always attended in the warm company of my brother, Michael. Once inside we actually saw little of each other; we knew we would meet again at the end and assess the changes. We were there for support, not guidance; inside, it would all be up to me. Outside, the crowd would be milling about: some were attired in an array of outlandish garb and others dressed in plain jeans;[4] some were selling and buying tickets, buying and selling and ingesting controlled substances; many seemed to be meeting old friends and partaking in the party atmosphere that all of these detailed events and more produced. The Grateful Dead were a cultural phenomenon about which I am certain dissertations have been and will be written. Good for them; they all deserve each other. To me, these concerts were my introduction to a safe madness. I have learned in my life—and to a large extent at these events—not to suppress madness; I have accepted that madness is an invaluable space for observation and learning. I have discovered that sanity is the toleration of madness: healthy living is the capacity to bear the tensions that doubt and uncertainty and dissatisfaction and irresolution produce. The Grateful Dead concerts inspired that madness and showed how constructive it could be, how it could be managed and productively used. We—my brother and I—would arrive in a heightened state of anticipation, bearing our share of hallucinogenic substances that we would consume at carefully prescribed times in order to facilitate manipulated states of visioning. We—my brother and I—would wander pointedly amidst the crowd, smelling the scene, studying the faces, drinking the atmosphere. There was a party up ahead, and everyone knew it. Everyone was to be a part of it. The Dead were going to steal your face right off your head. Nothing yet had actually happened; it was all anticipation. But there was no doubt that a considerable event was about to occur.

There were two moments—not unconnected—that happened to me after ingesting LSD. The first was a moment of panic and occurred not long after eating the blot of paper. That anxiety always seemed to me connected to a lack of confidence that I would be capable of controlling the experience, that I would lose control, that I would lose myself—become, as it were, berserk. I regretted the meal awhile. The second moment occurred not very long afterward, as the hallucinogen began to take effect. I would experience a rush—like a great wind blowing my body from within. I would recognize this moment as the beginning of the trip, and I would tightly grasp the imagined arms of an imagined armchair and anticipate the takeoff. Hold on for the ride, as it were. And once it began, I was soon high above the earth, soaring, held aloft finally by the music.

I sit here in the basement in the quiet morning hours facing the computer. I've been thinking about this project for months now. Now, the blank screen terrifies me—I look at the status bar and acknowledge that I am on page one, position one. I stare blankly at the bulletin board before me, reading yellowed memos and aging notes; these are all in the past and I must move toward the future and there is nothing on the board that will help me. I grasp my coffee cup with an intensity that threatens to shatter the glass. I berate myself for accepting this assignment, for accepting any assignment. I could be working on lesson plans. I could learn how to write a lesson plan. I dust the top of my desk. I reformat the page and change the font. I clean the toilets down here. I look at the clock and estimate how long it will be until the family will awaken and I can go upstairs. I stare again at the blank screen—I don't think I can get out of this writing—and take a very deep breath. I put my fingers on the keys and write a first word, any word. That first word almost fills the page—it confirms the next word that determines the next, and so on and so on. I see a sentence or even two; I am comforted. Outside the wind begins to howl.

The opening strains of music send me searching for the identity of the song. It is both an anchor and a release. I know where I am and I don't know where I am going. The crowd begins to move and I begin to move in the crowd. I recognize the song. I close my eyes and respect the music. I feel safe. There is a pattern, I apprehend, to the band's arrangements: the Dead start on familiar ground—a song from the vast repertoire in a wholly recognizable form—and then during the song's rendition the band begins to wander off in directions unplanned and unknown. Connected as I was to the music—held aloft, as it were, by it—I would follow. From the familiar strains of "Jack Straw," or "Alabama Getaway," or "Uncle John's Band," the music would move into extraordinary patterns, and I would move with it into strange places. I was never afraid. There was always something that tied me to the place and to the music—a theme, perhaps, or a sound, or the good grace of the other participants—yet the music always led me to wander in places it itself had never been. The invitation was always to come hear Uncle John's band who had come to take his children home—but, in fact, it was always clear that the responsibility for that homecoming would ultimately be mine. The fact is that no one—not even the band—knew where we were going; all that we were certain of was that the journey would be taken. There was precedent but no certainty; it was a journey chaotically organized. We were confident that finally we would surface, finally we would return, finally we would come home—but it would have to be by our own resources: If I knew the way I would take you home, the band sang. We would visit incredible places and see fantastic things. It would, indeed, be a long, strange trip. And the home to which we returned would not recognize us or necessarily believe our tale. We would tell it anyway. We had to do so.

As I have said, there is a pattern to the band's individual arrangements, as indeed, there is to the concert as a whole. In the first phase there is much that is familiar and comforting; indeed, one could say that affection and careful caressing are produced in the Dead's structure. The first touches are vernacular and pleasant, and there is laughter and merriment in the activity. Embraced by the familiar and the joyful, we dance and laugh and bask in the gentle petting. I am comfortable and yet excited—my body moves with the touch of the music. I delight in the playfulness and seduction of the music. I'm getting what I know I want. The pleasure is all mine and immediate. Then the mood begins to shift, and a sense of tension develops as experiment and risk enter the arena; what was once familiar becomes stranger and stranger—curiouser and curiouser I think—and I am titillated by the movement away from the familiar and the resulting tension that this move produces. I am no longer certain what will next occur, what direction I might next be offered, though I feel remarkably unthreatened; I am in good care. Indeed, I am aroused by the attention this teasing movement suggests; I move to the seductive attendance of the music, attempting to find its touch, though it playfully eludes me. I follow it. Slowly the band continues its move away from the familiar; the subtle play of instruments continues to provoke and tease; the song is there yet, but now attending to it requires a different engagement, one that commands my full attention. I actively search for the familiar and the known, but they become less and less available. I begin to see what I didn't expect to see and did not know was even there for knowledge. This tension remains both uncomfortable and pleasant. The music pulls at my body to follow; I am intensely focused and I follow the notes, the lines, the rhythms, as the drums beat passionately and the guitar pulls on me as taffy on the fingers until the tension is unbearable and then in an instant the band explodes in concert and the crowd explodes with it and the tension breaks and I let go of my breath volubly and my body releases its tension and the band restores the familiar again in the sound and feel of the tune as the Dead gently return me to more solid ground.

As I stare at the screen, which slowly fills with my words, I am comforted by the company of my thoughts. When I write, I move from the familiar to the strange. I begin with what I think I know so that I may go to some place I do not know, though when I begin I always fear that I actually know very little; I panic to think that this nothing will not fill up the blank pages; I panic to think that if this nothing manages to mark over the pages, everyone will recognize the nothing I know. Slowly, as I wrap myself in the familiar, I sense the rumbling—unformed words, half-sentences, incomplete rhythm—that suggests the possibilities of movement away from the familiar, safe center. I am pulled by the prospects I can yet only anticipate; I make myself available for risk-taking, and I become anxious to know what it will be possible to see and feel from the work I am in the process of constructing. I dive into my words and produce new words that reflect thought; I compose ideas that were not there before. As I produce words and place them in contiguity, I make sense that I understand—though I can swear I did not know the sense I would make when I began. If I'd known then what I knew now, I'd have written something completely different. I start with my arms crossed and my head cocked to the right side. I stare defiantly at the screen and reread the ideas already visible. An idea hangs about like the fog in the fields behind my house, and I position my hands on the keyboard and try to give substance to the air heavy with moisture. My fingers move and I watch the screen, stopping occasionally to check the pulse of the work; I sense movement and pith: the lines bounce about as I write and rewrite and edit and reedit. All this movement is thought transformed into physicality and physicality recast into thought. My whole psyche forces up against my skin, like the powerful wind that blows through the screens of my windows. My entire body is made attentive and responsive to the back and forth, up and down movement of the screen; the tension increases as I rush to produce rain from this cloud before the sun dries up the fog. In a great burst I ejaculate the thought contained in words. I jab fiercely at the period key and sit back in the chair, my arms dangling at my side. I feel, actually, quite powerful.

As I write, I hear noises from upstairs. I look at the clock and realize that the day is about to begin upstairs. I save what I have written—save it as well on a backup disk—and push the keyboard back in under the screen. It has been a good morning's writing. And I sense emotional drain. Thank goodness there are peanut butter and jelly sandwiches to make. I will empty the dishwasher and set the table and prepare breakfast. I ascend. I wonder if they will recognize me.

Later, after the break, I will return to the writing. There will be a sameness about the madness, though it be madness nonetheless; at the end of this later session I will take the work out on my daily run, where I will jog some yet-stuck thoughts into words and begin work on the next day's labors. I will run through some problems that today's work made clear. I will prepare some problems that other days will need to resolve. Tomorrow will be much like today. And so on and so on until the work concludes.

I leave the concert exhausted—I am drenched in perspiration and my muscles ache. I have been to strange places and have seen remarkable things. The world outside the concert hall appears an unfamiliar place—it is certainly not a Grateful Dead concert, and, besides, we have changed.

Metaphor Two

Perhaps males (at least a great many of them) have always been jealous of the birthing process. To bring life out of the body, to sustain the life in the body as it prepares for independence, is a mysterious and wonderful event from which males biologically are excluded. We must look at women with envy—perhaps that is why childbirth is described in Genesis as burdensome and painful rather than as beautiful and miraculous. It must be for this reason that men have attempted for so many years to control the birthing process, and in the language of the process have made themselves the deliverers of newborns and, by such positioning, have rendered the birth mother invisible. I think it may be that many of our (male) images concerning the creative process derive from our envy, our fear, and our awe of birth. I cannot help thinking about how I work in terms of the birthing process.

There is a story I have carried about with me for a number of years concerning Michelangelo and the creative process. It is an apocryphal story, but I love it anyway. And like all apocryphal stories, it is only partly untrue. Exactly what part of the story is untrue, I am not certain; but nevertheless, I am comforted to know that not all of it is untrue. In his fictional biography of Michelangelo, Irving Stone (1996) has the sculptor describe how it is he is able to create out of a block of coarse stone his delicate, polished figures of his sculptures. Michelangelo contends that when he views a piece of stone he can actually see the figure entrapped in the block of marble, and that it is his design to free that figure. There is, at least, some historical validity to this piece of fiction: Michelangelo is one of the few Renaissance sculptors who actually went to the quarry to choose their own stone.[5] I imagine Michelangelo drawn to a certain piece because he actually could see a figure within it, the image in his mind to which he would, as it were, give birth. In any case, it is in a sense a birthing process to which Michelangelo refers; as a sculptor he will bring out a body from within the body of marble.

Hanging on my wall are postcard reproductions of Michelangelo's series of sculptures known as *I Prigionieri*—the prisoners. The series consists of four works, all full-sized figures and all in a seemingly unfinishedness. That is, each of the four figures is a representation of a male form emerging out of the marble in which it has been imprisoned. Each form is portrayed in a particular stage of emergence; only partly released, each is only partly free of the marble. These are rough-textured sculptures; whole sections of the marble remain seemingly untouched, the figures only partly chiseled and all incompletely realized. Nevertheless, they are to my mind, finished pieces; I see this series as an attempt to enact the process of birthing ideas, of embodying thought. I am accustomed to thinking about the creation of a piece of stone sculpture as the making of form, but Michelangelo's pieces seems to suggest that a form already exists that begs for release; ironically, what form the figure will take is apparently unknown until its release. Remarkably enough, what identity these sculptures may assume upon release remains unclear; after all, these figures have yet to come fully out of the stone blocks. Once the figures are free, who knows how their bodies will be set down? These sculptures represent to me the struggle to produce the work rather than to embody the finished idea. In this series of figures Michelangelo has represented the process in the product! And the product displays a glorious, agonizing, and painful series of events.

It is this difficult labor that I see in the four prisoners. They each exist in various states of emergence from the stone; Michelangelo has portrayed the act as agonizingly strenuous, even a bit ungainly and awkward, even a bit painful, though the sculptures themselves are magnificent. Though they struggle in terribly graceless poses and contorted stances to wrestle free of the marble prison, there is yet inordinate beauty and dignity in the struggle. The torsos and limbs of each figure are in various states of egress, though in all the figures the feet and parts of the hands and heads and faces remain entrapped. One, an older man (he is full-bearded),[6] seems to be pushing his way out the stone by the strength of his massive chest and arms; his head, of which only the front is free of the stone, is thrown back on his right shoulder as a result of the tension the struggle demands, and his neck muscles and tendons are stetched and tensed. His left arm remains still wholly entrapped in the stone, but the muscles in the arm are tensed as they struggle against the intractable stone. His front torso pushes out of the stone, and his stomach muscles show signs of great exertion. His emerging muscle-thick right leg is crossed awkwardly across his left leg at the knee; his front left calf is visible as it supports the efforts of the head and upper torso for release. A second figure, a clean-shaven younger man, covers his brow and right eye with his left arm as if embarrassed at being seen too early, still within the graceless and awkward process of development. Or perhaps this younger man is resting after previous exertion; perhaps he is asleep and he covers his eyes against the intense light of the world. His muscles are less developed than those of the first, older man, and his smooth-skinned face betrays the hint of a smile. The thigh and calf of his left leg step out of the stone, though his right leg remains wholly entrapped. A third figure, heavier it would seem than the rest, seems to be wrestling with the block of stone that still covers much of his head;

his eyes and the top of his nose are all one can see of his head and neck area; his eyes are closed with the tension of the struggle. It is clear to me that he is straining to release his head—to pull the heavy weight of stone from his head: He appears to be twisting the rock free from his head or twisting the head from the rock; his head turns at a ninety-degree angle to his shoulders. His left leg is almost entirely emerged and yet stands solidly and tensely for support; his right leg, only the upper thigh muscles visible and tensed, rises out of the stone as if stepping out of deep water. Only threads hold his upper body to the stone—perhaps he is trying to pull the huge marble off and over his head. Last, the oldest-seeming man struggles in what might be the final stages of emergence; his head is cocked almost onto his left shoulder, and his left leg, as if it had been stuck in a muddy swamp, is tensed as he essays to lift it finally out of the stone. The bottom of his right leg steps out of the marble block as if stepping out of high, thick grass. Both his feet are still encased within the stone. He is the closest to total egress—he alone is almost free. His upper torso and back are completely released from the marble, and his left arm hangs free to move. He stands freely, completely unsupported by stone. His neck is bent and almost resting on his left shoulder, and there is on his fully-bearded face a look of determination and resignation. This figure alone of all the figures wears a semblance of garments—on his right and left upper thighs a cloth seems draped, though it seems to have fallen in the struggle to emerge. Or perhaps in the emergence he is about to cover himself with it—like Adam in the Garden after eating of the fruit of the Forbidden Tree. His right arm remains still entrapped above his head in the block of marble, but he is apparently wrestling to pull away these last weights of stone that still rest on the back of his head and neck.

These figures are not at rest but are, rather, portrayed in various stages of an extraordinary struggle (my romantic notion) to free themselves from the unformed stone. Though some critics have claimed that they are merely unfinished works by Michelangelo, to me there is nothing incomplete about them. They epitomize to me the struggle of ideas trying to be born; Michelangelo's productions have given me insight into the process. It is obviously a messy and painful process. I sometimes wonder who these figures might be once they have emerged, but I am content to know that this knowledge is not available to me. Rather, what remains clear in these figures is that even Michelangelo could not be certain of who they would be upon release. If he had known their identities before he began the work, then the act of creation would have been no more difficult than cracking an egg. But the image in the faces of these figures is of struggle. It is the struggle of the creative process. It is work.

I sit in front of the computer with my fingers on the keyboard. I want to write something about how I work. I have some vague sense of what this is about. There is an idea inside, but it must be given form; it is work to which I have committed myself—for which I might one day be committed—but to which I now look to with strength. I know that I will learn something in the process, but I do not yet know what it will be. Oh, it is a messy, disorderly, and dirty process in which I engage. I burp and fart and eat; I drop crumbs and dribble coffee. I walk around with my head in blocks of stone trying to release the idea. I pull at my skull and push in the sides of my head in the attempt to squeeze out the word that will form the idea. I talk *sotto voce*; I smile; I scream aloud. I squint and yet cannot see the full face of the idea—but I recognize its forms. I think I can go on.

The Metonymy

I stand here at the window preparing Emma's lunch: a peanut butter and jelly sandwich, some carrot slices, two cookies, and some chips. Too much salt and sugar and a little nutrition, but prepared with bottomless love. I look out at the gray morning sky—it looks like rain, but in Wisconsin, at this time of year, that is not a likely occurrence. I wish it would rain—I like the rain. It neither wholly sullies nor thoroughly cleanses, neither wholly chills nor fully warms. The rhythm of the rain comforts me even as it threatens. Unlike the snow, the rain insists on its presence by its drumming: it demands attention. Dylan sings, "The rainman gave me two cures, and he said, jump right in, the one was Texas medicine and the other was just railroad gin." I have been down in the basement again this morning. I like the idea of the rainman; I need the cure, but it don't come easy.

I think of the Grateful Dead (1970) who, too, sing of the rain and what I've been doing down there in the basement: "Maybe you're tired and broken, your tongue is twisted/With words half-spoken and thoughts unclear/What do you want me to do, to do for you, to see you through?/A box of rain will ease the pain, and love will see you through . . ." I don't know what I'd do without that box of rain.

Oatmeal or corn grits? I think I'll go wake the children.

Notes

1. I am not so romantic as to consider my dying down here in the basement glorious; rather, I prefer to consider the descent part of the epic nature of existence: necessary to salvation.

2. This first cup of coffee is crucial. It must taste just right or the morning is unproductive. It is always strong. After my guests have sampled my coffee for the first time, they almost always request tea.

3. I do not think I was as young as I should have been.

4. We called them dungarees, but alas, when I used the term in a class recently, no one understood what I meant.

5. I am grateful to my colleague Claudia Smith for this information.

6. As I continued to reread this I think that Michelangelo has portrayed for me images of men in various stages of life. I've got to stop rereading this paper and move on.

References

Gilman, P. (1992). *Something from Nothing.* Ontario, Canada: North Winds.

Grateful Dead (Hunter, Robert and Lesh, Phil) (1970). *Box of rain.* Ice Nine Publishing.

Poe, E. A. (1967). *The Complete Poems and Stories of Edgar Allen Poe.* New York: Knopf.

Stone, I. (1996). *The Agony and the Ecstasy.* New York: New American Library.

Chapter 12

Contrariety and Commitment: Wedding Passions

Lance Ternasky

Active, persistent, and careful consideration of any belief
or supposed form of knowledge in the light of the grounds that support it,
and the further conclusions to which it tends, constitutes reflective thought.
(John Dewey, 1910, p. 6)

The function of the school is not merely to conserve
the values of the past, but to provide for the continuous reinterpretation
of our cultural heritage so as to make it the servant
and not the master of our lives.
(Boyd Henry Bode, 1940, p. 297)

The opportunity to examine and document one's own generative process is something of a gift. As a teacher of applied philosophy, most of my work occurs within academe. I do not sculpt or dance. For me, then, the invitation to write this chapter serves two principal purposes. First, it allows me to explore what many of us (I think) take for granted. We often become so enamored of our projects that we overlook the means involved in their production. My fixation on the ultimate birth of an idea conceals the equally important gestational phase. It seems that we seldom consider the foundations of our creativity.

Second, the exercise serves an essential pedagogical purpose—a purpose adeptly noted by Mary Belenky.[1] Belenky captures one of the most unfortunate aspects of the typical exchange between teacher and learner. In this conversation, teachers adroitly present the distillation of months or years of their work to students who may well come to view the process as almost magical. While they are permitted to view teachers' sophisticated constructions, students have no idea how these ideas came to be. The problem is compounded when teachers then ask their students to *critique* these ideas with which they have just become acquainted. Given this state of affairs, students may well come to view teachers and their productions as beyond the pale of mortal men and women. Scholarly work then comes to be seen as exalted—a practice that only special people are capable of performing. At core, we diminish our students and their creative capabilities by withholding from them both our successful strategies and also our false starts, wrong turns, and disappointments.

Having accepted the editors' invitation, I was faced with the task of contemplating and eventually describing my process. I found myself wondering at the conclusion of the contemplative phase whether it was possible to trade my process in for one more appealing. I sensed that my model was atavistic and, thus, hopelessly unevolved. Equally distressing, it initially seemed only marginally informed by the more progressive discourse and commitments I regularly espoused in my classes. To my chagrin, I concluded that my generative process is fueled by antagonism, conflict, and a certain up-againstness. *Contrariety* seemed necessary for my creativity.

Admittedly, the notion that learning or insight attends contrariety is hardly novel. Every undergraduate education major knows the progenitors of such an orientation and could readily associate the idea with both ancients and moderns (most would recall Hegel's movement from thesis through antithesis to synthesis). Given this, we might be inclined to conclude, mistakenly, that the process was similar for all those dependent upon contrariety. Upon reflection, it seems likely that considerable diversity can be found in the ways in which persons actually engage such a model. This paper is an unapologetic attempt to explicate my personal variant.

Let me begin with a story that I find compelling: the Hebrew scriptures story about Jacob at the Jabbok.[2] During a sojourn, Jacob reaches the banks of the Jabbok. As evening approaches, he sends his entourage and all his possessions across the stream and remains alone on the opposite side. As night settles, Jacob finds himself locked in a wrestling match with "a man."[3] The contest continues all night, and as dawn nears, the being insists that Jacob release him. Jacob refuses and eventually suffers a dislocated hip for his persistence and obstinance. Even so, Jacob will not yield until he has received a "blessing." Just before sunrise, the being finally acquiesces and provides Jacob with his boon.

I find this story revealing because Jacob's behavior resembles the way in which I struggle with ideas. Like Jacob, I find that I must distance myself from people and possessions during creative periods. While a part of me genuinely believes that camaraderie and dialogue would advance my purposes, I have always needed isolation in the early stages of an idea's development. This is not to suggest that I can separate *entirely* from my various associations, but it does suggest that I must temporarily bracket these connections.

The need for seclusion is born of quite pragmatic considerations. I have never developed the capacity to be polyphasic; my proclivity for distraction has forced a certain single-mindedness. I seemingly can attend to just one pressing idea at a time. Further, I have learned that there are certain inherent dangers in prematurely presenting new ideas to a wider world. New ideas are fragile and demand stringent protection from assorted threats (including "constructive" criticism from colleagues) if they are to mature. Until fully formed, they must be shielded from the external intrusions that may result in a stillbirth or murder. Developing ideas are treasures that initially must be hidden if they are to avoid being pillaged; and, for me, this requires protective nestling.

Consider, next, Jacob's wrestling match. Unless opponents are unevenly matched, an end to the contest seldom arrives quickly, and the advantage frequently shifts. In similar fashion, an idea does not take shape facilely but develops in spurts and with attendant setbacks.[4] It is only fitting to describe the process as wrestling, and thus as both trying and exhausting. Although there are certainly occasions when "victory" appears near, I seldom experience the bliss that some of my colleagues describe in recounting their productive periods. For me, the contest with an idea has always been labor.

There is, fortunately, more to the story. If it were simply labor without reward, one might question the motivations of the wrestler. But the story tells us that a "blessing" attends the struggle, and it is this that continues to draw me back into the fray. Now, some may view Jacob's blessing as his *just* reward: the spoils of victory. My interpretation is somewhat different. For me, there is no sense of *actual* conquest in the struggle. The blessing is given not because the battle has been won but because one remained tenaciously engaged. The blessing is granted not because one wins but because one struggles—it is a matter of recognition, not recompense.

This tenacious engagement is characterized by certain attitudes. Intimacy, exclusivity, and hyper-attentiveness typify the relationship between a person and an idea, even as contrariety reigns. We might even say that the idea and the person are *wedded* in some sense. Less charitably, we might call such engagement obsessive. Regardless of the appellation, we find these characteristics operating with Jacob. He is relentless and absorbed. He does not offer his opponent a respite, nor does he suggest that the contest continue at a more opportune time. Certain pivotal opportunities only rarely present themselves, and on these uncommon occasions, both reticence and a cavalier attitude are best eschewed. Seriously grappling with an antagonistic idea seemingly compels me to *marry* it.

If we are fortunate, the blessing follows the tenacious engagement, but even this comes at a cost. Were the blessing a matter of remuneration, the agreed upon exchange at the end of the contest would satisfy the conditions of the relationship—a relationship one could thereafter conceivably ignore. The case is different with Jacob. Jacob leaves the encounter marked (i.e., wounded), and such encounters are not easily forgotten.

The process is time-consuming—at times *all*-consuming—and leaves us with psychic reminders. I can easily recollect major insights and breakthroughs, as they are etched in memory. And even though they continue to inform my thinking and practice, they are often accompanied by a bittersweet awareness that the event has passed, and that I have been profoundly affected by it.[5]

At this point, an observer might charge that my creative experience is little more than *preoccupation* with my own spontaneous, short-lived, idiosyncratic constructions. From the outside, struggling with philosophical ideas may look more like obsessing about irrelevancies. Songwriter Edie Brickell tells us that philosophy is nothing more than "the talk on a cereal box [and] a walk on the slippery rocks."[6] And on occasion, my students have asked, "Who could care about this? Why?"

Such perceptions reveal the uneasiness novices feel when they are confronted by the affection that specialists display toward their vital ideas. But wedding the antagonistic idea that often seems like "the other" requires that one press deeply into an area. A friend once described this process as "exhausting the well." His thinking was that one might bypass meaning if one moved too quickly or too capriciously. His goal, like Jacob's, was to hold tightly, over time, to an idea until it had revealed its core.

As a teacher, I must still defend my process from the non-specialist's impression that it is simply overspeculation. Toward this end, I have found one of Alfred North Whitehead's distinctions helpful. In laying out a philosophy of education, Whitehead asserts that true learning begins with "romance." In saying this, he acknowledges what many effective teachers intuitively know: the learners' imagination must be captured before they will endure subtleties. They must in some way enter into a relationship with an idea; otherwise, they will be resigned to lifelessly reciting lifeless details. But Whitehead realizes that romance is not enough. Attraction and infatuation may be essential, but they can hardly sustain life or intellect. Consequently, true learners will eventually delve deeply enough to specialize—to begin developing what Whitehead calls "style."[7]

For Whitehead, style embodies the aesthetic qualities of "attainment and restraint." It might be called artistic precision, and "the love of a subject in itself and for itself, where it is not the sleepy pleasure of pacing a mental quarter-deck, is the love of style as manifested in that study." But even this is not enough, for "above style, and above knowledge, there is something, a vague shape like fate above the Greek gods. That something is Power."[8] If we follow Whitehead's thinking, true learning—and for my purposes, creativity—eventually terminates in power. For both of us, the creative process is not complete until it takes root or gives birth. The creative process is empty until it does something in a lived life.

The introduction of Whitehead might appear to conflict with the meaning I associated with the Jacob story. As I have used him, Whitehead is promoting a decidedly instrumental quality for the learning/creative process. In contrast, the Genesis story seems to possess an intrinsic and distinctly individualistic focus. Here, it is almost as if something beyond self beckons, and the mention of "blessings" appears almost egoistic. It might seem that the struggle with contrariety was largely motivated by hedonism: we struggle with ideas chiefly because of the pleasure generated by the skirmish.

Now, while I am not inherently opposed to hedonistic motivations, this view does not cohere with my creative process, for a purely individualistic focus entertains a form of dilettantism that I personally reject. This form is problematic not because of its superficiality (something I endorsed with "romance") but because it connotes a dabbling of the sort that suggests, "I am the center of the universe, and I want all I can get."[9] The chief danger here is that one simply begins *collecting* insights. Rather than considering beauty or value, I may simply be taken by the notion of receiving a gift. Again, this in itself is not troublesome unless it prevents me from developing Whiteheadian style—style that permits me to utilize knowledge and creativity for purposes greater than self.

I do not want to suggest that the absence of style insinuates self-absorption. While this is possible, it is just as likely to be the result of an inability to contend with contrariety. Experience suggests that many a dilettante simply lacks strategies for selecting from among several antagonistic ideas/positions. If insight or inspiration comes to us unexpectedly and is often "contrary to," then inevitably dilettantes would be faced with the difficult task of choosing between rival goods. If they lack a means of choosing, then they may well resort to a museum model that collects and catalogues but avoids *assessing* potentially oppositional notions. They may even view such a stance as admirable, given a need for openness to diversity and awareness of their own fallibility.

The implicit danger is that the indecision prompted by indiscriminate respect for alternative positions may ultimately lead to myopia, malaise, and an inability to act; and these are detrimental characteristics for those who embrace style. If style leads to power, then vacillation following from a principled uncertainty thwarts its development. What is needed is a mechanism for selecting between the rival notions that ineluctably accompany contrariety. We must choose something besides eclecticism if power is to take form. But how do we accomplish this once we have acknowledged both that competing conceptions exist and that we may be mistaken?

There are a number of ways in which we could do this, but one I am fond of is contained in the advice to the religious devotee.[10] David-Neel recounts the guidance offered to one struggling over which spiritual discipline to embrace. The story suggests that we should behave like an eagle trying to decide with which sheep to abscond. The eagle, it is said, examines all the sheep and, realizing that it can take but one, simply selects. In like fashion, pilgrims, recognizing that they cannot practice all disciplines are admonished to consider each and then wed one. The story proclaims that those equally open to all possibilities may be erudite and knowledgeable, but they will wander aimlessly until they choose. The faint-of-heart and the ambivalent may be quite impressive, but they will lack power, for there is no power without passion, and there is no passion without commitment.[11]

Once again, however, my process seems faced with additional difficulties. How do we commit to what appears an arbitrary selection, and after committing, how do we maintain an attitude of contrariety that views the learning/creative process as oppositional? In "On Liberty," J. S. Mill offers certain thoughts that have helped me escape from a potential impasse. In this piece, Mill argues for the ongoing need for critical deliberation. He tells us that we risk losing an insight if we silence an idea or ignore its claims before giving them serious consideration. He claims that even in an absolute falsehood we may well find a seed of truth. But more importantly for my purposes, even if an idea or principle is absolutely and eternally true, Mill argues that it must still be challenged, probed, and questioned. If we fail to do this, the *truth* may become prejudice or dogma or fall into desuetude.[12] *Sans* contrariety even toward that which we most fully endorse, we sacrifice memory and a vital source of inspiration.

Now, what this means for my process is that contrariety demands that I commit even as I continue to question the commitment. The difference between this approach and that of negative power, however, is that here the questioning takes place from *within* the commitment rather than from outside it.[13] This move is critical for me. If the analysis only comes from an *external* source, then it may well take the form of assault. "Objective" critics are compelled to find the soft underbelly, but since they are not "invested," they have no compelling need to preserve or perfect. Their criticism need not call persons or principles to self-reflection: they are free to objectify and dismiss. At best, such critics hold hubris in check. At worst, they function as unconscious executioners.

In contrast, contrariety from the inside demands a different set of motivations and actions. A popular philosophical image is that developing working and workable philosophy is much like building a boat while afloat. Consequently, if we are *truly* committed both to the idea and to contrariety, then we are compelled to seek ways to sustain both. Rather than looking for the weakness that will sink the argument, our internal critic seeks ways in which to perfect the flawed craft. Now, if we were committed only to the idea, we would expect untenable or indefensible ideas to be preserved indefinitely. Such ideas would slip into dogma, and adherents would scramble to find justification for their continuance, even if this meant relying on sophistry. If, however, we embrace both commitment and contrariety, then the unworkable or inexcusable idea will need to be abandoned. But here again, abandonment from the inside does not mean relegating an idea to the back of the closet shelf. If an idea has sufficient power to extract an initial commitment, then it very likely possesses certain components that continue to warrant consideration. Even if its flaw is that it is fundamentally mistaken, understanding the original attraction invests the idea with a certain current value. When necessary, abandonment from the inside invites us to harvest even from refuse. The marriage of commitment and contrariety permits us to dig out meaning from sources the external critic may well disregard.

Further, to marry an idea while we continue to wrestle with its nature makes us responsible for the ensuing relationship. Responsibility here means acknowledging the mutuality of creativity. As in any salutary relationship, unilateral behavior is seldom characteristic of growth. It is only in the most unhealthy of relationships that one party is expected to do the growing while the other snipes from the sidelines. The same applies in the contrary encounter with an idea. If we approach an idea as if it were only something to be understood or controlled or remade, then the prospect of creativity falters, for when truly wedded, the idea and the person will effect change in each other. Ideas powerful enough to secure a commitment demand reciprocity. Such ideas may be molded, but they demand tribute: the thinker must also be altered. The resulting marriage is distinguished by the evolution of *both* parties.

For some, wedding ideas might intimate something of mystical union. It may even smack of the sentiments contained in, say, the writings of certain eastern mystics or Carlos Castenada.[14] Although such an understanding may be appealing, it runs counter to my experience. Contrariety seemingly does not permit enmeshment or dissolution into bliss because the idea always remains "the other." Because of this, I find myself simultaneously attracted to and repelled by it. Rather than this serving as a cause for alarm, however, the resulting push-pull nature of the relationship provides the dynamic tension that keeps the essential conversation alive. While *union* may be charged with promoting a sweet slumber—contrariety feeds the fires of creativity.

Finally, my creative process turns on two pivotal commitments. The marriage of contrariety and commitment demands both skeptical passion and passionate skepticism, and I find that I cannot relinquish either. The former acknowledges that while we must marry the idea, this does not mean that we become one with it. The passion may be fervent, but we still embrace something other than self. Passionate skepticism is essential because we are wont to fall in love with our ideas, and we therefore risk additional layers of self-deception. Skeptical passion compels us to be honest about the relationship. Passionate skepticism holds the parties accountable to themselves.

In the end, I am left with a process that is initially solitary and typically trying. Although they are probably the exclusive product of my collective experience, the ideas with which I wrestle exact tribute even as they reveal seemingly cloaked aspects of themselves. The insight born of such encounters must be protected during its formative period, but eventually it must be married. It is only within the bonds of intimacy with an idea that one can delve deeply into its meaning, and it is only with such commitment that the possibility of power emerges. The passion that attends this marriage is fueled by the tension between contrariety and commitment, and this pair serves as the fire and flux in my crucible of creativity. Nothing emerges from the crucible unscathed; both the idea and the thinker are fundamentally altered by time spent in that vessel. Having been altered, both are poised to comment, challenge, and effect change. Ultimately, it is this need to inform the lived lives of real people that sparks my creativity.

Notes

1. See chapt. 10 of Mary Field Belenky, Blythe McVicker Clinchy, Nancy Rule Goldberger, and Jill Mattuck Tarule, *Women's Ways of Knowing: The Development of Self, Voice and Mind* (New York: Basic Books, 1986).

2. Genesis 32:22–32

3. This being is sometimes considered to be God or another celestial creature. I associate the being with aspects of Jacob himself.

4. William James's depiction of progress as the periodically halting and somewhat variable movement of a "thin line of flame advancing across a dry autumn field" captures the essence of the process for me. "A World of Experience," *Essays in Radical Empiricism* (Cambridge, Mass.: Harvard University Press, 1976, p. 42).

5. On the basis of the preceding discussion, one might imagine that I believe that ideas, like Athena, emerge full-grown and in full armor from the head of Zeus, or that they are *a priori* entities external to self-specific items simply awaiting discovery. Although I understand both perceptions, neither is what I intend. One wrestles with oneself. And although one can never definitively know what form it may take beforehand (and contrary to certain foundationalist epistemologies), insight percolates into consciousness only through layers of one's own experience.

6. Edie Brickell, *"What I am"* (New York: Geffen Records, 1988).

7. Alfred North Whitehead, *The Aims of Education and Other Essays* (New York: Free Press, 1929, pp. 11–14).

8. Ibid. (p. 12).

9. Such an orientation coincides well with Harvey Cox's description of certain persons as "gluttons for experience." See his *Turning East: The Promise and Peril of the New Orientalism* (New York: Simon and Schuster, 1977).

10. Alexandra David-Neel, *Magic and Mystery in Tibet* (New York: Kendall, 1932).

11. I am not suggesting that an ambivalent person cannot have a dramatic impact. What I am suggesting is that such a person exerts only what one might call negative power. This is not the power of fruition or creation. Negative power is perhaps better viewed as constraint. It serves as the brakes on experience. It corresponds well with one of William James's many distinctions. James noted in "The Will to Believe" that people typically fall into one of two categories. They are either seekers of truth or avoiders of error. Negative power is best understood as aligning with the latter. See William James, *The Will to Believe and Other Essays in Popular Philosophy* (Cambridge, Mass.: Harvard University Press, 1979).

12. John Stuart Mill, *Three Essays* (Oxford: Oxford University Press, 1987).

13. For a detailed account of such thinking, see Henri Bergson, *The Creative Mind: An Introduction to Metaphysics* (New York: Wisdom Library, 1946).

14. Consider, for example, "[A] warrior chooses to follow the path with heart. It is the consistent choice of the path with heart which makes a warrior different from the average man. He knows that a path has heart when he is one with it, when he experiences a great peace and pleasure traversing its length." *A Separate Reality* (New York: Simon and Schuster, 1971, p. 262).

Chapter 13

On Lemmas, Theorems, Corollaries, and All That

Mike Siddoway

Meditation, withdrawal or abstraction
from clamorous assailants
of the senses and from demands for overt action,
is as necessary at the reasoning stage,
as are observation and experiment at other periods.
(John Dewey, 1910, p. 209)

Theory is the lifeblood of science.
(Boyd Henry Bode, 1940, p. 283)

If one is asked to think of a mathematician, there is a stereotype that would probably come to mind—part accountant and part disheveled wanderer. The former notion I've seen many times elicit a single wide-eyed shake of the head. The "disheveled" doesn't matter. Wanderers we are, but through a terrain so exotic that one doesn't get far without a total effort. And then the theorems might come; and strangely, when they do, the place that looked so dark and different at the outset simply blends in with all the rest that's known, and one looks again into the strange world in which one has learned to maneuver.

So how do we move from an open problem to its resolution? I'll wend my way through an account of a problem that I grappled with for three years in the late 1980s. But there's plenty to talk about before we get to that story. I won't state the theorem I was trying to prove, but I will say that it belongs to the realm of algebra and deals with how a basic algebraic object called a module breaks down into simpler indivisible parts. (This is, in general, a very old problem in mathematics and is akin to showing that any integer can be written as a unique product of prime numbers, where a prime number is an integer that is divisible only by itself and one. For instance, 30 can be written uniquely as the product of the prime numbers 2, 3, and 5.)

Any mathematician who tells you about what they do will use the word "work" at some point. I'll get started with a few comments about "working mathematically."

In the Don Delillo novel *Ratner's Star,*[1] a young math whiz, Billy Twillig, is brought into a think tank to decipher a message thought to be from a planet in another solar system. Dr. Softly, one of the old-timers at the institute, tells Billy very matter-of-factly, "You're a mathematician, you work till you drop" (p. 305).

Certainly, achieving results in any discipline requires a great deal of work. Something else is meant by the term in mathematics.

I got a taste of this other meaning early in my career when talking to a professor while I was working on my PhD at Tulane. We were discussing the work of a fellow student, Lige Li, who had spent over a decade in prison in China during the cultural revolution before entering the United States to study. Li is a brilliant mathematician and works extremely hard. I mentioned this during our conversation and was met with a reaction that might have followed my having said "He has ears."

The professor said plainly, and with no guile, "He's a mathematician!" and we quickly moved on to other matters. There was simply nothing to add on this count. In this most abstract of all the arts, in a discipline that requires many years of training before one can begin to listen to its great symphonies, work does not mean the usual "keeping at it." If one is to create anything in this transcendent domain, nothing short of total immersion will suffice.

My first excursion into this other world took place in Chicago. I had a fancy math undergraduate degree in hand and thought I would smoothly make the transition to the next level of difficulty. I knew graduate school promised to be a far more demanding experience, but had no idea that the trials ahead would more closely resemble those of a drifting wild-eyed medieval monk than those of an overly studious, narrowly focused . . . well . . . nerd.

Mathematics is not a profession; it is a calling. It is not, for me at any rate, classical and tweedy. It is Ornette Coleman, Saint Francis, Kenneth Rexroth, the Beats, and the swirl of hockey. It is solitary, twisted, and fierce like the badlands of my eastern Montana childhood. It's all or nothing. For Joyce, "The Dead" were those making do somehow after an initially minute turning in their lives. To the great, and most adrift of all mathematicians, Paul Erdös, "the dead" were erstwhile mathematicians, those lifted from the waters of theorems.

My days in Chicago were the beginning of my baptism. I've been immersed, more off than on, ever since. But always, the call to be lost in it all, to work till I drop, sends tremors through my most non-mathematical days. As with all things spiritual, "the called" aren't abandoned, but they sure can get sidetracked. ("sidetracked" = "chair." That's the only equation I'll burden my readers with. You can also make what you will of its premonitory tone.) For eight ferocious years in Chicago and New Orleans I was far from shore and held by the tumult of this great abstract river, and for seven days in 1987 I hit a stretch that nearly tore me asunder before revealing a result surpassing anything I'd imagined possible when the journey began.

When I arrived at Northwestern in the fall of 1980, I was most struck by my fellow students. They were the most off-beat bunch I'd ever been around, and their collective ability for mischief and mathematics would be hard to match by any incoming class at any university. It was clear in our first meetings outside of class that the year ahead would be completely unpredictable, and that the monastic approach I had assiduously adhered to at Notre Dame while an undergraduate would not work in this crowd. There was too much mathematics to learn from this ragged bunch to justify hiding away and getting by. If my fellow mathematician (and Montanan) Ted Koczynski had learned his chops in this company, he would probably have gone down the same iconoclastic road, but he would have mailed shaving cream bombs instead of the lethal variety that a wry sense of humor would have precluded.

There were five of us who eventually became inseparable. We all had apartments at the beginning of the year, but this nod to respectability (and good sense) was soon shed. I'm not sure who lived where after the third month or so. We were constantly on the move; often taking the train into Chicago to find a café where we would be left alone to work, and our coffee cups would be kept full. (By the way, Paul Erdös defined a mathematician as "a machine that turns coffee into theorems." We did all we could to keep this definition current!) The table we occupied was soon piled with papers. The talk was not only of mathematics, but if it had been more gab than it was, these intense sessions wouldn't have gone on through the winter and into the spring. We were consumed with mathematics. I didn't have a place to live after Christmas and was spending my nights in my office or on some friend's floor. It didn't seem important at the time to concern oneself with a room of one's own. My rootlessness was certainly my own choice and was at least a little contrived, but I was undeniably gripped by the beauty of mathematics.

When we weren't wrestling with some theorem, we were more likely than not busy talking about literature or poetry, and there were not a few poems written by our post-beat circle in the year we spent together. Over these peripatetic months it became clear to me that creating mathematics, like composing music or writing a poem, was an art, something beautiful to be passionate about. This is not at all to suggest that my undergraduate years had been less intense mathematically or bereft of the depth of the discipline. I worked extremely hard and laid a great foundation for my graduate studies, but I really had only a vague sense of the richness of the field.

A subtle shift occurred during my stormy year at Northwestern. The transition that took place between my spartan undergraduate years and my more Rabelaisian introduction to graduate school was clarified for me while reading an article in *The New Yorker* about Mikhail Baryshnikov.[2] The story recounts, in part, Baryshnikov's return to Latvia to perform in the hall where he had first begun to dance. He is not outwardly sentimental about the reunion and makes the trip, one he claimed for many years he had no desire to attempt, reluctantly.

He begins to warm to the enterprise when working with his old teachers, and he finally delivers a spectacular series of solo dances to culminate his visit. The author explains the gathering power of his crowning performance by noting, "He had returned home at last, but the home wasn't Riga; it was ballet" (p. 47). I learned in that tempestuous year at Northwestern that mathematics was my home. It would take me another six years to learn how to live there and to plumb the outer reaches of its lands, and the lessons of course go on. But no matter how far I'm removed from mathematics, I am drawn to its rigors, and I know the peace that attains to the passage and, once arrived, to the struggle that brightly fires the days lived there.

Romantic those times were and revelatory, but not in the end conducive to getting through coursework and qualifying exams, let alone solving an open problem and writing a successful dissertation. And there were other stirrings that reached a crisis in the course of my Chicago bohemian idyll. How does one square a life intensely devoted to the study of the most abstruse, otherworldly questions imaginable with the very real suffering and injustice that any random walk through the city reveals in abundant detail? I'd found my home, but it wasn't clear that I could justify living there.

I've always been a voracious (though slow) reader. All through my hell-bent training as a mathematician I've been accused (both self-accusations and the usual variety) of spending too much time with books outside of my studies. There have been stretches over the years when my worn over-burdened satchel has contained books and periodicals in four languages. There's always a math book in there, and a paper or two, but it might take a minute to find them. The "crisis of faith" that waxed during my time at Northwestern was certainly aggravated and abetted by much that I read. Aleksandr Solzhenitsyn begins his novel *The First Circle*[3] about a mathematician and political prisoner named Nerzhin, with the words, "And Who Are You?"

How do you reconcile the pursuit of your art with the world as it is? In the Bertolt Brecht play *Leben des Galilei*,[4] Galileo laments having set a standard for the scientists that follow him for buckling under the dictates of authority. Thomas Mann and Joseph Campbell went back and forth about the role of the artist in the face of tyranny, Mann contending that art should work directly to oppose evil; Campbell vehemently disagreeing, holding that art is above extremism of both left and right and should be pursued purely, at all costs, ideology be damned. Mann the German novelist, Campbell the American liberal arts college teacher. Well, I can't stomach Campbell's view. I couldn't back then, and the intervening years have only fortified my abhorrence for support of the stand that Brecht's Galileo vilifies.

Herbert Mehrtens, a German historian of mathematics, has written a number of articles about mathematics in Germany during the Nazi years. He mentions that many mathematicians lost their jobs for racial and ideological reasons during the years before World War II.[5] By 1938, twenty-six of the ninety-five full mathematics professors in Germany had been expelled. Otto Blumenthal, publisher of the (German Mathematical Union) journal *Jahresbericht*, was denounced by the general student council at his university (Aachen) and fired from his post. He would die in 1944 at the Theresienstadt concentration camp. There was even a journal named Deutsche Mathematik, which appeared from 1936 to 1943, that promulgated an Aryan mathematics.

What is the role of a mathematician whose colleagues are being removed from their posts because the state deems them undesirable in some way? If a colleague is fired because she or he is Jewish, shouldn't all mathematicians put down their pencils and pads and say

"No! We'll not stand for this!" What did my friend Li's colleagues do when he was denounced and sent to prison in communist China for being an intellectual? This is precisely the point Brecht made in the play I cite above. Why isn't a strong sense of moral outrage a part of the way scientists go about their work? Why can't we say, looking back on World War II, "The Nazis tried to co-opt thinkers of all varieties; but of course, the mathematicians told them to go to hell!"

The answer is that we want to be left alone, with what little time we have, to work on our theorems. Galileo didn't want the additional hassle that making a stand would have brought on.

Another debate that has raged since the end of World War II, was whether the German physicist Werner Heisenberg and the rest of the atomic bomb research group he headed deliberately slowed their progress because of their misgivings about the Nazi regime or were simply stumped by the problem and gave up. Thomas Powers' book *Heisenberg's War*,[6] and *Operation Epsilon: Farm Hall Transcripts*[7] obtained by eavesdropping on the German researchers at war's end, reveals that ideology had little to do with their work one way or the other. They tried their hardest to build a bomb, and failed. If there were any doubts about the Nazi program, the scientists readily submerged their doubts and got on with their exciting work. They, like many scientists, maybe most, didn't give a whit about the consequences of their demanding work. But not all.

There are many examples of scientists/mathematicians who think hard about how their work affects the world around them. Ted Koczynski left his post at Berkeley in part because he objected to training students who would use mathematics in dubious industrial applications. Joseph Rotblat, a British physicist who worked on the Manhattan Project, which developed the first atomic bomb, resigned when he learned that the German atomic bomb program had ended in failure. He was the only scientist to leave the program when the threat that had led to its formation was removed.

The most ironic example of the conscientious scientist is that of Albert Einstein. In 1914, the imperial government of Germany issued a "Manifesto to the Civilized World" signed by "ninety-three German artists, poets, historians, philosophers, scientists, musicians and clergymen"[8] which supported the gathering German war effort leading up to World War I (p. 100). A countermanifesto, against the rising tide of militarism, was organized by Georg Friedrich Nicolai, professor of physiology at the University of Berlin. In all of Germany, only three scholars agreed to sign this dissenting declaration. One was Einstein, who had just arrived in Berlin from Switzerland. Another who signed, Otto Buek, stated, "We have overestimated the courage and integrity of German professors" (p. 101). Of course Einstein's activism took another turn when he later supported (then lamented) the construction of the atomic bomb in light of reports out of Germany that Heisenberg's team was close to a solution.

The point I am trying to make with this somewhat lengthy digression is that mathematics, demanding and abstract as it is, must not occur in a vacuum. In order to do mathematics, one must find a way not to enter completely into the exotic terrain of its splendors. For me, the price of staying only there is too high. Dostoyevsky said, "Life begins on the other side of despair." He says, not that life is "lived" there, but that it "begins" there. Maybe I'm fishing a little here, but this gets at the ferocious balance that I try to strike between mathematics and "all the rest." Mathematics is a sort of rarefied despair. We mathematicians are stuck 95 percent of the time. I find out so much about "going on" from the theorems I struggle with. It is important to me that the lessons I learn in my work carry over to the days I live and the battles I fight. The goosebumps I get when I solve a problem are not abstract in the least; and I pray they are only the smallest hopeful sign of how my work will make me a better human being.

I don't intend to imply that the most egregious examples of moral failure occurred in Germany in the 1930s and 1940s. Robert Jay Lifton is correct when he couples the story of the German medical community during World War II[9] and American Scientists working in the nuclear weapons industry today.[10] The lesson from all this is that all scholars need to ask how their work fits into the world. We live very privileged lives. At the least we need to ask ourselves how we can use our talents to make the world better. The answers will vary widely; there is no set course that will work for everyone. Scientists, at root, are not in the habit of seriously facing the consequences of their work. I knew I couldn't proceed with my education before addressing these issues. After leaving Northwestern, I spent two years away from academia.

There is no need to go in to any detail about the years between my leaving Northwestern and my return to graduate studies at Tulane. I taught at a Franciscan high school on the south side of Chicago as well as night school at Northwestern, did some community organizing on the west side, and worked in a few cafés where I'd once abused coffee privileges as a student. My vocation as a mathematician became clear over this time. I decided to go back to school and finish a PhD. Nothing new there. What was new was that I saw teaching as a way to keep a balance in my life as a mathematician. I couldn't wait to get back to school. I decided to study algebra and hoped I could work with a famous Hungarian mathematician at Tulane. As at Northwestern, I had a teaching assistantship, but I viewed the teaching very differently after having taught adults at night school and inner-city teenagers at Hales Franciscan High School. My first year went very well. I passed my preliminary and oral exams and was admitted to candidacy. Then the real work started . . . solving an open problem.

In 1985, my adviser and I began discussing projects I might work on. I think every student wonders how she or he can possibly solve any open problem, let alone one which others have worked on and failed to solve. After so many classes and so much "known" mathematics, it didn't seem possible that there could be that much more "out there." I passed this thought on to my adviser who said, "We know practically nothing! Unsolved problems are nearly all there is to mathematics!" He gave me some papers to read and recommended a book or two. One paper in particular caught my eye. I would work on generalizing the last theorem in that paper or showing that no generalization existed for most of the next three years. And I mean "work" in the mathematical sense. I'd returned home at last. As dance was the hearth that Baryshnikov found on returning to Riga, mathematics was where my fires burned, and New Orleans was the stage where my solos would crash or soar.

"Solos" is apt. I am a very private mathematician. Most of the discussion I carry on amounts to mumbling to myself while pacing some space I happen to be in. I did talk to my adviser a great deal during those years, but really no one else. "Crash or soar" doesn't really fit at all. Filling a page with Warholian repetitions of "crash *and* soar" would be closer to the mark. Every day there was some euphoria, every day some stomach-induced giving away at the knees. Most nights were spent in the mathematics library and days away from school walking through the city mulling over some problem. At times these wanderings were so trancelike that I would "come to" and not realize where I was. I listened to jazz continuously when working at home, finding the work of Roland Kirk, Pharaoh Sanders, Ornette Coleman, and other avant-garde artists most in tune with my mathematical thoughts. I swam a great deal as well, setting aside an hour to swim and getting lost who-knows-how-many-laps-after-beginning in some fine technical point I couldn't get past. There were times that I woke up at night consumed with some part of the problem . . . nightmarish alterations of symbols juxtaposed with revelation. I would leave my desk at school after filling every available blackboard space with my work, only to return after waking, long before first light, to add some improvement to the board I'd left only a few hours before.

The first year and a half was spent whittling away at the problem in lower dimensions. My intent was to prove a theorem in two settings which allowed for any arbitrary dimension. Though some progress was made, the theorem I'd hoped to generalize gradually appeared to be either false or beyond my abilities. I began to look for counter-examples, examples showing the generalizations I sought weren't possible. This effort too came a cropper after a long summer. Some soul (and gut) searching got me back on track, and buoyed by some positive results in the fall of 1987, I again set to proving the theorem.

Well into the third year of working on this problem, and five years into my studies at Tulane, I was really nowhere near a solution. Teaching was my salvation. I was as subterranean as any Kerouac character as far as my mathematical life was concerned, but, I was saved by my students from the emptiness that had befallen me at Northwestern. And I had students in so many places! I taught my courses at Tulane and also traveled to the St. Thomas housing project on Saturdays to work with an incredible group of high school students. I taught several courses at Xavier University of New Orleans, and I even had some less formal (though most intent) students among the New Orleans café habitués. I read a lot too. There wasn't a *New York Review of Books* that I didn't read from cover to cover the whole time I was in Louisiana! Many of these were as full of my mathematical scribblings as my notebooks, and resembled the bizarre manuscripts of Kenneth Patchen when I finally set them out by the side of the curb.

In October 1987 I began to worry that I was not going to be able to finish this beautiful problem. I had perhaps enough to write a thesis with some related results I'd proved, but I felt deeply that the whole project would be a failure without these theorems. Then all of a sudden, toward the end of the month, as New Orleans finally began to reveal hints of autumn, I woke in the middle of the night after a feverish day of work and realized that I had solved both of the generalizations I had worked so hard to prove! For the next week I carefully went through all the details, keeping myself to the most exacting scrutiny I could muster. There were times when I thought it had all fallen apart, only to somehow have the "beauty of it all" save the day. This is when you begin to realize you've found something that really matters. From a seemingly desiccated wasteland, a nascent, glowing creek sprouts out of the infinite dark, and doubt though you must, the flood breaks and the brilliant blinding waters rush through you. How about that?

Well, that's about it. Maybe one last thought from one of my favorite writers. Perhaps Samuel Beckett wasn't writing about a mathematician in *The Unnamable*,[11] but there are words I once read there as the light began to fail on a winter's day as I walked home to the apartment I kept while on a long mathematical stay in Germany that made, and make me wonder still, if Sam didn't know the deep ways of lemmas, theorems, corollaries, and all that. "I've just crawled out, perhaps I went silent, no, I say that in order to say something, in order to go on a little more, you must go on a long time more, you must go on evermore" (p. 364).

Notes

1. Don Delillo (1976). *Ratner's Star*. New York: Vintage Contemporary Classics (1989 ed.).

2. Joan Acocella (January 19, 1998). "The Soloist," in *The New Yorker*.

3. Aleksandr I. Solzhenitsyn. (1968). *The First Circle*. New York: Perennial Library (1990 ed.).

4. Bertolt Brecht (1955). *Leben des Galilei*. Berlin: Suhrkamp.

5. Herbert Mehrtens (1989). "The Gleichschaltung of Mathematical Societies in Nazi Germany," *Mathematical Intelligence*, vol. 11, 3.

6. Thomas Powers (1993). *Heisenberg's War*. New York: Knopf.

7. Thomas Powers (1993).*Operation Epsilon: The Farm Hall Transcripts*. Introduced by Sir Charles Frank. Berkeley: University of California Press.

8. Martin Gilbert (1994).*The First World War, A Complete History*. New York: Holt.

9. Robert Jay Lifton (1986). *The Nazi Doctors*. New York: HarperCollins.

10. Robert Jay Lifton and Eric Markusen (1990). *The Genocidal Mentality*. New York: Basic Books.

11. Samuel Beckett (1959). *The Beckett Trilogy, The Unnamable*. London: Picador.

Chapter 14

Many a New Thing

Skip Fox

> This function by which one thing signifies or indicates another,
> and thereby leads us to consider how far one may be regarded
> as warrant for belief in the other, is, then, the central factor
> in all reflective or distinctively intellectual thinking.
> (John Dewey, 1910, p. 8)

> Apart from mind the world is just a vast machine
> operating blindly and heedlessly according to mechanical laws.
> When mind appears on the scene, an entirely new set of phenomena
> enters into the picture. The mind chooses and rejects,
> loves and hates, admires and despises, remembers and forgets,
> makes guesses and blunders—in short, it does things
> of which there is in the material world not a trace.
> (Boyd Henry Bode, 1940, p. 37)

My sense of engagement in the process of writing poetry is embedded in my sense of form. Form is the occasion of possibility. An occasion provisionally and fluidly bound by circumstances in which we are allowed to participate when we give ourselves over to an understanding of the confluence that flows between and through a series of contiguous states, ideas, experiences, phenomena, etc. The "antithetical center," H. D. called it (Doolittle, 1972, p. 33), from which dolphins swim.[1]

In this definition, as nexus, I read or extrapolate the following ideas:

1. That the poem is an activity which requires the poet's fullest engagement.
2. That this activity is participatory, since the poet is not an outside arbiter but participates in the energies of the poem. In a very real

sense, the poet follows these energies. As William Carlos Williams wrote, "The poet thinks with his poem, in that lies his thought, in that itself is the profundity. . . ." (quoted in Creeley, 1989, p. 572).

3. That in the poem anything goes because the contiguous is *whatever* is present at the time of writing (any series of states, ideas, and so forth) and cannot viably be predetermined. As Lyn Hejinian (1996) wrote,

> Work is retarded by . . . a desire, which is anticipation of its certainty, and hence a desire impossible of satisfaction, in the future despite the grand decision to pull it present. (p. 2)

Any "certainty" projected beyond the current engagement, if insisted upon, will "retard" its process. And the poet had best be aware of what is going on, not sprawled out before a map of what he or she meant to mean.

4. That forms as previously defined (sonnets, couplets, odes, and so forth), established conventions of meter and rhyme, and even distinctions of genres (the lyric, narrative, elegiac, and so forth) will be used, if at all, in ways different from what a shortsighted view of tradition seems to dictate. Poets who follow the mandates of tradition in a pedestrian manner employ form with the belief that there is an organic correspondence between the structures, repetitions, and rhythms of formal poetry and the body or language of the artist. Many experimental poets also feel this connection between the processes of the poem and the body or language of the poet, but their sense of this connection as well as their notion of form is not so narrowly defined. Poets who don't look to the work of the past merely for a dictionary of patterns or a grammar of ornament, or as a way of publicly positioning themselves within the context of an exterior authority, might discover what earlier poets did *within* the formal prescriptions: the deeper sounds and rhythms of the work, the music in the phrasing of nuanced ideas and psychological states, and so forth. Other supporters of tradition in a simplistic sense claim that the purpose of art is to give form to life, to rein in chaos. But I believe that art is an extension of life, revealing new imaginative possibilities with which we might engage. In this sense, art *is* life, and in a fuller way than what we commonly mean: that through art the artist comes to participate with the world's processes more and more intimately.

5. That the only way to get the activity right is by willing to be wrong. If the poet thinks of competence as the ability to skillfully

replicate the good poetic qualities of other poets' work, to master a period style; then to achieve a level of competence is to abdicate the full responsibilities at hand. Desiring competence will distract the poet from his or her own involvement in the process, since it appeals to an exterior condition.

6. That there is no authority other than the poet's own. Who else can enter the confluent other than the poet at hand? As Robert Duncan (1973) wrote, poets must be the author of their own authority, if their authority is to have any foundation. Someone once asked Robert Creeley, "Was that a real poem or did you just make it up yourself?" (Creeley, p. 577). How else to answer, except "yes"?

7. That the poet goes, as Duncan said, where his recognitions are, where his deepest sense of becoming might be realized. And the recognitions are individual, fluid, and intuitive. The poet's reading, personal and artistic associations, and attentions, are also so "governed."

8. That freedom, open attentiveness, and energetic engagement are the predominant senses the poet has when engaged in the process. The two great contemporary metaphors for the writing of poetry, dance and play, correspond to all three senses.

Hilda Doolittle's "antithetical center" is central to my sense of the poet as following the poem. There is no center to the process if we mean by that something capable of being isolated, willed, articulated, or stabilized. No form or center other than that which the poem, itself, finally is *as* it is during the creative process. And yet poets sense, even from the first, an undefinable, fluid center which they increasingly realize as they follow the directives of the poem, a center which cannot be articulated except through their own continuing activity. The so-called formal properties of a poem (length of line, regularities and irregularities of sound and rhythm, or even the overall shape) are insignificant when compared with this desire and ability to follow the poem at hand and to intuitively realize this center. Any center deliberately projected and then willed into being will "retard" the poem with the sense of a "certainty," to use Hejinian's terms, a sort of pseudo aesthetic feedback from a future which doesn't exist.

As Joe Napora wrote (1997), "How possible is it to know the consequences of an act based on the narrow interests that propel the will?" What are these interests that ultimately impede the poem? They are various and include the desire to project the self into a public arena, the need for stability, the vertigo when looking into a fluid universe of incomprehensible energies, and so forth.

But even when the poet is not beset with these confusions of the spirit, there are, of course, other impediments to participation in the process. The chief of these, for me, is self-consciousness. Certain aspects of the self become a screen through which all else is filtered, a screen whose active principle is an inordinate concern with how others will see me: "How will I take myself in terms of how others might take me?" But as Charles Olson noted (1965), the self in the poem should not be prioritized; it should be present but only as any other object in the field of objects, any other contiguity in the occasion of the poem. Poets consider only marginally, if at all, how they will be taken by others.

Writing is concurrent with the source of the poem; thus, the source cannot be experientially considered as prior. What might a source be? Almost anything. The poet thinks of something of a certain order and in that moment is already writing. Typically, for me, these orders come from a few areas, which are impossible to generalize. The only way to describe or define those areas is by example, not by generalization. (Many of the examples of ideas, information, energies, and perceptions concerning the origin of a poem also apply to those that contribute to its continuing process.)

Sometimes I am fascinated by certain subject. It might be arcane or commonplace; but rarely, to my knowledge, is it what anyone else has attended to, at least in the way that is attractive to me. It has the effect of a song I can't get out of my head. I wonder why all the stations aren't constantly playing it, and I wonder why entire shelves of the library aren't devoted to it, why the best ancient and modern minds have not written extensively on the subject. The subject might mean nothing to anyone else; that's the poem's job. It could be something as simple as, How does the mind feel about the body as it ages? Or, What is it to see the body as it really is (not necessarily within current psychological or philosophical theories)? Or, What does the presence of our awareness of mortality increasingly provide us? How does it intrude on a daily basis? What are its contours? Sometimes an idea from an unrelated observation in a book will stimulate a poem. I remember reading in, I think, a book on forensic science about the typical person's reaction to seeing a corpse: the pupils immediately dilate, even faster than the corpse's did, and then, even more quickly, constrict to pinholes. We see, perhaps, the form but not the thing itself and are instantly at full attentiveness. Quickly, we realize that we have encountered great anomalies, and we beat a retreat. The book implied that our immediate withdrawal is not a socialized response but an entirely human one, in which we admit that we can find no reconciliation of death with all of our other realities. All this takes place without thinking. Whether or not my depiction of the "classic layman's corpse response" is accurate, and whether or not I have correctly posited its implications, I find this set of responses attractive and possibly indicative of other human responses or, at least, I find it artistically interesting to place this set against other human reactions. Thus begins a poem.

Sometimes reading a book or several books, as a whole or in part, will generate a poem or portions of a poem. For me, though, a book of poetry has yet to have this effect.[2] Usually, it will be books that have nothing to do with poetry, books on philosophy, archaeology, anthropology, cognitive science, religious history, myth, and so forth. And even when texts prove generative, they have no precedence over other contiguities (things heard, seen, thought, and so forth). Very occasionally I will search out a certain book because I think it might be generative. This method has rarely proved effective. Useful reading for me is more serendipitous, desultory.

Sometimes a poem will begin with a fairly complex idea, one which disturbs or haunts the poet from various angles. At the inception of this idea, the poet is already engaged—even when he or she has yet to write a word—and the idea gains in complexity as it runs through the conscious mind a few times a day, but always, it seems, running in the background. For instance, I once thought of a person, a character, as an archetypal figure, but since I suspect the nature of archetypes, I began to think imaginatively of a figure outside of narrow archetypal definitions, even beyond the metanarrative, but also as a figure with a strange residual disturbance from something like a story or a dream of which the figure was a part. Naturally, it was most easy to see the figure fully in certain cruxes. I felt that these, too, were the haunting residua from something like metanarratives. Being in such situations allowed the figure to be most inventive so that it might, for instance, rescue a self which had been given to it not by the social world but only through this participation with a world that had been there all along. And through all this a third, a narrator, almost seemed to experience the event with the figure, for whom all this was like an experiential apparition. And a fourth, the poet, watched all three (figure, experience, and narrator) and each of their relations and energies. Concurrent was the figure's desire for the discovery of the self in an

American myth of discovery, both as I have it and as it is given in popular culture and history, and dozen things besides. With this type of idea, the first line begins someplace in the middle of the reckoning, usually immediately after the initial idea and always long before the complication has proceeded very far. And during the poem the idea finds further complication. Although the initial idea and the early complications are never truly left behind, they never become a plan beyond the poem but remain a continual part of its process by "way," not by "will," to use Napora's terms.

Or a poem begins with a scrap of overheard conversation. I once heard a coed, presumably referring to her name on a registration form, saying to her adviser, "The computer drops an *e*. Grates on my nerves." This became the first line of the poem. I thought about what she might truly be saying, which seemed to have something to do with social identity. That she is like others (she, too, has a peeve) and different (she has a *particular* peeve, and such a lovely minor one, at that, complete with its own music). And then I asked whether this overheard snippet of dialogue accurately reflected at least one way we find ourselves, today, in this culture. Surely this is not how people see themselves and their relation to others in any important way. It must be more than that, I felt, even if this might be one of many ways of identifying the self. What might be more viable notions of my own identity beyond the social matrix? And how might I sense their arrival? The original scrap of conversation is complicated, like the idea which begins other poems.

The same type of process occurs when the poet sees something or thinks of a line, and there is always this sense of being terribly attracted to, even haunted by, the scene or phrase, like the idea and the conversational scrap. Again, the so-called sources are never prior, in any meaningful sense, to the process of the poem; they are experiential and one with the engagement.

But such subjects as come from books, ideas, and so forth should not be taken as what the poem will ultimately be about. As Creeley wrote, "Poems aren't referential. At least not importantly so" (p. 490). So this "subject" should not be considered exterior to the poem, just as it should not be considered prior to the processes. The poem is not *about* these subjects in any usual sense. They are sources of energy in the occasion of writing, like everything else, and not some prioritized meaning or idea to which the poem directly or indirectly refers. The poem itself is the subject.

The poet realizes, then, that this idea or subject is just one of the active centers of the poem. Other centers are the overall shape as felt at any moment; the surface quality of words ("the tone leading of vowels," as Duncan (1973, p. 67) put it; the cut of the lines; the worlds that surround the poem ; the cultural resonances and the many ways to acknowledge and play with these; and so forth. When these centers, each of which has its own melodic line, coincide or relate in interesting artistic ways, and these are seen or felt in their shifts and musical correspondence and interplay with the melodic lines of others, the poet is involved in the process, following the poem.

There is also something which might loosely be called an agendum of a poem. For instance, "I am going to think at the very edge of the poem, and other texts will not significantly intrude." Or, "I am going to sit and think as deeply as I can about a certain type of words, things, ideas, or images, and I will read around as it comes to me, and the poem will be a melodic result of such thinking and reading." Or, "I'm just going to run around and get wet, taking whatever comes from a wide variety of contingencies, from the popular culture no less than the arcane." The agendum arises from the desires of the poem. For instance, it may call for nouns that seem to stand on their own, words that fly off the page, landscapes from a distance and then objects very close, a certain expansiveness, and so forth. In more general terms, the agendum also determines what sort of music there will be, what melodic correspondence of word, image, idea, sound, joke, perception, and apperception. But even this agendum has an origin in the process itself, occurs almost simultaneously with the incipient idea, the occasion of the poem, and is not properly the poet's own. The self is of the process at this point and so a participant in *its* policy; the self does not impose a policy of its own.[3]

Once in the confluent field, how does a poet proceed? One method of writing is an intense and prolonged engagement which allows the entire poem to be written during a single sitting, or a few sittings, i.e., in a relatively short period of time. Another method is extensive revision of an earlier piece. The poet writes an entire poem or a sizable portion thereof at one sitting and then revises it extensively, a process which could take anywhere from several hours to months. A third method, one which reflects the majority of my experience, is incremental development. The poet starts over at every point in the poem, writing each new line or phrase, and then thinks back over and over the poem before writing the next. This sort of poem might take a very long time to write. (There are probably many more methods and, perhaps, infinite shadings of varieties and mixtures in the practice of contemporary poets.)

The first type of process, writing an entire poem in one sitting, is most notable in poets who seem to share a sense that the fully attentive, and perhaps unmediated, mind in its activities is worthy of artistic attention. These poets would probably agree with Allen Ginsberg's observation, "Mind is shapely" (1962, p. 326). Frank O'Hara's "In Memory of My Feelings," Ted Berrigan's "Things to Do in Providence," Bernadette Mayer's Midwinter's Day, and Ginsberg's "Wichita Vortex Sutra," (which even makes continual reference to the singularity of its engagement) are fine examples of poems that arose through this process.

The second method, in which the poet writes an entire poem and then extensively revises it, is probably least employed by experimental poets, since the potential for discovery within such a process is not as apparent as in the other two. Experimental poets may feel they would be engaged in a uselessly repetitive activity without an imaginative engagement with the possible, the previously undefined. The original text seems too restrictive, since the poet takes its intentions as somehow sacrosanct, holding sway over the intentions that might arise within the present occasion of revision. Yet if poets look at their subsequent involvement with the text not as though they were finishing a piece of furniture toward some externally defined sense of perfection, but as the possibility of a coordinate engagement (of the present with the past *and* present concerns and energies of the text), the original text can become a ground on which further play or dance can occur with an originating energy.

This is hard to determine by simply reading others' poetry, but I believe that for most experimental poets the third type of process is most common, writing a poem over days or months during which the lines previously written are more or less "set" and the poet goes on from there, starting over and over as it were. Although I have written poems by the first two methods, the third is the one by which I have written the majority of my poetry and seems most true to my experience of discovery; that it is temporally incremental; that one chews over a problem, making bite-size progress over a period of time. For me, a fourteen-line poem written in this way make take up to five weeks, and a fifty-line poem may take over six months. At times, I feel like an inchworm over an abyss, but with a sense of where I have come from, which is, of course, constantly subject to revision. The low output that might result from this method might be frustrating, but as a poet who primarily writes this way, I know I have little choice, although I am currently engaged in separate projects which involve different methods and, therefore, can proceed on several fronts at once.

But even when I am working only on a single incremental poem, I am working much of the time. Although during my "daily life" I am not focusing directly on the poem all of the time, it is always present and provides something like a bass line in a jazz performance. I wake in the middle of the night thinking of the poem at hand; I write while I drive or run; I stop working on something else when I think of an idea or when I see, hear, or read something that strikes me in a certain way; and I take the poem out either literally, as in a notebook, or just in my mind. (I always have the entire poem memorized to the point where I stopped, even up to fifty lines of complicated text, without ever trying to memorize it.) Each time I bring the poem back up, I feel that I am reviving the earlier composition, reliving all of the coordinations of the active centers in their melodic correspondences. All of which, again, are subject to constant revision in the way I hear them, though they don't change on the page. These reevaluations, often radical, never overshadow or limit what might come. I learn that there are dozens of such reevaluations yet to follow and see them as provisional. But each reliving or recovery of the poem-to-date gives me the sense of a making a running start on the next line, phrase, or idea. I listen closely to these reevaluations, hearing echos of past readings in the line and finding new ones. I listen to see if the new thing will come into the poem and, if so, how. (It rarely comes in without modification.) This entire process, again, gives me the feeling that I am following the poem while holding the next thing in abeyance.

This entire activity, by whatever method, is far too complicated to call ordinary thought. The term many poets use is, of course, "intuition." But our culture's sense of intuition trivializes it. We don't see intuition as the clarifying force that it is. It is much more objective and illuminating than we normally consider, and it includes the ability to concentrate on a dozen or more things at once, feeling the melodic correspondences of all that has come before and reaching toward an extension of the melodies of idea, sound, image, cultural shading, and so forth. It includes deliberative processes as well as brief flashes of insight and feels almost visceral in its application. Maybe this is one thing Ginsberg meant when he wrote:

yes, yes,
  that's what
I wanted,
  I always wanted,
I always wanted
  to return
to the body
  where I was born. (Song, 1985, p. 112)

The times I have written entire poems or significant portions of poems by the first method, during a single sitting, have been exciting, but I don't tend to look back on the occasions themselves or the resultant works as being as important to me as the occasions of poems I have written incrementally. The former are not as open to new readings or reevaluations. They seem limited, not the result of a significant engagement during which I reentered an arena of significant concern over a period of time. The slower incremental poetry provides me with an experiential matrix in which the resultant work seems more deeply felt and thought. Further, the creative enjoyment of a prolonged engagement, hearing all of the different melodies of the piece at hand, far outweighs the frustration of a low output and the potential sense of hanging over an abyss.

So whichever way I have proceeded, I proceed until the end, although because of my involvement with the process at hand, I rarely focus on ending a poem. The agendum usually contains a sense how long the poem is going to be sustained. I also have a sense, when starting a series, of how many pieces it will contain and a vague sense of the length of each.[4] And I know the end when I see it. It seems I even sense its approach, and finishing a poem has nothing to do with exhaustion or abandonment. The end usually contains a resolution of the melodic lines and a sense that the poem can now exist on its own.

I don't want to give the impression that there aren't any compromises in my process. Occasionally I *do* have "end anxiety," the result of external concerns (how will others take this poem); and the work suffers in consequence. There are other sites of compromise as well. As previously described, I usually write in the flux of an artistic encounter, trying to understand and inhabit the confluence that flows between contiguous states, ideas, and so forth. But occasionally I will fall out of it somewhat. An entire line or phrase might be written that suits the poem at hand, but it will lack a word or two. The flux has become stabilized in terms of the line on the page, but there is a hole; and when I go to fill it, I no longer have the feeling of being involved in the confluence, of hearing all the various melodies and their shifting artistic relations. When I write such endings and fill such holes, I usually find myself working from a limited set of perspectives (usually intellectual and aural), rather than intuitively thinking of a dozen things at the same time. The line or word represents a compromise and always sounds jarring to me.

The longer I have written, the fewer the compromises. I feel as though I am coming increasingly closer to a state that is coordinate to the poem and its activities. I have also recently been writing several projects at the same time: a few essays; series of poems, letters, and notebook entries, all of which I take seriously. I begin working on one project, sometimes without even knowing why I chose it rather than another, and then find myself setting it down and picking up another because something I heard or thought or saw gave me a phrase, line, or idea which applies to another piece. In my available time these projects are "there," and at least one is usually calling to me. Their presence seems like a bass line, again in the musical sense, for much of my waking day (and probably my night), something just beneath my obvious levels of awareness, but I can always stop and find them there. Sometimes a poem broaches the liminal, intruding on my thoughts. Sometimes it's like hearing something in an adjacent room and becoming still to listen more attentively. At other times, of course, it's triggered by something read, heard, seen, or thought.

With several series, I don't feel as though I'm participating in different activities so much as the same activity on multiple fronts, all of which are part of a similar endeavor. At this point in my life, having several series is productive in another sense: I can listen to the currents between them, the relative and shifting melodies as they relate to each other in interesting ways; and as a result, I feel myself more involved in the total possibilities of poetry.

In poetry, one further satisfaction, usually in the process of the poem or just afterwards, is the awareness of deeper possibilities, of where I may be going, not just as a poet but as a person in a *life* of poetry. The dream is usually of ever-further engagement as the center in the self becomes more implicated in the antithetical center that is the heart of all poetry, the written as well as the yet unwritten. "To inhabit the deepening viabilities," I once wrote, and I would stand by that. Yet I know that such projections, as all others, are provisional, can never be insisted upon without a retardation of the process. And my experience bears this out. The places or states I have come to never match past projections, although they may contain aspects of them. When I look back from a certain "place," I constantly feel as though I could never have known that such a place existed or even could exist. The last lines from Ezra Pound's "The Tree" (1971) after his metamorphosis is complete, reads:

> Nathless I have been a tree amid the wood
> And many a new thing understood
> That was rank folly to my head before. (p. 3)

I have always loved these lines, and my appreciation of them has deepened over the years.

Notes

1. While I do not pretend to speak for anyone other than myself, placing my own experience in evidence, much of the following seems to apply, if I have correctly read their poetry and their testimony, to many modern and contemporary experimental poets. Likewise, I cannot pretend to speak for myself even a year from now. I may well come to think of the following as overly idealized or wrongheaded. However, my past experience with these ideas, that they have steadily grown and have made increasingly good sense, suggests that they will remain important, if not central, to my thinking.

2. Of course, reading other poets constantly informs the work at hand and may even stimulate work, but it has less of a direct influence, for me, on any given poem. Other poets primarily extend my sense of the possible.

3. Sometimes the impetus for a poem comes with a public agenda (e.g., the picture of a man with a briefcase standing in front of a tank in Tiananmen Square). Sometimes an idea will come with an agenda that seems too banal or not liable to complication; it lends itself too easily to a cliché, even a countercultural cliché, and many poets don't try to delve beneath the obvious. They amuse themselves by playing the idea out. In these cases, the poet's real job is to find the *poem's* agendum as it works through him or her, one which may include the more public agenda but which cannot be subsumed by it.

4. Other experimental poets whom I respect have no notion of the length of the poem at the beginning. Lacking this sense indicates, perhaps, a greater sense of freedom in the process than I have.

References

Berrigan, Ted. (1980). "Things to Do in Providence." *So Going around Cities: New and Selected Poems, 1958–1979*. Berkeley: Blue Wind. (pp. 256–257).

Creeley, Robert. (1989). *The Collected Essays of Robert Creeley*. Berkeley: University of California Press.

Doolittle, Hilda (H.D.) (1972). *Hermetic Definitions*. New York: New Directions.

Duncan, Robert. (1973). *Truth and Life of Myth: An Essay in Essential Autobiography*. Fremont, MI: Sumac.

Ginsberg, Allen. (1962). "When the Mode of the Music Changes, the Walls of the City Shake." In *The Poetics of the New American Poetry*. (Eds. Donald Allen and Warren Tallman.) New York: Grove (pp. 324–330).

Ginsberg, Allen. (1985). "Song" and "Wichita Vortext Sutra." In *Collected Poems, 1947–1980*. New York: Harper, (pp. 112, 394–411).

Hejinian, Lyn. (1996) (Preface). *Writing Is an Aid to Memory*. Los Angeles: Sun and Moon (pp. 1–2).

Mayer, Bernadette. (1982). *Midwinter Day*. Berkeley: Turtle Island.

Napora, Joe (13 November, 1997). Letter to author.

O'Hara, Frank. (1994). "In Memory of My Feelings." *The Collected Poems of Frank O'Hara*. (Ed. Donald Allen.) Berkeley: University of California Press, (pp. 252–57).

Olson, Charles. (1965). *Proprioception*. San Francisco: Four Seasons.

Pound, Erza. (1971). "The Tree." *Personae: The Collected Shorter Poems of Ezra Pound*. New York: New Directions. (p. 3).

Chapter 15

Through a Tangle of Branches: Reworking the Poem

Rebecca Luce-Kapler

> These imaginative enterprises often precede thinking
> of the close-knit type and prepare the way for it.
> (John Dewey, 1910, p. 3)

> This reconstruction of experience is something
> that the individual must do for himself.
> (Boyd Henry Bode, 1940, p. 297)

After basking in a rereading of Seamus Heaney's (1996) marvelous poem "Personal Helicon," I find myself whispering the first line: "As a child, they could not keep me from wells." And I wonder: what could I not be kept from while growing up on the farm? I open my journal and begin to write.

> As a child they could not keep me from exploring outside . . . I was often out by myself, imagining and thinking. There was the big old Balm of Gilead east of the house that had a wide crotch to sit in beneath large leaves—or rather—I think the tree was a Russian poplar . . . I vividly remember one summer evening sitting in that tree, its leaves rattling as a warm breeze blew. I looked back to where the sun was setting, the land stilling at the end of the day . . . I imagined multiple lives for myself and yet did not begin to imagine the one I am living now.

As I continue to write, I remember places that drew me over and over again: the chicken house with its nest boxes, the cows' trail down to the aspen woods bordered by Deer Creek, the meadow where I tried to stage plays with my recalcitrant sisters. Yet it was the tree to which I return, and my journal writing ends with a web that brings to the surface some of the ideas that linger around the poplar.

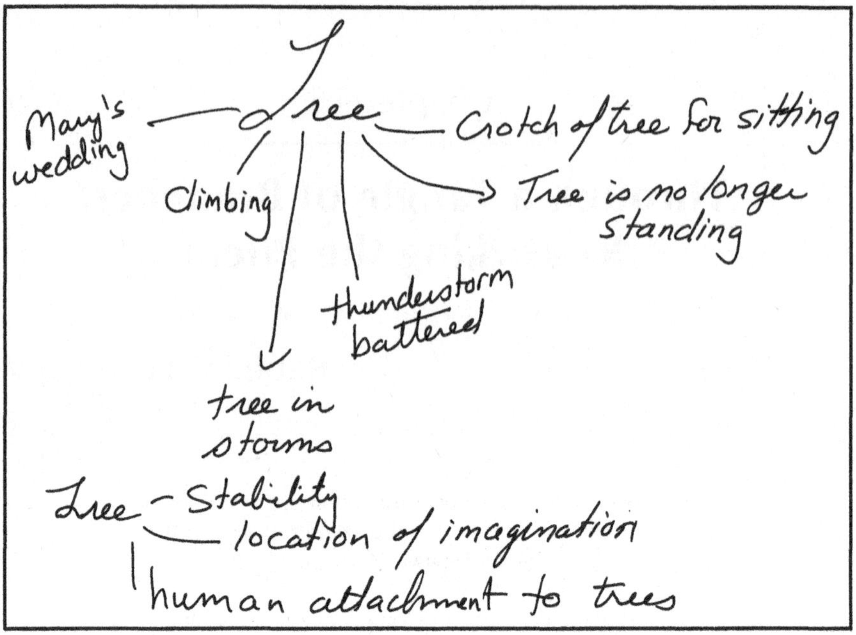

Figure 1

I realize that I am unwilling to break my connection with Seamus Heaney and have been searching for a possible entry into a poem through the journal writing. The tree offers the possibility: "location for imagination; human attachment to trees." After I create the web, a halfhearted stanza wobbles out to distinguish itself from the spill of words.

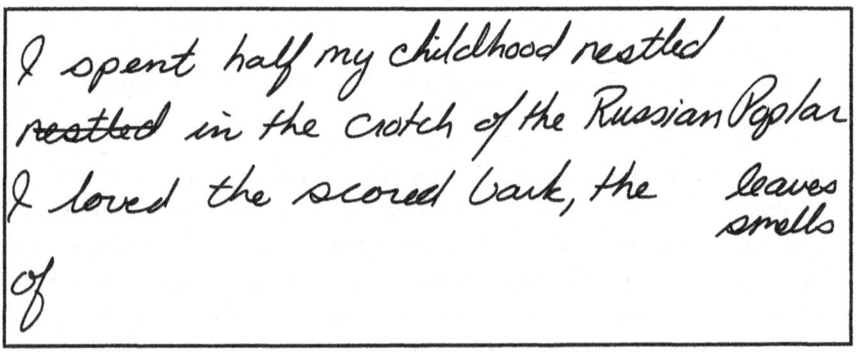

Figure 2

When or where does a poem begin? I try to identify a moment where the emerging writing begins to find form, where my life experiences assume a particular shape. Did the poem begin in that tree? In reading "Personal Helicon"? In creating a word web? Yes, I think. In all of those. I remember how sure I have been with my writing students in the past, marking what I claimed was the beginning point of writing with "prewriting exercises," then moving on to assigning their first draft and finally exhorting them to rewrite. But if I'm not sure where writing begins, how about the rewriting? There are no clear boundaries in this process. I return to work on the poem again, starting by reworking the first stanza and then attempting to write two more.

I spent half my childhood nestled
in the crotch of our Russian poplar.
I loved the scored bark, the broad, and bitter leaves
Smells of clean, woody flesh and greening

Once, in the summer, just at sunset
I climbed up its generous limbs
imagined the stretch of valley to the horizon hills
~~Was a po~~ my ~~life stret~~ unfld
(representing life line somehow)
→ The blizzard of cotton
~~Another tree remembrance~~

Figure 3

The lines are quickly drafted, some crossed out as I reach dead ends in my attempt to describe as succinctly and clearly as possible the memory of being in that tree. I can envision the texture of the light in the summer sunset; my fingers remember rough bark; and a faint memory returns of smells like sweet clover and crushed grass. As I search for the words to convey the sensations, I am reflecting on an experience that has been "written" and "rewritten" in my memory and that I am now trying to write on a page. I wander through language, choosing my words and rewriting the memory yet again, but I am not yet rewriting the poem. Not enough of the experience has traveled to the page for the rewriting of the poem to begin. The first stanza is but a moment's clearer vision for one small part of an imagined whole.

The language spills onto the page as my mind races ahead of my hand, sometimes flying down dark alleys that are realized only when the words are written. I am trying to find language for the feelings and intuitions that swirl about this tree; and in searching for that language, I sometimes stumble, trying one word and then substituting another.

I return to writing in my journal in an effort to realize the poem, and I finally ask myself a question that provides the impetus to continue the poem. I write:

What kind of mystical connections are there to trees?
taste the bark—beads of its sweat
my flesh grows into its white sweetness
swim up the root capillaries
exploding through green
feel the sun nourish me
strengthen my limbs from the bite of a woodman's ax wanting to dull the edge of his blade with the sticky saliva from my chlorophyll tongue, shaking my leafy
head in defiance. "Become Daphne."

This journal entry moves me beyond the sensory impressions of the experience to the deeper mythical implications that I felt but could not articulate before. I sense with this entry that I have discovered the center of gravity for the poem. Knowing this, I now finish the first draft:

I spent half my childhood nestled
in the crotch of our Russian poplar.
I loved the scored bark, the broad and bitter leaves,
Smells of clean, woody flesh and greening.

Once, in the summer, just at sunset
I climbed up its generous limbs,
imagined the mellow motes of last light
were choices I had yet to make.

The blizzard of tree cotton
that had earlier filled the sky
was subsiding, settling to the ground
like drifts of snow marking a new path.

I tasted the rough skin of the tree,
licked the beads of sweat from its runnels
until my flesh grew into its white woody sweetness.

I swam from the root capillaries
warm in the sap
and exploded into green
where sunlight could nourish me

Strengthened my limbs to resist
the bite of the woodman's ax
dulling his blade with sticky saliva
and shaking my leafy head in defiance.

Titles: Spending Time with Daphne
Tasting Daphne's Flesh
Another of Daphne's Daughters

With the first draft completed, could I now begin to rewrite the poem?

Moving into Rewriting

Our memory of an experience encompasses both the explainable, which we can describe in language; and the ineffable, whose reverberations we can only sense. Within the words of the first draft lie those inexplicable sensations, and it is with the desire to reveal experience beyond language that we return to rewrite, to write a poem rather than a cathartic draft. A poem, Octavio Paz (1992) suggests, is made of words but "for the purpose of containing and secreting a substance that is impalpable, resistant to definition . . . " (p. 77).

Through the work of rewriting, the heartbeat of the poem grows stronger, its unity more assured, and the writer can discover the beauty of the piece, the epiphany that James Joyce described in his unfinished novel, *Stephen Hero*:

> First we recognize that the object is one integral thing, then we recognize that it is an organized composite structure, a thing in fact: finally, when the relationship of the parts is exquisite, when the parts are adjusted to the special point, we recognize that it is that thing which it is. Its soul, its whatness, leaps to us from the vestment of its appearance. The soul of the commonest object, the structure of which is so adjusted, seems to us radiant. The object achieves its epiphany. (quoted in Grudin, 1990, p. 58)

The roots of my poem are deeply anchored in personal experience. My journal writing stirred the memories to the surface, and by exploring almost forgotten childhood obsessions, I returned to a summer evening when I was ten years old. The writing of the poem now has to move from my recounting and imagining of experience to a text where image, rhythm, and form work in concert to become a poetic and aesthetic experience for the reader.

Stepping Back

Rewriting seems to begin with a stepping back, a cooling off after the first heat of spilling our thoughts onto the page. I need a chance to clear my vision and to move away from my initial deep attachment to my words. Friedman (1994) tells the story about attending a poetry reading at a coffeehouse where a woman announced to the audience, "I wrote this poem this afternoon. . . . I hope I can read it before my throat closes up" (p. 76). The poem, Friedman says, was about loneliness and lying in bed at night with the heart pounding:

> She read it in a soft, breathy voice, and when she was done she looked up. We applauded politely. She blinked, then rose stiffly, as if her stomach were full of splintered glass, the disappointment palpable about her as she returned to her folding chair. Watching her I thought, I hope to God I'm different, although I suspected I was not. (p. 76)

What feels so forceful when one writes, Friedman continues, is not always forceful when it is read. Enraptured with my work, I may be unaware of the faults and inconsistencies that cause my readers or listeners to pause or stumble. Initially, I may write for myself, but in the rewriting I must remember that I also write for others, so I return to the text and position myself as reader rather than creator this time. I read, searching for the possibilities that present themselves: What images are evoked? What metaphors are suggested? What universal meaning reverberates through the words? But these questions require time for the emotional distance between ourselves and the text to grow. I think of the occasions when I have rushed students into presenting writing that has not had the luxury of distance. For them, the work still felt too close to their immediate feelings and thus was deeply personal and often private. No wonder they asked how I could assign a mark to something so intimate and so integral to their experience. A junior highschool student who was a subject in my master's research (1994) explained how he had learned to write "schoolly" as a way of dividing the "real writing" he enjoyed at home from the assigned work of the classroom. There often is not enough time given in schools for waiting, knowing that you will return to the writing, that such time is necessary to revision. Writers need that time: time to move from the one who originated the writing to the one who will discover its achieved version (Plumly, 1992, p. 244). The vision needs to clear for a re-vision.

I decide to put the poem aside for several days, but those days stretch into several weeks when my grandmother suddenly dies. I cannot bear the vulnerability of writing poetry with the deep sense of grief I am feeling over realizing that my grandmother's death has marked the end of a generation in my family. With that ending, a time in history to which I had access seems to close and my generation of siblings and cousins ages overnight. When I finally return to the poem the hopeful memory threaded through the lines jars me and I am more sensitive to the sensuous imagery. My grandmother spent most of her life regarding the sensual responses of the body as dangerous; and for a moment, this poem reminds me of the huge difference between our personalities. I crave more distance and so rewrite the poem in third person:

She spent half her childhood nestled
in the crotch of a Russian poplar.
She loved the scored bark, the broad and bitter leaves
smells of clean, woody flesh and greening.

The distance indeed widens; but with that, all pleasure in the poem disappears. I decide it should stay in first person, but the dissatisfaction I feel with this draft enables me now to approach the poem on a deeper level, searching for the patterns that will change it from a personal reminiscence to a poem, from catharsis to illumination.

The Palimpsest of Rewriting

The stepping back has begun the complex process of rewriting which van Manen suggests is one of "re-thinking, re-flecting, re-cognizing"

(1990, p. 131). My initial writing of the poem conjured up a memory of my attachment to trees. Now, however, I must return to the memory of that writing and reflect on it. The body is a palimpsest where the tracing of experience remains—both the experience of the tree and writing about the tree. In rereading the poem, I alternate between my memories of that time—the feel of bark against my skin, the sound of the wind in the leaves, the early evening light of summer—and the memories of writing. I wonder what impulse gave rhythm to the writing of the poem? How had I remembered the experience? What sensations was I trying to evoke? In the rewriting, these questions become important.

> Rewriting establishes the palimpsest and permits you to stay in touch with the first cause of the poem, regardless of the number of erasures, writings-over, transformations: the first impulse is the secret that will be revealed the more it is concealed through rewrite. (Plumly, p. 243)

By reflecting on remembered experience, I could begin rewriting the first draft and perhaps begin to realize or re-cognize the poem in that draft. The poem would be, as Charles Olson describes it, "energy transferred from where the poet got it" (in Lee and Miller-Kritsberg, 1994, p. 27).

I remember how, in the past, I brought sections of my work into class on overheads and modeled rewriting with my students, asking for their input and considerations. But never did I talk about how I return and reflect again on the experience I have just written about or how the texts I read in conjunction with the writing have influenced the work. Nor did I describe the desire to discover an aesthetic shaping of my experience so others would be invited in to consider their own experiences. I had not shown them what lies beneath the skin of my writing.

Before I write the next draft of my poem, I begin by reading "Personal Helicon" aloud to revisit the images and rhythms that had recalled a memory of childhood summers, gnarled trees, and rustling leaves. The poem begins:

> As a child, they could not keep me from wells
> And old pumps with buckets and windlasses.
> I loved the dark drop, the trapped sky, the smells
> Of waterweed, fungus and dank moss.

Something in the rhythm of Heaney's poem has called to me and reminded me of the trees where I spent hours as a child. In reading his work, I seem to have physically stored the felt qualities of his writing; and in rereading, this is recalled. "In writing poetry," Rilke suggested, "one is always aided and even carried away by the rhythm of exterior things; for the lyric cadence is that of nature: of the waters, the wind, the night" (1954, p. 112).

I write another draft of my poem, reading and rereading it aloud to hear the rhythms suggested by my reading of Heaney and my own words and line breaks.

ONE OF DAPHNE'S DAUGHTERS

I spent/lived half my childhood nestled
in the crotch of a Russian poplar.
I loved the scored bark, the broad and bitter leaves,
smells of clean, woody flesh and greening.

Once, in summer, just at sunset
I climbed her generous limbs,
imagined the mellow motes of last light
were choices I had yet to make.

The blizzard of ripened tree cotton
earlier blotting the sky
now subsided, settled in drifts,
a white pathway inviting footprints.

My tongue touched the rough tree skin
licked her beads of sweat from runnels
as my flesh commingled with
her inner/white woody sweetness.

I swam through root capillaries
washed in warm sap
and exploded into green
arching for sunlight to nourish.

I strengthened my limbs to resist
the bite of a woodman's ax
dulling his blade with sticky saliva
and shaking my leafy head in defiance
the shake of my leafy head defying
the shake of my leafy head a defiance

Discovering the Pattern

Beyond the personal experience of the poem lie the deeper patterns which were beginning to be revealed through my rewriting. By attempting to say exactly what I mean, I discover what I mean to say. Still, I find myself becoming confused by the words. What should I keep and what needs changing? I am losing sight of what is important until I remember what Richard Hugo said about poetry and words: "The words should not serve the subject. The subject should serve the words" (1979, p. 6). Perhaps what I need is to put the draft to one side and entirely rewrite the poem. From that process, what is important should emerge. I am again reminded of Hugo's advice to poets:

> When rewriting, write the entire poem again. If something has gone wrong deep in the poem, you may have taken a wrong turn earlier. The next time through the poem you may spot the wrong path you took. If you take another, when you reach the source of your dissatisfaction it may no longer be there. (p. 38)

I begin a new draft without referring to the old one.

ONE OF DAPHNE'S DAUGHTERS
I spent half my life nestled
in the crotch of a Russian poplar,
The feel of the rough, scaly bark,
the smell of leaves broad and bitter.

Once, at summer, just at sunset
I watched mellow motes of light
choreograph possibilities
of my life not yet lived.

The tree cotton blizzard
subsided, settled into
drifts of white fluff,
emptiness inviting footprints.

I tasted beads of sweat from
the tree bark's runnels,
merged my flesh into its
sweet white woodiness.

I swam root capillaries
soaked in sap
and exploded into green,
stretching my limbs for sunlight to nourish

Strengthening my trunk to
withstand the woodcutter's ax
dulling his blade with sticky sap
shaking my leafy head in defiance.

Now I have two versions with which to work. I consider the relationship between the two, trying to determine the important images and the particular words that surface again. Then I rewrite the draft stanza by stanza.

I spent half my childhood nestled
in the crotch of the bam tree.
I loved the scored, scaly bark,
the smell of leaves broad and bitter.

I return to the word "spent," since its sound is echoed in this stanza, which also are reminiscent of wind through the leaves of a tree. I realize, too, that an emerging awareness of sexuality is present in this poem, and the more specific word "spent" points to that sense. The second version also enables me to write the last two lines more tightly and to focus on the smell of the leaves as being the strongest scent rather than deferring to the odor of wood. I change the name of the tree, which is referred to both as bam (for balm of Gilead) and as Russian poplar in the district where I grew up. Besides, bam is what I called the tree as a child, and it does have a more evocative sound than Russian poplar.

Once, in summer, just at sunset
I climbed her generous limbs,
and imagined mellow motes of light,
choreographed choices I had yet to make.

This stanza becomes a blend of the two versions. In the second rewrite, an interesting word, "choreographed," appears which suggests the dancing of the light that I had imagined but had not said. "Her generous limbs" is an important phrase to me, although it didn't appear in the second version. I want to suggest the tree as having a feminine quality early in the poem and relate that to the girl's developing body, so I retrieve that image and keep the mellow motes which appear both times.

The tree cotton blizzard subsided,
settled to the ground

in drifts of white fluff
marking the emptiness of possibility.

Again, with this stanza, I think the second version helps me tighten up the first. I entirely delete the reference to "sky" which is not necessary because of the word "blizzard"; and I make my reference to a snowbank more oblique by using "white fluff" instead. From the words "new path" and "inviting footprints," I think I am finally able to describe in the last line what it is I am really trying to express, the ambiguity that is present when as children we consider our future.

My tongue touched the rough tree skin,
licked the beads of sweat from runnels
as my flesh commingled
with her white, woody sweetness.

This stanza has lost some extraneous words and has found a better phrase than "my flesh grew into" or "my flesh merged." "Commingled" seems to convey the effect I want more clearly. Also I have returned to the feminine pronoun rather than "its" for consistency and to remind readers of the gender I am imagining.

I swam up root capillaries
washed in warm sap
until I blossomed into green
arching for sunlight to nourish.

My limbs strengthened to resist
the bite of the woodman's ax
finally dulled by his frantic efforts
and the defiant shaking of my leafy head.

In the final two stanzas, I delete repetitions such as "sap" and one awful choice, "saliva." There is still something not quite right about the final stanza, however. I cannot seem to get the rhythm or the words right. I wonder if perhaps the stanza doesn't belong, but I resist that idea. I want the sense of strength and success suggested by this stanza. Daphne, of course, must spend her life as a tree, but I want to show that women have moved on from there. I decide to rewrite this stanza after leaving it for a day or two.

For me, the tree has become a symbol of the growing up of a young girl, with her connection to nature and the mythical past; but I continue to wonder about the woodcutter. As a symbol, is it too much?

W.D. Valgardson gives a warning about symbols: He writes, " I think one of the worst things any writer can do is impose symbols. That's a dreadful thing to nail them on. It should be like driftwood. You don't nail the knots on. The water washes and erodes and what's left are these hard knobs. That is the way that symbols should be. They rise out of the material naturally" (quoted in Hodgins, 1993, p. 211).

I realize that I have "nailed" on the woodcutter in my enchantment with the idea. I am overly pleased that I thought of him as deepening the allusions present in the poem, and my pleasure is a warning that this does not belong. As Ernest Hemingway advised, "You must kill your little darlings." The strength of the tree (and by association, the girl) has to arise from within that metaphor rather than from without. However, there still has to be some sense of this strength being in the world. I reread my poem and think about the sound of the wind that has guided some of my decisions, and how it was the sound of the wind through those bam trees that comforted me as a small girl in the darkness of my bedroom. Perhaps what needs to arise from the material is the wind rather than a woodcutter. My relationship with the tree is also my connection to the wind. "We take our identities from our relationships," Hugo writes, "just as the earth takes its configurations from the time of day, the position of the source of light. This is a warm, fluid world" (p. 8). I decide to rewrite the last stanza yet again.

> With my limbs thus strengthened
> and a defiant shake of my leafy head
> I would begin to dance
> with the coming of the wind.

At last my poem seems to find its shape and realize a sense of knowing that goes beyond words. The process reminds me of Lynn Emanuel's words about revision: "The choosing, and shaping, looking backward and forward, the sense of materiality and the sense one is working on *something* that already has its own shape and exists and can be altered—is something that confronts us moment to moment" (1992, p. 256).

I am now at the point of rewriting where the final questioning of the presence of words and punctuation can begin: the stage where I ask myself, "How little can be said and still convey the sense of wonder that I hope this poem can offer a reader?" Plumly writes: "The silence out of which a poem comes is part of its power, just as the words first written are inditements and indictments of what is possible" (p. 244). And van Manen warns us about overwriting and emphasizes the importance of leaving some things unsaid: "The silence of spaces is as important (speaks as loudly) as the words that we use to speak" (p. 113). Every word has to be considered, particularly connectives and transitional words that are often not necessary in a poem. At the same time, I must read and reread the poem aloud, feeling the rhythm through my breath, responding to my body. As I read the lines, can I breathe softly, like a quiet wind? Do I have to gasp before the end points, stiffening my muscles so that I lose the contemplative mood of the poem? Do the sounds of the words remind me of summer evenings? Can I smell the scents, hear the sounds, envision the sights of that moment?

Rewriting is always surprising. In working with each line and word, in reading aloud to hear the rhythm, I realize that the third stanza about the blizzard does not really belong. The idea of possibility and choice is covered in the second stanza. This third one is gratuitous, a hanging-on to the "reality" of my memory. The image does not add to the poem; indeed, it detracts from the sunset-lit atmosphere that I envisioned. In removing it, I feel that the poem reveals more clearly what I hope the reader will imagine and sense. Still, there is a sorrow in taking out a stanza at this late stage. In my living with and working through this poem, that idea has been there from the beginning; and as with all things to which we become attached, I find it difficult to let go. What if my instinct is wrong, I think. What if it really is better being left in the poem? But I know it is not better and so I must let it go, the words trailing away from the body of the poem. For now, the rewriting comes to rest:

ONE OF DAPHNE'S DAUGHTERS

I spent half my childhood nestled
in the crotch of the bam tree.
I loved the scored, scaly bark,
the smell of leaves, broad and bitter.

Once, in summer, just at sunset
I climbed her generous limbs,
imagined mellow motes of light,
choreographed choices I had yet to make.

My tongue touched rough tree skin,
licked beads of sweat from runnels
as my flesh commingled
with her white, woody sweetness.

I swam up root capillaries
washed in warm sap
until I blossomed into green,
arching for sunlight to nourish.

With my limbs strengthened
and a defiant shake of my leafy head
I began to dance
with the coming of the wind.

Acknowledgment

The author gratefully acknowledges the support of the Social Sciences and Humanities Research Council of Canada and the Izaak Walton Killam Memorial Scholarship for this research.

References

Emanuel, L. (1992). "In Praise of Malice: Thoughts on Revision." In R. Behn and C. Twichell (Eds.), *The Practice of Poetry: Writing Exercises for Poets Who Teach*. New York: HarperCollins (pp. 151–156).

Friedman, B. (1994). *Writing Past Dark*. New York: HarperCollins.

Grudin, R. (1990). *The Grace of Great Things: Creativity and Innovation*. New York: Ticknor and Fields.

Heaney, S. (1996). Personal helicon. WWW Document. Available: URL http://sunsite.unc.edu/dykki/poetry/heaney/personal.htm/

Hodgins, J. (1993). *A Passion for Narrative: A Guide for Writing Fiction*. Toronto: McClelland and Stewart.

Hugo, R. (1979). *The Triggering Town: Lectures and Essays on Poetry and Writing*. New York: Norton.

Lee, J. and C. Miller-Kritsberg (1994). *Writing from the Body: For Writers, Artists and Dreamers Who Long to Free Your Voice*. New York: St. Martin's.

Luce-Kapler, R. (1994). *Never Stepping in the Same River Twice: Teaching and writing in school*. Unpublished master's thesis, University of Alberta, Edmonton.

Paz, O. (1992). *The Other Voice: Essays on Modern Poetry* (Trans. H. Lane). New York: Harcourt Brace Jovanovich.

Plumly, S. (1992). "The Rewrite as Assignment." In R. Behn & C. Twichell (Eds.), *The Practice of Poetry: Writing Exercises from Poets Who Teach*. New York: HarperCollins (pp. 243–244).

Rilke, R.M. (1954). *Letters to a Young Poet* (Trans. M.D. Norton). New York: Norton.

van Manen, M. (1990). *Researching Lived Experience: Human Science for an Action Sensitive Pedagogy*. London, Ontario: Althouse.

References

Chapter 16

Writing with/in Leftovers

Delese Wear

Every judgment is analytic in so far as it involves discernment,
discrimination, marking off the trivial from the important,
the irrelevant from what points to a conclusion;
and it is synthetic in so far as it leaves the mind
with an inclusive situation with which the selected facts are placed.
(John Dewey, 1910, p. 114)

Education, in whatever form, is concerned with the improvement
of present living. The big issue is the question
of what constitutes improvement.
(Boyd H. Bode, 1940, p. 254)

I

A vibration starts up, vague and insistent.
(Neruda, 1975, p. 53)

A muse by any other name. A word flies by in class . . . it comes from the mouth of Kate, a beautiful blond goddess who moves with incredible composure through this world of big-boy science, formidable surgeons, and high-speed competition for grades and prime residencies. She will be a wonderful doctor—she is gifted in so many ways yet is surprisingly humble and has a social conscience and a genuine ease with all patients. She has just eagerly described how she thinks patients view her . . . and the words pause long enough above the conference table to be grabbed by Alexis, an African-American student whose presence can fill up an entire room. Even without words, she demands that you notice her. She seizes Kate's words and puts her own out there: *No way . . . that's not how it is at all for me. . . .*

Do you know how it feels to be mistaken, every time you walk into the room, for someone from housekeeping or an aide of some kind?

It's all over for me for the moment. I quit listening, even in this setting I love so much, and I'm spinning off somewhere else with their words. I think of Elizabeth St. Pierre's (1997) recognition that she, too, needs to be "smack dab in the middle of the action, in turmoil, in conflict, uncomfortable, nervous, and a bit out of control" before she can start thinking. How often for me this rattle takes place in the classroom, where a student's response to fiction we've just read, or to a description of a patient in the ER the night before, or to some disclosure about doctoring, sends me off. My body feels the vibrations, these words whizzing by that insist I pull them over for inspection. *What does Alexis mean? Why is it so insulting to be mistaken for a nurse's aide? Would Kate feel the same displeasure? Do patients ever make this mistake with Kate? What's the medicalized mix of gender, race, and social class?*

I think of William Carlos Williams, who spent his life on doctoring and writing, which are both dependent upon a "lifetime of careful listening." He describes how "we catch a glimpse of something, from time to time, which shows us that a presence has just brushed past us, some rare thing. What was that? We can't name it" (1984, p. 123). He's right—I can't name what is going on in my classroom right now. Words have brushed past me, and even though I return to our shared space around the conference table, the words are at play and I have already begun to write. I have no idea where this is going.

II

How swift my mind/how stupid my pen.
(Swenson, 1978, p. 80)

Beginnings. I now have some words mined from my students, and an idea is slowly forming. The idea is vague, and because of that vagueness I have an unquiet mind. I lie awake at night before falling asleep, thinking, thinking, thinking. When I run each morning, I can't wear the headset that fills me with the noise of music and news; I need the predawn peace to move words around, hoping to see a thread begin to weave itself, a form begin to gel, thinking of writers on whom I can draw, fragments of lines and phrases that carry images that say what I think I mean.

I make lists. I get a new manila folder and type a label with something remotely resembling the topic. I get busy not writing. I think a great deal about what the first sentence will be. I scan my shelves looking for places where the right words are hiding, but I don't know what I'm looking for. (As with the infamous definition of pornography: I will know it when I see it.) I order book after article after book, knowing I'll never read them all but believing that the answer is there, too. I take notes on everything I read, and I put all my jottings into my manila folder. When I open it up, I am surprised at how full it is getting and how many yellow sticky notes with amazing words, titles, quotations, and notes to myself are there.

I am unable to hold on to this unborn idea long enough to name it and inspect it. Yet it possesses me even as it keeps me at arm's length and makes me awkward and clumsy when I try to articulate it to myself or others. I know it has to do with some mixture of women and doctoring and power; women's relationships with each other as different kinds of caregivers; how women medical students' bodies are differentially coded with and by power in medical settings; how power moves back and forth between and among doctors and patients and all other caregivers; how power is slowly etched on the surfaces of women students' bodies as they move through medical systems so utterly dependent on unequal distributions of that and other sources of power.

III

The Muse bumped
against my window this morning.
No one was at home but me
and the baby. The Muse said
there was room on her back for two.
Okay, I said, *but first I've got to . . .*
(Waniek, 1993, p. 396)

I confess, it all sounds so lovely, the idea of passionate nights in the library stacks or sacred time set aside each day for writing; but I don't know what it would feel like, how it would be planned, how it could be integrated into the dailiness of one's life. I think of colleagues I have known—mostly men—who designate specific days or times for writing, who work at home because there are no interruptions, who call forth words and they appear on demand. For me, and I suspect so many women who have trouble setting boundaries, who are assigned and accept so many roles, and whose lives seem to be making one caretaking list after another: we write using leftovers. I write at stoplights on bank statements; I "stop writing the poem / to fold the clothes" (Gallagher, 1993). I try out word relationships at the kitchen sink with my hands in soapy water; I discard those words and begin to sketch others on a napkin at the coffee shop. Bending over my roses, I use mnemonics to memorize words I know I'll forget when the phone rings.

Often, it is background noise and the physical clamor of other responsibilities that produce the words, images, and ideas that work, for a while. I think of Christa Wolf's (1989) narrator in the novel *Accident: A Day's News*, who thinks of activities that many would consider a waste of time, but that become in some unexplainable way the nourishment for the birth of ideas and for tending to ideas: "Changing a baby's diapers. Cooking, shopping with a child on one's arm or in the baby carriage. Doing the laundry. . . . Sweeping the floor, mopping it, polishing it, vacuuming it. . . . Doing the dishes. Doing the dishes. Doing the dishes. Taking care of a sick child. Thinking up stories to tell. Singing songs" (p. 31).

Though I now have a life that does not include the immediacy and physicality of raising children, the background noises of my woman's life are still audible here in the apparent foreground of my deceptively clean, uncluttered kitchen; a laundry basket that now takes days to fill; a quiet phone. My children are still and always present to me; the kitchen is still the locus of my home and my work; the role reversal taking place between my parents and me occupies my time and worries; and, of course, the unending appearance of students at my office door is at once my greatest pleasure and my greatest distraction from extended time for writing, for the pursuit of that first sentence, for the honing of the idea that will form the work.

I am somewhere between fascinated and appalled by the neatness of so many of my (usually male) colleagues' "scheduled" writing time or other "protected" time for doing work that requires concentration: *"Every day between such and such a time I write,* they say. . . . *It's sacred time. . . . No interruptions allowed. . . . No phone calls. . . . Secretary (or wife) protects me. . . ."* I do not understand how such compartmentalization is possible or even desirable, even as I recognize how it figures in productivity. I think of Richard Feynman, the Nobel prize-winning physicist, married to a woman who had tuberculosis for seven years. The story goes, that on the day she lay dying he drove to her bedside (he'd been working several hours away developing the atomic bomb). She died, so he went back to the work site. He describes the scene upon his return: "When I got back. . .they asked me what happened. 'She's dead. And how's the program going?' They caught on right away that I didn't want to moon over it" (quoted in Gergen, 1992, p. 134).

Who *are* these people?

IV

You've got the poem cornered. It gives up, lies down, plays dead.
No more resistance. How easily you could take it into your teeth
and walk off with it!. . . So you stand above it, sniffing its fur
poking and pushing it, turning it over. Suddenly you see that
its eyes are open and that they stare at you with contempt.
You walk away with your tail between your legs.
When you return the poem has disappeared.
(Mueller, 1986, p. 49)

I am in search of an image, a metaphor, a way to help me think about how I write. At present I'm tentatively, suspiciously drawn to rhizomes: *My* story of Kate's and Alexis's stories connects to other students' stories, to a medical school memoir I just read, to my daughter's friend's sister's story: not a global rumination on women and medicine and power but a "potential sum of *local* descriptions" (Eco, 1986, p. 82). Rhizomes, according to Eco, can be viewed only by the inside:

> At every node of it no one can have the global vision of all its possibilities but only the local vision of the closest ones: every local description of the net is a *hypothesis*, subject to falsification, about its further course; in a rhizome blindness is the only way of seeing (locally), and thinking means to *grope one's way*. (p. 82)

Similarly, my life (and its various nodes, including mother, teacher, wife, adviser, daughter, committee chair, friend, *and* writer) makes sense when I think of it rhizomatically.

I am in a constant state of interruption, physically, emotionally, intellectually. I always begin again with leftovers.

Bam! Driving to work I connect two points: Alexis's displeasure with being mistaken for a nurses' aide, and the description offered by Deepak—another student totally unrelated to Alexis and Kate—of always being considered a foreigner because of his brown skin ("Yes, I speak English," he responds in his thick Tennessee drawl.) And here comes another thought nudging its way in, this one from a paper I'm working on that examines the ritual of the white-coat ceremony in medical education. This is when students receive their doctorly apparel to remind them that compassion and humility are at the heart of medicine, and it sets them apart from other health care workers. Where might these points converge in my writing?

Rhizomes help me to think about these interrupted connections. Unlike the root systems (foundations) and growth patterns of trees (branches of knowledge), which build "vast conceptual systems that are central, unified, [and] hierarchical," rhizomes "thwart unities . . . pluralizing and disseminating, producing differences and multiplicities, making new connections" (Best and Kellner, 1991, p. 99). Rhizomes are subterranean stems, not roots that regulate growth; they "connect with other lines in random, unregulated relationships" (p. 99). I am attracted to this image even though it feels too nihilistic; my writing may be unregulated, but it is not random.

It's a new day. I'm writing in a restaurant—coffee and toast after a long run. The background noise—Muzak, clink of glasses, low talk of patrons and servers is comforting. I read everything I've written so far, and I'm surprised at what I read. Was that me? A few images and sentences please me; a few make me cringe. Mostly, I'm uneasy because I don't know where to go next. This writing that refuses the outline is giving me nerves.

I think how this writing in restaurants is, in many ways, part of the same never-ending writing project that threads the years of my life together: my first diary; notes (often intercepted) to my best friend in seventh-grade math class; my tenth-grade English assignment on *To Kill a Mockingbird* (pretend you're Scout); E-mail messages I send to friends, students, colleagues, my children away at college; book chapters on how I write; grant proposals to fund my work; and syllabi that I take as seriously as book chapters and grant proposals.

V

Every time Trudi took a story and let it stream
through her mind from beginning to end,
it grew fuller, richer, feeding on her visions of those people
the story belonged to until it left its bed

> like the river she loved And it was then that
> she'd have to tell the story to someone.
> (Hegi, 1994, p. 73)

Writing this, writing this way, has evoked the old ghosts: *Exactly where do you get off, thinking that stories of your experiences are adequate or useful on any theoretical or practical level?* It is a tired question, based on so many take-for-granted beliefs about making knowledge. Alice Walker chides me: "Really / you've got to be kidding. Other / women have already done this / sort of suffering for you" (1991, p. 262).

I want to "write lives"—both my own and others'—so that my writing "matters" (Richardson, 1990, p. 10). I think of the personal theorizing that has mattered most to me: Jane Tompkins's brilliant, audacious essay, "Me and My Shadow" (1989), in which she confessed how tired she was of "the conventions that keep discussions of epistemology, or James Joyce, segregated from meditation on what is happening outside my window or inside my heart" (p. 123); Hélène Cixous's "Coming to Writing" (1991), which characterized her writing as a way of "never becoming resigned, consoled; never turning over in bed to face the wall and drift asleep again as if nothing had happened; as if nothing could happen" (p. 3); Nancy K. Miller's *Getting Personal* (1991), which validated how self-narrative and critical argument could be joined in one braid; and more recently Laurel Richardson's (1997) *Fields of Play: Constructing an Academic Life*, which she called a "critical ethnography of the self" (p. 2) and Carolyn Ellis's (1997) "Evocative Autoethnography," which concentrates on "telling a personal, evocative story to provoke others' stories and adds blood and tissue to the abstract bones of theoretical discourse" (p. 117). These continue to make a difference to me because they have directly influenced the writer I am always becoming. They make a difference because of the *stories* they tell, each disclosing lapses, connections, and what otherwise might be. They inspire me because of their substance and style, the fleshy personal narratives they use instead of the solid gray mortar of disembodied abstract argument.

Everywhere I am unabashedly a voyeur. No, that's too polite a description: I have to work at not staring. I am endlessly fascinated by the way people look, walk, talk to each other, dress, touch each other, laugh, move, think out loud. I eavesdrop on personal stories being told around me at the lunch table, on the bus, and (like Patricia Williams) in clothing store changing rooms. With these affinities, I admit to what Laurel Richardson characterizes as "yawning my way" through so much "scholarly" or "academic" writings *except* those that use the personal story as a tool for teaching or theorizing. But finer distinctions must be made here, as bell hooks (1995) notes:

> I don't think of *personal* and *personalize* as the same thing. For me, *personalize* means that you see everything as coming back to your ego and to your narcissistic construction of self. . . . I have found those details often to be what grabs people, and it's what makes theory seem (as it does for me) to have concrete application. When you tell a story about how you use an abstract idea or a bit of theory in a concrete situation, it just feels more real to people. (p. 109)

In addition, these writers, I think, come cleaner than the seemingly author-neutered texts so prevalent in most academic writing. *Of course* the students I choose to write about, the classroom experiences that form my stories, and the self-disclosures I make are half-truths, wildly skewed attempts to make visible some of the selves inhabiting my body that choose what and how I write. Jane Flax writes, "If we do our work well, 'reality' will appear even more unstable, complex, and disorderly than it does now" (1987, p. 643).

My thin skin is useful because stories are rarely trapped for too long. I imagine my colleagues in basic science as those rubbery plastic Gumby-like characters who have the outline of hands that push out from inside their bodies but never break through the skin. They don't fool me by such control and containment, by their passive-voice masks, by their refusal to talk about their relationship to their data, or by political climates that directly influence what kinds of research they seek funding for, all influencing what knowledge is "made" and what is not. Their own personal stories are right smack in the thick of their peer-reviewed articles, abstracts, and grant proposals.

This is not to say that storied writing—explicitly personal, that is—is somehow more reflective of a "true" or objective reality, out there, just waiting for readers like me to see it and know it as I do. As I write, I am creating and discovering the view from right here. *My* windows, *my* walls, *my* vision of what's around the corner, what's possible. Not an innocent location, by any stretch. Indeed, as Donna Haraway describes such writing, it is actually polluted. This is cyborg writing, which is taken up in a kind of "gleeful, critical, angry spirit." According to Haraway it resists, "authoritative writing practices that try very hard to produce the kind of masterful 'I', a particular kind of authority position that makes the viewer forget the apparatus of the production of that authority. I think cyborg writing is resolutely committed to foregrounding the apparatus of the production of its own authority, even while it's doing it" (p. 49).

A cyborg writer tracking rhizomes—to the extent they can be tracked, kept, ordered: perhaps that is "how I write." No. I am *not* a cyborg; I am a fully fleshed, very mortal woman in the middle of her life still seeking a way to write with intelligence and ethical purpose, in a way that people will find interesting and will connect to their own lives and projects. Any cyborg worthy of the name would have figured out how to do this by now.

VI

> A work in progress quickly becomes feral.
> It reverts to a wild state overnight.
> It is barely domesticated, a mustang on which
> you one day fastened a halter, but which now you cannot catch.
> It is a lion you cage in your study. As the work grows,
> it gets harder to control; it is a lion growing in strength.
> You must visit it every day and reassert your mastery over it.
> If you skip a day, you are, quite rightly, afraid to open the door to its room.
> You enter its room with bravura, holding a chair at the thing and shouting,
> "Simba!"
> (Dillard, 1990, p. 527)

Fumbling with my belt loops this morning as I dress, I realize how out of control this writing has become and how I can't seem to escape it. Writing this has become a little like "The Lady or the Tiger?" all over again, only now I find dozens of doors with all kinds of unknowns lurking behind them, waiting to pounce on me even if I just peek. Lately I've been searching for the door that will help me understand my writing as an ethical practice, but I'm struck by the notion that probably all academics must surely believe that their writing has some implicit ethical dimension. That is, don't they all assume that whatever form their writing takes, whatever the methods they use to "make" knowledge, whatever their discipline is, its purpose is to influence or change how those who read it will think, theorize, create, and so on?

This again brings to mind Maxine Greene (1987), who describes how Bruner's characterization of two modes of thought, "each providing distinctive ways of ordering experience, of constructing reality" (1987, p. 9), helped her understand thinking by means of narrative.

One mode of thought is constructed by a "well-formed" argument (my colleagues' craft of persuading other investigators that their methods, data, and interpretations are trustworthy); the other by a "well-wrought" story (my attempts to fill narratives with fully human subjects who know, think, and feel—or don't). And if my writing is indeed an invitation to pull up a chair, the kinds of stories I tell must be tempting enough to warrant even polite consideration of the invitation. They must be stories that people would want to eavesdrop on, straining to hear (in spite of themselves, a little embarrassed at their curiosity) what happened or didn't happen next, who said what, what people looked like/wore, how they felt. It is the lure of stories that moves us to keep Toni Morrison on our nightstands and to sneak looks at the *National Enquirer* in the checkout line. We think in stories; we live in stories; we create and use stories to make meaning of our lives.

Ultimately, as Maxine Greene shows me both in her writing (grounded so often in literature, in story) and in the story of her extraordinary life, we are all "condemned to creating our lives as meaningful" (p. 12). My commitment to writing—to writing narratives about my experiences as a woman in a medical academy, which always include stories about students, classrooms, curriculum and other faculty members, is such an effort, I think, a life that tries to "create change, to lessen oppression, [and] to assist in the development of a more equitable world. . . . "[It is] a search for an ethical way to 'be' in the personal/professional nexus that shapes our lives and in the texts we seek to present and re-present" (Tierney and Lincoln, 1997, pp. viii, x).

VII

"What, leftovers again?"
(Siblings Tracye, Delese, Sam, and Rachel Wear,
to their mother, Frances Wear; Mogadore, Ohio, circa 1964)

I read what I've written for what seems to be the hundredth time, looking for a pattern, a theme, some cohesiveness between parts. Mary Gergen reminds me that "traditional narratives demand an end point, a goal. Certain rhetorical moves are required by custom—concentrating on the goal, moving toward the point, putting events in a sequence, building the case (no tangents, please)" (1992, p. 133). I've done all this to a point, even though my "rhetorical moves" are jerky at best, overlap or circle back on each other, and remain unfinished. I've tried to build a collection of stories about how I write, and I have included a vague introduction, a description of some of the problems of writing narratively, a respectable number of references to make my points (and to show how much and who I read: the predictable legitimization by citations). I have included stories about my experiences that incorporate writing this particular narrative and a few that typically form the fabric of my other writing. With no resolution in sight, I repeat over and over Gergen's words, which gently tell me not to worry: "Let us not stick to the point! Let us improvise!"(p. 142).

Freed from the pressure of closure for the moment, believing that writing narratively allows me to write stories that are *partial* (Richardson, p. 28), I return to the stories I have started about students but have stored away. But when I open up the refrigerator, these and dozens of other leftovers come pouring out. What can I do with them all? What kind of stew can be made from them? Do I need to use them all? How long will they keep? Whichever ones I decide on, preparing them involves seasoning, combining, stirring, and, of course, repeated tasting. I'm not just cooking for myself and my own tastes; I have obligations, especially to women and others marginalized in the whole medical/health care mélange. The "fact" that increasingly large numbers of women are entering medicine does not speak for itself without interpretation. Rather than reciting promising statistics about this trend, I want to find stories that tell of "the gaps, the broken glass, the unpainted walls, the pallid faces, the empty shelves. They are too often obscured or denied" (Greene, 1994, p. 447).

Some stories do it better than others, whether classroom incidents, asides and snippets of conversation, secrets students tell in my office, E-mail messages, words and phrases from students' writing, overheard conversations (the one going on outside my door). Some may stick to me more than others because of the mood I'm in—the way my daughter sounded on the phone last night, the story I read in the newspaper this morning, the news I just received of a friend's denied tenure. I'm struck by how indeterminate and fluid writing really is. I think of how Bourdieu characterizes writing (when it is done well) as the art of "necessary improvisation" (quoted in Polkinghorne, 1997, p. 11). Embedded in social life, writing cannot be "accomplished on the basis of rules, recipes and normative models" (p. 11) because we cannot have policies and prescriptions for every possible circumstance in which we find ourselves—including writing. Instead, according to Bourdieu, we *improvise*, and our improvisation is marked by "pause, interval and indecision" (p. 11).

For now, I put back the unfinished story of Kate and Alexis who are presently eclipsed by Sandy, a first-year student whose earnestness and almost visceral spiritual qualities fascinate me. Why Sandy? Maybe proximity. At last night's Women and Medicine dinner I sat next to her and listened to her experience of the dreaded first year of medical school, pleased to have a chance to get to know her better. When the time came for the only agenda item—voting on the nominations for the Gender Equity Award—it happened. Out of her intelligent, reflective, compassionate mouth came the words, "I think we should always have two awards, one to a female faculty member and one to a male, so that no one thinks we're favoring women."

I was overwhelmed with disappointment. Sandy, in some attempt to be fair-minded, had put forth a suggestion that we should honor a male who may or may not be deserving of recognition for the sole purpose of avoiding the charge of—gasp!—gender bias among *women*, who still endure huge social and economic inequities in the hierarchies of U.S. medicine. I looked around the table, waiting to see if anyone else heard her comment in the same way I did. Instead I saw nods; these gifted, hard working, highly focused women have arrived at this location, not by making waves but through intelligence, diligence, and practicing the high art of accommodation to the rigid system holding U.S. medicine in place.

Suddenly, there's no more room in the fridge. Unwilling to throw anything out (wasteful, my mother says), I've used up all my Tupperware and plastic wrap to store these leftover stories, and now they all need to be re-examined and puzzled over for their possible uses. Some need to be eaten to make room for more. Which ones? Is this the one I should choose, for now, the one that works best in the task of writing for social change? If I unfold this particular story more fully, connecting it to other stories illustrating women's and other marginalized students' contradictory experiences as doctors-in-training, will it work on behalf of creating more just, more humane, more nurturing environments for all students?

I see I must improvise.

VIII

> I know you are reading this poem as you pace beside the stove
> warming milk, a crying child on your shoulder, a book in your hand
> because life is short and you too are thirsty.
> (Adrienne Rich, 1991, p. 26)

Now, after writing about *how I write* (meaning, *in what way do I write*), I realize how intertwined that question is with another: *why I write*. In fact, let's try this analogy: *How I write* is to *Why I write* as *Form* is to *Content*. That is, inseparable. This awareness unfolded as I wrote this, which is to say that writing this paper was indeed a method of inquiry (Richardson, 1994). *How I write*, I came to realize, was a lot more complicated than describing the mechanics, logistics, and aesthetics of writing, a process-oriented inquiry that writers such as Annie Dillard (1990) and Nancy Mairs (1994) have so richly described.

I have come to realize more fully just how much of my writing has been for two communities—intended readers I must have conceived before I decided how I would write. For the first group of readers I write narratively about my own experiences and those of my students and colleagues so that they might "fill in or compare their experiences and provide their own sensitivties about what [is] going on. . . . [to allow them] to feel the specificity of my situation, yet sense the unity of human experience as well" (Ellis, 1997, p. 131). Such writing, I believe, is more likely to achieve this end when it is full of the candor, uncertainties, tentativeness, and self-doubt that are all enmeshed in the telling of a good story. This is a community of readers conceived narrowly as the academic medical community, and more broadly as women who find themselves patients of physicians educated in the United States. I want the stories I write to hit readers' homes, to reflect their experiences, to make them feel not crazy, to help in our collaboration against regimes of power and exclusion without being "expelled" from our various communities (Pinar, 1997, p. 93). As such, I work to build skills in "storytelling, in meaning-sharing, for groups and persons who are not now a part of our narrow circle of critics" (Tierney and Lincoln, 1997, p. 50).

Second, I write for what Yvonna Lincoln calls a "policy community," which may or may not include the first community. I write to broaden or alter images and to inform or possibly change routines, practices, and habits in a very public sense for those who have been denied a means of expression, or whose expressions are not considered important. My intent is to watch what's going on and write about it as a person with a history, feelings, and political intentions; I want my writing to reach the hands of the people in charge.

I knew this, vaguely, before I started this, but the process of writing has brought it more out in the open—sometimes slowly, as in the frustration of trying to remember the title of a song over a period of hours or even days; or sometimes unexpectedly, as in the free-floating line from May Swenson's long-forgotten poem that suddenly appeared without my summoning it when I began writing this paper.

What I really didn't know was that I'd come to think of leftovers as descriptive of how and what I write—in leftover time with leftover stories that stay with me after the moment when I live, hear, read, or witness them. My mother's presence stands with me at the kitchen sink after meals: "*How can you throw that away? Why, there's enough of that for another meal!*" (Of course, this is the woman who is known to save a tablespoon of applesauce, or a dollop of mashed potatoes: "*potato pancakes for your father.*") In saving stories—in trying never to let them get away until I decide to use them or throw them away—I have become, for now, the writer I am.

I stuff the stories of Alexis and Kate and Sandy and Deepak back into the refrigerator. They'll come out again, I suspect, to be used singly or together, but for now I cannot imagine how.

References

Best, Steven and Douglas Kellner (1991). *Postmodern Theory: Critical Interrogations*. New York: Guilford.

Cixous, Hélène (1991). *Coming to Writing and Other Essays*. Cambridge, Mass.: Harvard University Press.

Dillard, Annie (1990). *The Writing Life*. New York: HarperPerennial.

Eco, Umberto (1986). *Semiotics and the Philosophy of Language*. Bloomington: Indiana University Press.

Ellis, Carolyn (1997). "Evocative Autoethnography: Writing Emotionally about Our Lives." In W. Tierney and Y. Lincoln (Eds.), *Representation and the Text: Reframing the Narrative Voice*. Albany: State University of New York Press (pp. 115–139).

Flax, Jane (1987). "Postmodernism and Gender Relations in Feminist Theory." *Signs*, vol. 12, (pp. 621–643).

Gallagher, Tess (1993). "I Stop Writing the Poem." In Florence Howe (Ed.), *No More Masks!* New York: HarperPerennial (p. 354).

Gergen, Mary (1992). "Life Stories: Pieces of a Dream." In George C. Rosenwald and Richard L. Ochbert (Eds.), *Storied Lives: The Cultural Politics of Self-Understanding*. New Haven: Yale University Press (pp. 127–144).

Greene, Maxine (1987). "Sense-making through story: An autobiographical inquiry." *Teaching Education*, vol 1, 2 (pp. 9–14).

Greene, Maxine (1994). "Epistemology and Educational Research." *Review of Research in Education*, vol. 20 (pp. 423–464).

Haraway, Donna (1995). "Writing, Literacy and Technology: Toward a Cyborg Writing (Interview with Donna Haraway)." In Gary A. Olson and Elizabeth Hirsh (Eds.), *Women Writing Culture*. Albany: State University of New York Press (pp. 423–464).

Hegi, Ursula (1994). *Stones from the River*. New York: Simon and Schuster.

hooks, bell (1995). "Feminist Praxis and the Politics of Literacy: A conversation with bell hooks." In Gary A. Olson & Elizabeth Hirsh (Eds.), *Women Writing Culture*. Albany: State University of New York Press (pp. 105–140).

Mairs, Nancy (1994). *Voice Lessons*. Boston: Beacon.

Mueller, Lisel (1986). "Stalking the poem." In *Second Language*. Baton Rouge: Louisiana University Press (pp. 49–50).

Miller, Nancy K. (1991). *Getting Personal: Feminist Occasions and Other Autobiographical Acts.* New York: Routledge.

Neruda, Pablo (1975). *Memoirs.* (Trans. Hardie St. Martin.) New York: Farrar, Straus and Giroux.

Pinar, William F. (1997). "Regimes of Reason and the Male Narrative Voice." In W. Tierney and Y. Lincoln (Eds.), *Representation and the Text: Reframing the Narrative Voice.* Albany: State University of New York Press (pp. 81–114).

Polkinghorne, Donald E. (1997). "Reporting Qualitative Research as Practice." In W. Tierney and Y. Lincoln (Eds.), *Representation and the Text: Reframing the Narrative Voice.* Albany: State University of New York Press (pp. 3–22).

Rich, Adrienne (1991). *An Atlas of the Difficult World.* New York: Norton.

Richardson, Laurel (1990). *Writing Strategies: Reaching Diverse Audiences.* Newbury Park, Calif.: Sage.

Richardson, Laurel (1994). "Writing: A Method of Inquiry." In Norman K. Denzin and Yvonna S. Lincoln (Eds.), *Handbook of Qualitative Research.* Thousand Oaks, Calif.: Sage (pp. 516–529).

Richardson, Laurel (1997). *Fields of Play: Constructing an Academic Life.* New Brunswick, N.J.: Rutgers University Press.

St. Pierre, Elizabeth (1997). *Circling the Text: Nomadic Writing Practices.* Paper presented at the American Educational Research Association, Chicago, March 24–28.

Swenson, May (1978). "The Wonderful Pen." *New and Selected Things Taking Place.* Boston: Little, Brown.

Tierney, William G, and Yvonna S Lincoln (1997). *Representation and the Text: Reframing the Narrative Voice.* Albany: State University of New York Press.

Tompkins, Jane (1989). "Me and My Shadow." In Linda Kauffman (Ed.), *Gender and Theory: Dialogues in Feminist Criticism.* Oxford: Blackwell (pp. 121–139).

Walker, Alice (1991). *Her Blue Body Everything We Know.* New York: Harcourt Brace Jovanovich.

Waniek, Marilyn Nelson (1993). "Levitation with Baby." In Florence Howe (Ed.), *No More Masks!* New York: HarperPerennial (p. 396).

Williams, William Carlos (1984). "The Practice." In Robert Coles (Ed.), *The Doctor Stories.* New York: New Directions (pp. 119-126).

Wolf, Christa (1989). *Accident: A Day's News.* (Trans. Heike Schwarzbauer and Rick Takvorian.) New York: Farrar, Straus and Giroux.

Chapter 17

"Whatever Gets You Through the Night" (John Lennon, 1974)

Susan Edgerton

Thinking begins in what may fairly enough be called
a forked-road situation, a situation which is ambiguous,
which presents a dilemma, which proposes alternatives.
(John Dewey, 1910, p. 11)

Whether we are willing to admit it or not,
we find ourselves engaged in a class struggle,
and in this struggle there are no neutrals.
Devotion to the ideal of democracy requires us to be partisans in the fight.
(Boyd Henry Bode, 1940, p. 294)

When I was nineteen I read Joan Didion's *Slouching Towards Bethlehem* (1968) for the first time for a class in expository writing at the University of Texas. I still remember the instructor, who was a graduate teaching assistant; I remember her name, her face, and her long red hair, and her voice as she questioned the validity of my claim that everyone is *morally* obligated to spend an entire lifetime furiously learning as much as she or he possibly can. (I did not know at the time that I would be a teacher.) I credited her then with teaching me how to write. All I can say for certain now is that she moved me. I am always reminded of her when I read Didion. For me they became almost the same person, though all I know of Didion is from book cover photos and written words. Together they conjure an image of pinch-faced reserve, an awkward grace, pale freckle-faced red-haired withdrawal that drapes an explosive, surprising, raging, passionate mind. (An explosion always yells, "Surprise!") These qualities I believe I observed in my teacher, though all I know of her is what I made of her in one semester at age nineteen. So maybe she is still working on my writing.

Didion wrote about her own process, informing the reader that the pain of writing *Slouching Towards Bethlehem* "kept me awake at night and so for twenty and twenty-one hours a day I drank gin-and-hot-water to blunt the pain and took Dexedrine to blunt the gin and wrote the piece" (1968, p. xiii). Having been considered a fine student and fine writer throughout my substandard schooling, I was confused by Didion's words. How can just sitting down and writing be so horrible? But the words stuck with me. Maybe because I was taking writing-intensive classes in philosophy, government, and English in a much more competitive environment than my high school had provided, and I was experiencing criticism of my work for the first time. That was painful; but still, I couldn't fully appreciate Didion's remarks. She was not a student; she was, after all, a successful and respected writer. Why was writing painful for her?

Writing often hurts me now, twenty-three years later, and it has hurt for some time, even when it "hurts so good." Why does it hurt and how do I do it, now that I am no longer officially a student but someone who has published and does publish her writing? I agreed to address questions about my process, but I will tell you at the outset that, not unlike Didion's, some of my process is what many would call pathological. And I refuse to write fully about that. Perhaps, though, what I do say will render me so transparent that a perceptive reader (and I'm sure you are one) can know anyway. Indeed, I've just given part of it away: paranoia. Writing, for me, is paranoid. Judgment, it seems, is omnipresent and never-ending. Aside from private journal writing, my work is judged no less than when I was a student. And the judgments are often harsher than those that any teacher would have issued.

This year I was a program section chair for the American Educational Research Association conference and served on a search committee at my university for four tenure-track positions. As I sifted through the sixty-odd proposals I got for the conference, the three blind reviews on each of them and the sixty-odd job application folders, and heard myself and my colleagues comment on our lives and works, the intensity of judgment in academic life became sharply focused for me. Is the pain of writing for public scrutiny unjustified paranoia, or is it reality-based fear? And so what if we judge and are judged? Is that truly worthy of fear? By what strategies, besides or in addition to gin and Dexedrine, might someone such as I or Didion work despite and through the pain of fear and failure?

Didion also wrote, "[I] am so physically small, so temperamentally unobtrusive, and so neurotically inarticulate that people tend to forget that my presence runs counter to their best interests. And it always does. That is one last thing to remember: *writers are always selling somebody out*" (1968, p. xiv). Indeed. However, it is not unreasonable to suggest that Didion never managed to sell anyone out with her writing more severely than she has done to herself. In *The White Album* she offers us a psychiatric report on herself:

> The Rorschach record is interpreted as describing a personality in process of deterioration with abundant signs of failing defenses and increasing inability of the ego to mediate the world of reality and to cope with normal stress. . . . In a technical sense basic affective controls appear to be intact but it is equally clear that they are insecurely and tenuously maintained for the present by a variety of defense mechanisms including intellectualization, obsessive-compulsive devices, projection, reaction-formation, and somatization, all of which now seem inadequate to their task of controlling or containing an underlying psychotic process and are therefore in process of failure. (1979, p. 14)

The report goes on at some length. She adds, "The tests mentioned . . . were administered privately . . . shortly after I suffered the 'attack of vertigo and nausea' mentioned in the first sentence [of the report] and shortly before I was named a *Los Angeles Times* 'Woman of the Year.' By way of comment I offer only that an attack of vertigo and nausea does not now seem to me an inappropriate response to the summer of 1968" (p. 15).

I see Didion doing something that I believe I also do with some frequency in my writing: she offers herself up sacrificially, albeit with rationalizations, to the readers who may judge her and who are often judged by her, as a kind of preemptive strike against her own fear. We are like the band *Devo*: when asked why they did a Muzak recording of themselves, they answered that they wanted to do it to themselves before someone else did it to them. We are also like my partner, who, as a child, once grabbed a bar of soap and jammed it into his mouth, after uttering obsenities, before his mother could do it to him. Somehow, striking out at oneself and exposing one's vulnerability feels liberating (in a sick sort of way). Some of us know there will be many readers who are fascinated by our scab-picking, and who would surely pick the scabs for us if we didn't do it ourselves. We pick our scabs and bleed our histories.

But fear of judgment and failure is not the whole story about the pain of writing. Perhaps the thought of judgment provokes a certain kind of reflection; perhaps the intense self-scrutiny that is part of writing is a response to fear of judgment. But I believe the pain is linked to something deeper. I believe this because even my private writing brings about, or is often enough drenched in, a kind of pain. When I write I feel forced back upon myself, into caverns of consciousness otherwise avoided, face to face with my own foibles and contradictions. Why do it, then? Do I need to say to you, reader, that pleasure and pain are complicated, mutually implicated; that they defy dualistic thinking? Probably not. That observation, like the image of the struggling artist, is a cliché.

Where are the pleasures? Writing is as natural, as ordinary, and as involuntary an act as noticing or paying attention. I compare it to vomiting. While it succeeds and accompanies a horrible feeling, doing it is inevitable and provides dramatic relief. That characterizes *one* of my writing selves, at least. But there are also moments when a spirit of fun is the lead personality. This happens for me when I "see things." Things become other things. My cat giving birth to kittens as I obsess over five chapters that will be my dissertation in my hot one-room Baton Rouge apartment—five chapters, five kittens; the first one the most difficult, the final one late and runty. (I saw it, and then it happened.) Fireworks in Chinatown visible from my forty-fourth floor one-room apartment in Chicago as I obsess over the revision of that same dissertation-becoming-book, fireworks for *me* because I have written another sentence. Cottonwood seeds floating like snow in the ninety-degree, 90 percent–humidity air around a Mississippi River plantation home in Louisiana. Then, the air turning cooler with a breeze that knocks down leaves so they hit the ground simultaneously, like students conspiring to drop pencils at the same time while the teacher (writer) is mentally elsewhere. (Hey, what just happened?) There is no coherence, no narrative floating through my "line of thinking," and no line of thinking floating through a narrative. Stories come in snippets or snapshots, even from the novels I read to help me sleep and think and write. Incomplete sentences. Probably why I liked Annie Proulx's *The Shipping News* (1993).

Sometimes I get so thrown by events that I cannot face the pen or screen for days at a time. Last year it was months, until one day I realized that the only sentence I'd written aside from necessary correspondence was, "It's summer in Lower Michigan, and the flotsam and jetsam have taken to the frothy air." (Brilliant, huh? It was hot and humid, and my house is not air-conditioned.) During those non-writing months, however, I was wielding a hammer, crowbar, or paintbrush, "writing" what would become my home environment. From Jacques Derrida I learned that writing takes a multiplicity of forms and can become manifest through music, hitchhiking, visual art, a stick in the sand, motorcycle maintenance, or pig farming.

So, when it comes to writing, I don't often have a deep sense of wasted time anymore. This is partly because of Derrida's lesson, and partly because there can be no wasted time for one who experiences everything as material. Indeed, this is part of the pleasure of being a writer. Recently, I wrote a paper in which I used journal notes taken to record a conversation I heard while standing in line for my driver's license in Shreveport, Louisiana, in 1985. Waiting in line for a dose of Foucauldian or Kafkaesque bureaucracy need not be a waste of time! But given this approach to time and writing, a certain fragmentation is inevitable. The work is scattered across scraps of paper, napkins, notebook or folder covers, deposit slips, receipts, book margins, catalogues, and calendars.

I think I only recently noticed my sense of no-time-is-wasted as something other than "normal" or universal. At my institution there are many meetings. By my count, last semester I sat in meetings for thirty to forty hours a month. We all complain about them, myself included. But I noticed that, while I don't like being there so much, I seem to hold no regrets or sense of loss such as I've heard some others express. It is all material. (Colleagues beware!) The material is unorganized; it resembles my sock drawer and my day planner, but it moves in at the darndest times nonetheless.

On the other hand, I start to feel that time's a-wastin' when it's time to sleep and I cannot drop off, or I wake at three or four in the morning. So I have a rule: no matter how much work there is to do (and it is endless), no matter the density of stress and responsibility handed to me, my insomniac time is my own. If I'm to be awake when I need to be asleep, by God, I will read whatever I please. ("Whatever gets you through the night.") In this way I've read many a novel that feeds my work and my soul. Insomniac time is not a time to read or write about curriculum theory, cultural studies, or elementary social studies. Besides, nighttime is when my terror awakens and needs taming. I feel: Fear about the virtual, the not-yet . . . "bourgeois" fears including—fear of criticism, fear of loss, fear of pain, fear of failure, fear of the abyss of meaninglessness. I am running so as to avoid entering that dark cave of denial that beckons each time I'm still—like at night, as soon as the lights go out. The ringing in my ears transmutes into judging voices, chiding me for dirty deeds from my past, for duties unfulfilled, for lack of insight, love, wisdom, integrity, perseverance, ingenuity, energy, empathy.

Job-related work is not the antidote indicated.

I read novels in which there are sentences that floor me, especially when a sentence is the first of the book or of a chapter, such as, "They shot the white girl first" (Morrison, 1998), or "When I was three and a half years old, Ruthie Ericson fed me twenty-seven baby aspirin while I was sitting on the toilet" (Smiley, 1992, p. 277). I read novels that often help me sleep at night, but sometimes keep me up all night. Jane Smiley's *A Thousand Acres* should have had a warning label. Entrusting my sleep to that novel for 200 pages or so, I was duped. On a night I most needed my sleep, after page 200 or so, the family pathology in that story hit the shop fan like a spray of ice water, keeping me up all night to finish the novel and disturbing my sleep and waking hours for days after. I zombied around, repeating to myself, "Don't you think it's about time for you to grow up?" (This was not in response to my reaction to the novel; . . . it was about what I had learned from the novel.) "The best-laid plans . . ." I thought I needed to take care of job stress, relax, and sleep, when in fact what I needed was to just grow up.

So I am trying to write in a disciplined way right now, but I fidget and my mind wanders. Suddenly, I am remembering a girlhood friend who got into her car and turned on the motor in a closed garage. We were in our teens, and she had just given birth to a child whom she left in the care of her parents, with whom she was intensely angry. Was this the only way she could story her life for them? Suppose she had been a writer? . . . And for a moment I consider the simplicity of her act. What keeps most of us from the garage? Is that part of the drive to write? To have a voice in the tug of war against our own self destruction and destruction by others? A voice with which to do battle?

There's a vantage point it takes so long to find, where you can see how all the pieces fit as you watch them fall apart (Bruton, 1992, performed by Willie Nelson and Bonnie Raitt).

Non-human natural beauty offers the only imaginable escape from this madness. I try to get out in a beautiful natural setting once a week for several hours. This doesn't always happen, but when it does I know I feel the difference. It is impossible for me to either fret or strut in these settings. It is impossible for me not to worship there. It is impossible for me to write without this.

The task of writing, for me, involves moving back and forth between pen and paper and computer, between pleasure and pain. I have a pen fetish. What is this about? I think I need the tangible and the aesthetic sense of my fingers around a pen, my hand sliding along paper. Reading and writing are sensual. Rachel, my then three-year-old niece, once helped me to see the fundamental sensuality of this world, when I read to her. She lay next to me in my sister's bed as I read Annie Dillard's *The Writing Life* (1989). The words were well beyond her experience but as one little hand held a bottle in her mouth, the other reached up to touch the words on the page I was reading. It was a graceful and purely sensual touch, an appreciative touch, not a child's effort to point out words for the benefit of an adult.

Although my writing is made possible by the immensity of the world and the experience of the sensual, nevertheless when I write I shamelessly project. My personal experiences, epiphanies, catharses, become the world. How else could I entitle a book *Translating the Curriculum: Multiculturalism into Cultural Studies* (Edgerton, 1996)? At the time, cultural studies provided *me* with a means of bridging and gathering in my own scattered parts. How arrogant to ascribe to that intellectual movement the privilege of superseding another, (multiculturalism)? But what else can I do?

Anne Lamott, in her book about writing, *Bird by Bird*, told us that "good writing is about telling the truth," that people want to write so as not to be silenced any longer. Our truth is our experience:

> Remember that you own what happened to you. If your childhood was less than ideal, you may have been raised thinking that if you told the truth about what really went on in your family, a long bony white finger would emerge from a cloud and point at you, while a chilling voice thundered, "We *told* you not to tell." But that was then. Just put down on paper everything you can remember now about your parents and siblings and relatives and neighbors, and we will deal with libel later on. (Lamott, 1994, p. 6)

Luckily for me, it is not considered libel to defame an intellectual and social movement.

Writing reminds me how much I forget. Until moments ago I had forgotten that I have read books and articles about writing much as many people read self-help books, two by Annie Dillard, two by Natalie Goldberg, one by John Lee, one by Anne Lamott, one by Milan

Kundera, numerous articles by numerous writers. I've devoted so much time to "graphomania" (Kundera, 1986). This is big business! What could I have funded with the purchase price of these books?! How much writing could have happened in the time I spent reading about writing? Have I forgotten what I am here for? Or have I ever known? Uh-oh. Here comes schizophrenia (sung to the tune of "Here Comes Peter Cottontail").

The fascination with self and exposition of same sinks into shame, then bursts forth, Phoenix-like, as fury. And I am raging, forever raging. The situations in Iraq, Chiapas, Cuba, and elsewhere, and my government's genocidal practices in these worlds; the abysmal coverage by mainstream media here; economic disparity that widens every day; the fact that the food lines in this country are filled now with working poor; prison labor; union busting; child labor; children tried as adults; sweatshops; environmental degradation; nuclear waste and weaponry; and most of us just keep on buying, keep on wanting more, keep on ignoring, keep on numbing up and dumbing down. Suddenly this very project feels narcissistic to me. My energy is needed elsewhere.

Yet, to begin to see these issues as connected . . . Chiapas and Iraq and Cuba to a local labor dispute, to the increased demands on all of us for fewer rewards (this is even being felt in academia, sometimes presented as the Ivory Tower sheathed and protected by the mantle of "academic freedom"), to environmental degradation, to the politics in our private homes and communities (war is rape is battering is war; violence is everywhere and takes many forms), is to begin to see truth. But it is a road paved in rage, even if sometimes righteous rage. I have to find the hope and the love to keep me from that closed garage. Obviously, hope, love, and some amount of rage are required for doing "the work," for remaining mobile, for avoiding paralysis. And I have to write in order to find hope and love, and to channel rage. Paradoxically, this process that provokes so much fear and loathing (writing) is also one of the only ways I know to deal with fear.

My fears—my neurotic, obsessive night terrors—are also intimately linked with my courage. Courage, I now understand, exists only in the face of fear. I shall *not* go to the garage! Instead I'll pick up my fountain pen, my stylus, my sword, my paintbrush, my shovel, my hammer, my walking stick . . . *whatever gets me through the night* and enables me to do what I believe I am here for. And I'll pull up my socks, put on my combat boots, take deep breaths, trudge through the shit, and try again and again to listen, hear, be heard, love, write, fight, play, and act. What else is there? I am not being tortured, I am not starving, I am not struggling with poverty. Most of the people in the world face at least one of those horrors. There is work to do, even if it only amounts to "wheeling my little pushcart out into the marketplace of ideas" (Zinn, 1994).

References

Bruton, T.S. (1992). "Getting Over You." On Willie Nelson CD. *Across the Borderline, 1993.* Produced by Don Was. Columbia Records

Didion, J. (1968). *Slouching Towards Bethlehem.* New York: Delta Books.

Didion, J. (1979). *The White Album.* New York: Farrar, Straus, and Giroux.

Dillard, A. (1982). *Living by Fiction.* New York: Harper and Row.

Dillard, A. (1989). *The Writing Life.* New York: Harper and Row.

Edgerton, S. (1996). *Translating the Curriculum: Multiculturalism into Cultural Studies.* New York: Routledge.

Goldberg, N. (1986). *Writing Down the Bones: Freeing the Writer Within.* Boston: Shambala.

Goldberg, N. (1990). *Wild Mind: Living the Writer's Life.* New York: Bantam.

Kundera, M. (1986). *The Art of the Novel.* New York: Grove.

Lamott, A. (1994). *Bird by Bird: Some Instructions on Writing and Life.* New York: Anchor.

Lee, J. (1994). *Writing from the Body.* New York: St. Martin's.

Lennon, J. (1974). *Walls and Bridges.* Produced by John Lennon. Apple Records.

Morrison, T. (1998). *Paradise.* New York: Knopf.

Proulx, A. (1993). *The Shipping News.* New York: Simon and Schuster.

Smiley, J. (1992). *A Thousand Acres.* New York: Fawcett Columbine.

Zinn, H. (1994). *You Can't Be Neutral on a Moving Train: A Personal History of Our Times.* Boston: Beacon.

Chapter 18

How I Work

William F. Pinar

Nor is theoretical thinking a higher type of thinking than practical.
(John Dewey, 1910, p. 142)

Every individual . . . possesses a variety of selves.
(Boyd Henry Bode, 1940, p. 115)

I

Some such rhythm of the unconscious and the conscious
is involved in all fruitful thinking.
(John Dewey, 1910, p. 215)

Understanding has to with relationships.
(Bode Henry Bode, 1940, p. 242)

How do I work?

I begin the day by making an entry in my diary or journal. I think of my early pieces on *currere*, written in 1973 and 1974, how I would read, say, Virginia Woolf's *The Voyage Out*, marking passages that struck me in some way, making a text of those, then juxtaposing them with my diary. I hesitate to use that word, although it's not entirely wrong: after all, I do list events, as a diarist might. But for me the events I wish to list are primarily psychological, events that occur on the edges of everyday activities. For these I have to focus on the inner life, my subjective experience of what has happened in the world. They're not the same, psychological events and activities, but they're not completely distinguishable either. My experience of the world constitutes in large measure my inner life, and my inner life has everything to do with how I am in the world.

So, each morning, within minutes of waking, while the coffee is brewing, I make a diary entry. I start mundanely: date, time, weather conditions, and then I free-associate, more or less. Sometimes things have happened and I am the journalist; at other times I've a vague sense of something going on with me for which I have at first few or no words. If there has been a dream I can recall, if it seems curious or in some way noteworthy, I record that. I may review the events of the day before. Ordinarily I conclude with what I see ahead for the day. Ten to twenty minutes have passed and the coffee is ready.

Often Jeff and I rise at the same time. Because the first few hours of the morning are working time for me, he moves to the kitchen, where he sometimes watches the news. Soon he moves outside, where he surveys the flowers he has planted over the past two years. We wave at each other through the study window. The birds—cardinals, wrens, hummingbirds, a hawk as I write this, and of course sparrows—fly by, the small ones stopping to eat at the feeder outside the window. Jeff placed it there, to give my eyes a place to rest, away from this computer screen. He also built floor-to-ceiling mahogany-stained bookshelves in the study. My study is Jeff's gift to me, and that fact allows me to feel close to him even while submerged in my work, which I am nearly every morning, seven days a week (unless there is a guest or we're traveling).

The first hour or two is given to writing. I wake up—drinking my three cups of coffee—writing. It's Saturday, February 21, 1998, as I write this; and this morning I awoke early, just before five, and while I wanted to sleep more, unfortunately my mind settled on what I had to do. Now I'm not performing some fantasy of the martyr to work; it's that Jeff and I have just returned from a two-week vacation, mind you, and, among other things, the copyedited manuscript of *The Passionate Mind of Maxine Greene* was here. The copyeditor wanted it back by the end of the week, which was yesterday. No chance of that, first because we have just returned and second because LSU is now closed for Mardi Gras until next Wednesday noon. So I have a few days, but this morning I felt I had to see how much needed to be done, if I needed to bother the contributors or if I myself could supply whatever information was missing.

So this morning, because I was tired, because the Maxine Greene collection called me, I didn't write, that is, I didn't write in the book on which I'm working. But—it's three hours later, nearly 8 a.m.—and I am writing, a first draft of this attempt to think about how I work. This is a rare morning as I usually write in *Strange Fruit*, the first volume in the *currere* series I envision. I am determined to finish it by this time next year. The first and final sections are near the first draft, but the middle section remains distressingly unformed. But this morning I will think about how I work; this afternoon I'll return to the book.

By the time I have consumed three cups of coffee, ninety minutes or so have passed, and the writing is over, for the morning. I take a short break, eat something (I'm trying to diet, well, a little, so this morning it's not much), and return to the computer to take notes. This morning I'm taking notes—as I have done for maybe two weeks—from Saidiya V. Hartman's *Scenes of Subjection: Terror, Slavery, and Self-Making in Nineteenth-Century America*. The passages that struck me will help—as I see it now—with the opening chapter of that troubling middle section, as well as with a major methodological concern: voyeurism. You see, there are chapters on lynching and prison rape; how can I write and teach in ways that are not prurient, scopic, in some indirect way exploitative of the suffering of others? Hartman is helpful here, having faced this dilemma herself in depicting scenes of subjection.

As usual, several books are stacked up, already read, waiting for me to take notes. Most of these are library books, and I use the bookmarkers—usually just blank pieces of paper—to note the information I need to find the passages that initially struck me. I write "initially" because I sometimes find they don't strike me during the note-taking phase, and so I pass them by. I want to pass them by because this book, like *Understanding Curriculum*, has become too large for my taste. Now another sixty to ninety minutes have passed, and I'm ready for another break. Often I walk about the yard, admiring what Jeff has planted, and if he's working outside—he often is; that's his work—we chat about this plant or that. The gardens are the world which he built and which we occupy together. While he generously listens to me when I feel I must discuss, for instance, curriculum matters and I listen to him discuss, for instance, his family (left behind in Virginia), the world we share is "the forest," our term of endearment for our dwelling-place. Returning to the house after twenty minutes, I shower, and then I begin to read, usually for an hour. Then—when I'm not on sabbatical, as I am this term—I go to the office.

During the afternoons I'm not teaching I work on the collections I edit. There always seems to be one underway. In January I finished a reader on "Twenty Years of the Journal of Curriculum Theorizing" entitled *Contemporary Curriculum Discourses*. The book features pieces from the early years—one of Flo Krall's first ecological pieces opens the collection—but emphasizes work since the late 1980s. Royalties will go to the journal. Now, as you see, I'm working on *How We Work*, a collection I am editing with Marla Morris and Mary Aswell Doll. Keeping projects restricted to separate places—the book I'm writing at home, the books I'm editing at the office—helps me keep them separate in my head. Of course today is different; I'm working on "how I work" at home. That vacation has left things a bit topsy-turvy.

It was a fine vacation. Jeff loves sea water, as do I; we sea-bathed (as we say) each day, for hours at a time. The trip was a retracing of my steps of twenty-six years ago, when, after completing my Ph.D. dissertation, I treated myself to two weeks in the Caribbean. First, a transitional two nights in St. Thomas; then a week of camping at Cinnamon Bay on St. John; then another transitional period, three days at Cane Garden Bay on Tortolla. Because I was determined to take a "real" (not working) vacation, I didn't take a computer, although that decision provoked a bit of neurotic anxiety. I did take four books (which I promised I would read only when I wasn't playing in the sea) and the printout of that unformed middle section of *Strange Fruit*. I read three—Jessica Benjamin's *In the Shadow of the Other*, Mary Helen Washington's *Invented Lives*, and *The Black Male in America* edited by Doris Wilkinson and Ronald L. Taylor. I worked my way through much of Dewey's *How We Think*, from which we took the title for this collection.

The Benjamin book—several years ago Madeleine Grumet gave me *The Bonds of Love*, but it hadn't worked for me then—was exciting. It restates, in abbreviated form, important differences between object relations theory and Lacanian psychoanalysis, between psychoanalytic feminism and feminism identified with various strands of poststructuralism, concluding with an outline of a psychoanalytic theory of the "other." Reading the book on St. John, I was sure it would be a chapter in the first volume; but now that I'm back, now that I'm experiencing anxiety over the length and thematic complexity of the book, I'm sure I'll save it for one of the analytic volumes. I've three of these planned at this point, one on the conflations between "self" and "nation," a second on "representation" and the role of the contemporary intellectual, and a third on psychoanalytic theory of self-division and the construction of "others." Benjamin will help me there.

II

To be playful and serious at the same time is possible,
and it defines the ideal mental condition.
(John Dewey, 1910, p. 218)

Today—it's Friday, six days later—I'm at the office. I've meetings with Toby Daspit, a Ph.D. student working on his dissertation; and Vikki Hillis, a Ph.D. student directed by Bill Doll, who is editing Dwayne Huebner's collected essays. Today may be the day Vikki turns the manuscript over to me. Before Toby arrives I take advantage of a few free moments—the E-mail list was low today, for a change—to write here. Of course I can't always manage to begin writing (or reading or note-taking) when a brief segment of time presents itself, but today my energy is steady and calm, and I feel some pressure to keep going. Mary and Marla are basically finished with their part of the job; now it's up to me to bring the volume to a conclusion. Not completely, as they will want to see what I've written here, also the introduction (which I started for the book proposal), and the sequencing of the pieces. They may disagree, want revisions, etc. But the pressure has begun to build (inside me, not from Mary or Marla) to produce something to which they can respond.

Vikki just called. She had computer problems yesterday, and she has postponed the meeting until noon on Monday, at our house. The kitchen table, to be precise. That seems like a fine place to pass the manuscript from her hands to mine. Not only has Vikki edited the manuscript, communicating regularly with Dwayne; she has also scanned it. (Several of his early pieces were in mimeo form only; none was on disk.) There were more than a few references she wanted to include, names probably unfamiliar to present-day readers but well-known thirty years ago, like Harry Stack Sullivan, for instance. This collection has been three years in the works. I asked Dwayne's permission to collect his essays sometime in late 1994 or early 1995. While I am vague about when the project started, I do remember that while teaching at the University of Virginia in autumn 1995 I was reading everything he had written over a nearly thirty-year career. I wanted to publish everything, but that would have been a fat book indeed. Finally I settled on thirty-five pieces; it will be fat enough. Then I wrote the introduction and by early 1996 Lawrence Erlbaum, the publisher, had the manuscript. As mentioned, none of Dwayne's essays was on disk, and Lawrence Erlbaum Associates found that when they added the cost of typesetting the long manuscript—and it was considerably longer than the book they had agreed to publish—the economics of the project no longer worked for them. So I agreed to have it scanned in Baton Rouge. I had known Vikki Hillis from class; she's a B.A. graduate of Hampshire College and had worked for a time in art education with Karen Hamblen. A woman with a conspicuously creative intelligence, Vikki was willing to edit the manuscript after scanning it. It was a larger project than either of us imagined, and it has taken nearly eighteen months to reach this stage. Dwayne is wonderfully relaxed (or is appearing to be so) about the delays, but I am very eager to see the book in material form. That will happen later this year or early next year. I am excited already.

Now that Vikki has canceled, I can leave the office a bit early, swim in the LSU pool, take a brief nap, and enjoy a second work segment beginning around four I would guess. Typically, Friday nights are quiet for Jeff and me, and today will be no exception. Tomorrow too will be a full day, since I treat weekends pretty much as I do weekdays, except that, during my sabbatical, I make every effort to spend time in the office on both Saturday and Sunday. With no interruptions, it's possible to move quickly through the week's memos, regular mail and E-mail. It's early March, which means spring in Baton Rouge, and we may go to a nursery or two on Sunday (that means no office, so I must finish everything on Saturday) to see what's available. We've decided to cover the hill in azaleas—there are no hills in Louisiana; this was a barrier built by the Army Corps of Engineers to protect the neighborhood in case the bayou behind our house floods. Last summer Jeff planted impatiens all over the hill (it's approximately twelve to fifteen feet high and runs almost the length of our north side, approximately eighty feet long); and it was, before the hot sun and a dry August and September wilted quite a few of them, an astonishing array of color. We're not confident they'll come back—although with only one frost (and a light one at that), they should—but they don't hide the weeds very well. So, the plan now is to replace them with azaleas. It will take several years for them to cover the hill, but when they do, color will cover the hill once again.

III

Holding the mind to a subject is like holding a ship to its course;
it implies constant change of place combined with unity of direction.
(John Dewey, 1910, p. 40)

It's a week later now, and we did buy azaleas, maybe thirty of them. Not enough to cover the entire hill, but a start. And "spring" disappeared in a cold snap that required us to move all we could into the heated greenhouse. A few things left outside were damaged, but the azalea blooms remain, as do the daffodils. Could have been much worse. Vikki and I did meet on Monday; she's very close to finishing now. Like most graduate assistants, however, she also teaches undergraduates, and so this week she is swamped reading midterm papers. Next week, we think. Next week is Toby's dissertation proposal hearing. I've finished taking notes from Hartman's book; today I may finish with Mary Helen Washington's. It's sunny and cold; the office isn't sufficiently warm for me to stay long. I'll write a few lines more then head for the pool. Then the nap, then the second segment of working. These days, that's how I work.

References

Benjamin, Jessica (1988). *The Bonds of Love: Psychoanalysis, Feminism, and the Problem of Domination.* New York: Pantheon.

Benjamin, Jessica (1998). *In the Shadow of the Other.* New York: Routledge.

Bode, Boyd Henry (1940). *How We Learn.* Boston: Heath.

Dewey, John (1910). *How We Think.* Boston: Heath.

Hartman, Saidiya V. (1997). *Scenes of Subjection: Terror, Slavery, and Self-Making in Nineteenth Century America.* New York: Oxford University Press.

Huebner, Dwanye (1999). *The Lure of the Transcendent: Collected Essays.* (Ed. Vikki Hillis. Collected and introduced by William F. Pinar.) Mahwah, N.J.: Lawrence Erlbaum.

Krall, Florence R. (1979). "Living Metaphors: The Real Curriculum in Environmental Education." Journal of Curriculum Theorizing, vol. 1,1 (pp. 180–185). Reprinted in William F. Pinar, Ed. (in press). *Contemporary Curriculum Discourses.* New York: Peter Lang.

Pinar, William F. Ed. (1999). *Contemporary Curriculum Discourses.* New York: Peter Lang.

Pinar, William F. Ed. (1998). *The Passionate Mind of Maxine Greene: "I Am Not Yet."* London: Falmer.

Pinar, William F. (in preparation). *Strange Fruit.*

Pinar, William F., William M. Reynolds, Patrick Slattery, and Peter Taubman (1995). *Understanding Curriculum.* New York: Peter Lang.

Washington, Mary Helen. Ed. (1987). *Invented Lives: Narratives of Black Women 1860–1960.* Garden City, N.Y.: Doubleday/Anchor.

Wilkinson, Doris Y. and Ronald L. Taylor. Eds. (1977). *The Black Male in America: Perspectives on His Status in Contemporary Society.* Chicago: Nelson-Hall.

Chapter 19

A Truthful Tale About How I Work

Petra Munro

The exercise of thought is,
in the literal sense of that word, inference;
by it one thing carries us over to the idea of,
and belief in, another thing.
It involves a jump, a leap, a going beyond
what is surely known to something else accepted on its warrant.
(John Dewey, 1910, p. 26)

A democratic philosophy of education
rests on the faith that if the oncoming generation is given
an opportunity to see the basic issue, democracy will win.
It must win on these terms or it cannot win at all.
(Boyd Henry Bode, 1940, p. 297)

March 9, 1998
6:52 am

"We write to taste life twice"
Anaïs Nin

I am a writer. I am? A writer is someone who is not me. A writer writes with ease. A writer writes with ideas flowing steadily from her pen. A writer has a pool of rich, varied words. A writer is clever with words. A writer has a burst of inspiration and then writes madly for days, not leaving her room until a complete, perfect manuscript is done.

When I write I know that I must start months in advance of my deadline. I know I will need to do multiple drafts. My first drafts are mere free association. I cannot write a detailed outline and then sit and write. I do not know what I want to say until I am doing the writing. It is in the writing that I learn what it is that I want to say. My first drafts are just to find out what I am thinking. Once I know what I want to say, I begin the tedious but rewarding work of editing and crafting the writing. I am on many levels a terrible writer. I do not know how to use commas or apostrophes or how to spell. I constantly have to remember not to put the verb at the end of the sentence (a habit I developed because I learned German as a first language). Often I pay a professional editor to edit.

I have also come to rely on a writing group. I have learned much about my writing through having others critique it. I meet in a writing group once a week. At the moment we are four women, all academics, but from various fields. Each week two of us present our work. We begin by having the two writers who are not presenting that week report on their progress. Then each writer has an hour to use as she pleases. I always read my work out loud. It is when I read out loud that I hear my sentences go on forever. I become aware of using the same word three times in one sentence. And yet, I also become aware of the rhythm, the flow, the power of what I write.

My week revolves around the writing group. I began this practice in graduate school. Five of us began a research/study/writing group to support each other in our doctoral program. It was an extremely powerful experience (see Jipson, Munro, Victor, Froude-Jones, and Freed-Rowland, 1995). Our writing in that group addressed our struggles as teachers to work for social change. Putting into words, on paper, those feelings I had carried in my body made them real. To have others read them and nod, cry, say amen, say go for it, tell us more about this, was a profound experience. What was most surprising was that my colleagues said, "Your writing is best when it is your own voice, when you speak from the heart." As a history and political science major in college I had spent years learning to write in an objective, distant voice. Writing meant being outside my body, saying what others thought. I had no thoughts.

Writing empowered me. I came alive. It was a way in which I could name my world, make my world real. For others, writing was seen as a luxury, a bourgeois extravagance that detracted from the real work of political activism or the relational work of teaching. Whereas writing slowly became my priority, for others it was relegated to any time that was left over after "real" work was done. I suppose a central issue for me has been to legitimate my writing as something that is useful or meaningful in the broader scope of my political work. I am not under the illusion that my writing will change the world. On the contrary, I realize that what I write is often highly specialized, read by a minuscule number of people, the journals in which I write probably have a circulation of only five hundred people, and, often, it is addressed to an audience of like-minded people. What difference does my writing really make? I do see my writing as a political act. Perhaps it is political only because it keeps me sane. But I do believe that naming the world is a political act. To name my world as a woman is to write against the patriarchal script that maintains that experience is universal.

As a political act, I now claim my writing time first. As I look at my weekly calendar on Sundays, I block out my writing time first. I put a long arrow through the morning hours and in large block letters put WRITING. The writing group time is always in pen. I make no exceptions to any demands that might conflict with the writing group. I reason that, since I am an academic, one-third of my job is research, so therefore one-third of my time should be devoted to writing.

In my own mind, writing is not the most important thing I do (I love to teach and work with my students), but it is what keeps me sane. And because women are not supposed to be writers, I emphasize that part of my identity. I value the writing and the role it plays in my life by making it a priority. My mornings are devoted to writing. It has taken me years actually to practice what I preach. To take myself seriously as a writer has meant putting writing first. It has meant adhering strictly to my scheduled writing time and learning to say no, to say that "I have another commitment" when students, colleagues, or department chairs want to schedule meetings during that time. I have become brutal. However, to rearrange my schedule, to give in to other demands would be tantamount to devaluing myself, to writing myself off.

This does not mean that I don't feel selfish. I do. But I know that when I have committed a morning to writing, and taken care of myself, I am better able to focus on and work with others.[1]

During my first years as an academic, I struggled to take myself seriously as a writer because I did not consider it real work; but I am now comfortable in a routine that validates and honors my identity as a writer. When I began my tenure-track job at Louisiana State University, I put writing last. Teaching and committee work ate up my week, work ate up my life. Only evenings and weekends were left over for writing. Even then, I couldn't enjoy the writing because by the time I came to it, I was exhausted.

I write most mornings now. I begin my day with meditation, and by seven or eight o'clock I am at the computer with my second cup of coffee and a bowl of oatmeal. Oatmeal is my comfort food; I think it eases my anxiety about writing. I work on a small laptop, a Macintosh power book. It is small and compact, it doesn't take up much space. I work on what used to be my dining room table. I love having a big work space, with minimal clutter. The laptop is nice because it doesn't take up much space. My desk/table is in front of a window that looks out onto my back yard and a large live oak tree.

I usually put on some classical music (Mozart). By mid-morning when I am getting sluggish, I usually switch to something faster (in my case that means Van Morrison). In addition to music for inspiration I also have several items/pictures on my desktop. I have several postcards of artwork by Georgia O'Keeffe. They remind that what I do is art. I am an artist. Because her work is so deeply rooted in her experience as a woman and expresses female experience and symbolism, it keeps me aware of why I am doing what I do. I also have a postcard of Margaret Mead. I am not sure why Mead. The lone anthropologist. She wrote in multiple genres.

March 9, 1998 9:03 am

Have just returned from my midmorning walk with Maggie, my dog (actually a puppy). Just got my third cup of coffee and put on my Cecilia Bartoli CD. My walk is also part of my morning writing routine. I usually can sit only about an hour or hour and a half before I need to stretch both my body and my mind. Walking gives me time to digest, to mull, to reconsider. I walk to a grove of trees in my neighborhood, next to a convent where there are the twelve stations of the cross. The grove of trees reminds me of the Celtic sacred grove. For some reason the trees remind me of the larger picture. As I walk through this grove, I assess whether I am remaining grounded, rooted in my writing; am I remaining true to my heart?

What I thought about while I was walking was the fact that I have a very rigid routine about writing. And yet, within that routine there is a lot of murkiness. I do not use an outline; I do not censor my writing; much of it is free writing. Every time I stop writing and want to go back to correct, change, erase, I remind myself to keep moving, just keep writing. The contrast between this free-flowing writing and the strict routine I keep struck me as interesting. I need the routine in order to be free to write, to think, to imagine.

So where was I? Ah, Margaret Mead . . . not sure why she is on my desk. I have other postcards as well; of the cathedral in Norwich, of Hildegard von Bingen, of pictures from Carrow Abbey. These items were collected during my sabbatical in the fall of 1997, when I did research on medieval women religious, primarily mystics. I learned that Hildegard von Bingen (1098-1187) wrote six books, that Julian of Norwich wrote the first book in English vernacular, and that Mechthild of Magdeburg wrote the first book in German vernacular.

A long tradition of writing among women.

My own history of writing—as a young girl/journals.

March 11, 1998 7:24 am

Having my oatmeal and coffee. This morning I am listening to Pachelbel. The sun is shining and the dog has been out. Yesterday I did not write. It was my teaching day, so I spent the morning preparing for class. I did think about what I still wanted to or needed to write, about how I work. Much of that work does focus on taking myself seriously as a writer, as a creative writer, an artist. This is not always easy for an academic. Academic writing is objective, linear. One must "make an argument" and develop the argument in a logical and rational manner. Not only does this kind of writing obscure the messiness of life and the fact that we are human; it is also not challenging. I learned long ago how to write in this fashion. And yet, the master's tools will not dismantle the house. How I choose to write is a political act. What would writing look like that challenged the notion of objectivity, of the lone independent writer? How would writing look that invited readers to generate their own meanings, that did not provide neat, tidy answers?

One of my greatest joys as a writer is to experiment with writing styles that resist the normative expectations of academic writing. I have tried several modes. One of my first published pieces (Munro and Jipson, 1992) was a dialogue with my mentor and dissertation adviser regarding our experience of co-teaching a class and students' resistance to feminist theory and the use of fiction. We hoped to capture the ongoing negotiation of understandings, the intersubjective nature of how we come to know. We took this a step further in another piece (Munro and Jipson, 1997) in which we re-presented a taped conversation between ourselves as a means of presenting women's voices as pure text, as lived experience, in order to disrupt the devaluation of women's talk as gossip. In taking our experience of mentoring and friendship as a serious site of research, we hoped to disrupt what constitutes research and writing.

To push the boundaries of what constitutes writing when we take women's experience of representation seriously also prompted another project. This was a collaborative project (Adams, Causey, Jacobs, Munro, Quinn and Trousdale, 1998) in which several colleagues and I grappled with how to re-present the experiences of women teachers on the basis of their life history narratives. How could we represent the complexities of women's lives—the contradictions, complexities, multiple subjectivities, especially for women teachers, whose lives and representation have been circumscribed by dominant stereotypes. We decided to experiment with readers' theater. Again the text or script was composed of the actual voices of four women teachers. The interpretation was in what words we chose, how we juxtaposed them, and the staging. This was the kind of creative, intellectual writer's life that I had imagined.

This kind of collaborative work is often not considered writing, though. Writing is an individual act, done alone. Theater, conversation, or dialogue is not considered writing. Who has defined what counts as writing? Often my work consists of continually reminding myself that if I name it writing, it is writing. My work is often a matter of trusting my own definitions, creating my own definitions of what constitutes an act of writing.

March 12, 1998 7:23 am

This morning I have chosen Liszt and Grape-Nuts. Tomorrow is writing group, and it is my turn to share my work. I am wondering whether I can really present this to the group, since it is so rough. And yet, this is my writing process. This is how I work. I do not want to perpetuate the illusion that the words flow freely and perfectly the first time I sit down to write something. I am actually tempted to leave this piece as it is, with all its mistakes, as a way to show how I really do work. And yet I probably will not have the guts to do this.

I have been trying to remember my own history of writing. When did I start to write? When did I first think of myself as a writer? I have been "journaling" on and off since the seventh grade. I remember sitting in my closet and writing about how mean the other kids at school were. Expressing negative feelings was taboo in my family. We pretended to live the perfect suburban existence, to be the perfect, happy family. Writing, and reading, were my escapes. In high school I had a piece of writing published in the *The Wit*, the writing magazine. And yet, when I wrote that piece, a fictional piece based on a father-daughter relationship, I don't remember thinking about doing it as a writer. In fact, in high school, although I was straight-A student, I remember not feeling good about my writing, since I always had so many red marks on my papers when they were returned. My grammar was always bad, so I thought my writing must also be bad.

Throughout college, as a history major, I wrote term paper after term paper. I was excellent at research, doing notecards, organizing ideas, but never saw writing as a place where one could articulate one's own ideas. Or was it that I already knew that women weren't expected to have ideas of their own? My senior honors thesis, a reassessment of the Herero uprising of 1911 in southwest Africa, was criticized for not being Marxist enough. As I look back on it now, I see that on some level I was being critical of the overly deterministic analysis of a Marxist perspective, which obscured the complexity and contradictions of power relations. What I learned, though, was not to trust my own ideas.

My writing continued, however. After finishing my undergraduate work, I traveled in Europe for two years. I kept a detailed journal. In fact, this was when I began to envision myself as an artist. I was one more American going to Europe to seek inspiration to become an artist. Cafes, cigarettes, and my journal.

March 13, 1998 7:30 am

I began that journal on October 6, 1980, in Germany:

"I'm almost afraid to write in this book. I want my words to have meaning and be thoughtful. And at times I feel I am not thoughtful. It is a sign of my insecurity."

I have piled all my journals in front of me, next to the computer. I have just spent the last twenty minutes going through a trunk in which I keep my journals, letters, and memorabilia. I thought I would perhaps go through and find excerpts that reflected my emergence as a writer. And yet, as I read through my journals, I am not sure I want to share those writings. On one level, I don't want to read them; the experience is painful. What I am reminded of, though, is the fact that I have always written. Writing has always been a part of who I am. And yet, I continue to doubt that I am a writer.

October 13, 1976, DePauw College, Greencastle, Indiana

"I am still not a good writer, even though I really do try. Maybe I just wasn't cut out to write. So maybe I will stop now."

The reason that I am an academic is so that I can write.

March 16, 1998 8:25am

This is the second time that I write today's date. I started this entry at 7:21 a.m. and had written for about thirty minutes when the electricity went out. I had just done "save," but it was too late. I lost everything I had written this morning. When the electricity went out I took the opportunity to take Maggie for a walk. Went to the grove of trees in my neighborhood—thought about how the electricity going out was a good reminder of our (or my) illusion of control. In the past I probably would have gotten terribly upset and angry and been out of sorts the whole day. I suppose now I see it as an opportunity to tell another story about how I work. My work gets interrupted, erased, and reconstructed. The story will be told for a second time today. So, here goes.

It is Monday morning. Grape-Nuts and strawberries. I had thought I would write this weekend while the comments from the writing group on Friday were still clear in my mind. Usually, I like to write on Saturday mornings before my nine o'clock yoga class. Yet, this Saturday seemed to slip away from me. I don't beat myself up anymore for not working, even though I have said I will.

Writing group on Friday went well. Kate, Becky, and I carpooled to Doris's. After Becky and Doris reported on their progress, Kate read her paper on representations of the mother-daughter relationship in the work of eighteenth century women writers. As she read her well-crafted piece, I began to doubt my decision to read my unedited first draft. To ease my anxiety I ate two of the Pepperidge Farm cookies Doris had put out.

As I read my paper I realized that I was nervous. My voice shook as it does when I start reading a paper at a conference. I was both nervous and excited. There is an excitement about taking risks. For me to share my work, as raw as it was, was a risk. There was also excitement in the anticipation of how people would respond. And, yes, there was also fear, fear of having made myself vulnerable, of laying myself bare. When everyone laughed as I read the line about "Liszt and Grape-Nuts," I relaxed.

I am beginning to lose my concentration. Other thoughts—all the phone calls I have to make, preparation for class, going running—are starting to crowd into my mind. I have a full week and am anxious that I will not find or make sufficient time for writing. I will need to just carve out at least an hour every morning. I can make the time. I deserve that gift.

March 17, 1998

March 18, 1998

March 19, 1998 7:20 am

Class preparation, reading students' dissertation proposals, and grant work on the oral history project I run have eaten up my last two days. There is also an incredible "Women and Film" conference going on at LSU. Trinh Minh-ha is here—no way will I pass up a chance to hear her talk. I struggle to balance and make choices. However, this morning I have decided that all else is on hold for three hours so that I can write. Tomorrow is writing group and since Doris will not be there, I have half an hour to use as I please. I would like to share my ongoing work on this piece.

I am still digesting the feedback from last Friday's writing group. I had prefaced my reading of the piece to the group by telling them about the nature of the book project and that I was considering actually leaving the piece in its original state as a means of really showing how I work. There was enthusiastic support for telling the truth about how I work. I insisted, "Are you sure?" The consensus was that I should correct spelling and commas but leave most of the long sentences, the repetitions, the sentence fragments, the jottings. . . .

What about some of the contradictions and tensions, though ? Becky pointed out how interesting it was that my computer almost seemed to disappear on my large desk. She turned my attention to page four where I described my writing space. I had used "small" and "doesn't take up too much space" twice. What did this signify? Was I submerging my work? In not taking up "too much space" how did my act of writing replicate the patriarchy's desires? Or did the large open space of my desk signify my claiming space, my right and desire to inscribe?

Another contradiction seemed to be the tension between my desire to dispel the myth of the lone writer (a male construction) while simultaneously recreating that icon in my morning rituals. As Kate suggested, it seems that women writers have few alternatives to the image of the male writer. Either we are lone writers or we are not writers. And so, I struggle to create a writer's life in my own image. Sometimes I choose to collaborate. At other times, I take up the identity of the lone writer. I still hang out in cafés drinking coffee, writing in my journal, or editing my work. I like to bring my writing into a public space. A woman writing, carving out a space. In the act of writing I inscribe gender. A gendered identity that resists either/ors, that appropriates and disrupts, that transverses. . . . How I work is full of contradictions, and that is what makes it my work. In my writing, how I write, where I write, what I write, I hope to continually displace any unitary notion of what it is to be a writer.

The other contradiction that became apparent to me in how I work is the binary opposition I produce in talking about writing either as political (male) or as art (female). On one level I am complicit in reproducing gender as binary, as fixed, as unitary. And yet, at the same time I am suggesting that I am both. How I work is full of contradictions. How I work is continually to engage those contradictions rather than to erase them, rather than make them invisible. To smooth them out would be an erasure of self. How I work is not so much the act of writing, as the work of continually negotiating a gendered self in/through writing.

March 20, 1998 6:52 am

Oatmeal with raisins. I am editing what I wrote yesterday this morning. In rereading it I realized what I wanted to say. Also, as I listened to Trinh Minh-ha speak yesterday the whole notion of embracing contradictions and unknowingness as sites which open up spaces to rethink what constitutes agency and what counts as political was clearer to me.

March 20, 1998 8:45 am

I have just finished editing yesterday's work. It is no longer the original. I suppose it never was. Now we come to the end. In the writing group I had pondered how to end this piece. I thought about going back to some of my journals and finding another juicy quotation about my writing. I have not looked at the journals since last Friday. I have told several people this week that it was very painful to reread my journals. I don't think they are meant to be reread. I needed to write them, but for the process of writing, not as something I would read in the future or would use to reconstruct or understand my life. They have served their purpose. I will line them up on my bookshelves (which line my study walls) as a reminder that I have always been a writer. I don't need to construct myself as a writer. I have always written. I have always inscribed myself and the world through words. But it is not the words that are important. It is inscribing my life through/in writing that draws me to my work, that takes me to my chair, in front of my window, to the computer on that large desk almost every morning.

March 24, 1998 7:06 am

I have just finished correcting spelling and commas throughout the piece. But I have left most sentences as they were in my original version. The writing group meets this afternoon, so I will share the second half of this piece with them. One final edit, then, and the piece can go to Marla, Mary, and Bill. This is an arbitrary ending. Writing on a piece never really ends. I could go on refining, editing, deleting, tightening, . . . I am anxious, though, to return to my next major writing project, *Engendering Curriculum History*. I am excited about the challenges in writing that book. I hope to write a history of curriculum theory which is non-linear, which resists a narrative of inevitable progress, and which disrupts the notion of the individual subject as the center of history. In so doing I want to show how curriculum history has been complicit in the production of a normative subject that is unitary, male, western, and heterosexual. The task seems overwhelming at times . . . so tomorrow I will make my oatmeal, take my walk, and look out my window and write.

Note

1. When I read this piece to the writing group, I crossed out this paragraph. In reading it out loud I realized that I was uncomfortable in admitting that I put myself first. My unease in revealing my own "selfishness" seemed a reflection of gender norms that maintain that women should take care of others first. In the discussion group related to the idea that writing was a way of taking care of oneself. In the spirit of presenting this piece as my first draft, I have left it in.

References

Adams, N., T. Causey, M. Jacobs, P. Munro, M. Quinn, and A. Trousdale (1998). "Womentalkin': A Readers Theater Performance of Teachers Stories." *International Journal of Qualitative Studies in Education.*

Jipson, J., P. Munro, S. Victor, K. Froude-Jones, G. Freed-Rowland (1995). *Repositioning Feminism and Education: Perspectives on Educating for Social Change.* Westport, Conn.: Bergin and Garvey.

Munro, P. and J. Jipson (1992). "What's Real: Fictions of the Maternal." *Journal of Curriculum Theorizing,* vol. 10, 2 (pp. 7–28).

Munro, P. and J. Jipson (1997). " Deconstructing Wo/Mentoring: Diving into the Abyss." In N. Paley and J. Jipson Eds., *Daredevil Research: Re-creating Analytic Practice.* New York: Peter Lang (pp. 201–219).

Chapter 20

Upstairs

Lewis Putnam Turco

Reflective thinking is always more or less troublesome
because it involves overcoming the inertia
that inclines one to accept suggestions at their face value;
it involves willingness to endure a condition
of mental unrest and disturbance.
(John Dewey, 1910, p. 13)

A person is supposed to be the same self
throughout all the variety of changing experiences.
Is this just a suspicion, or are we entitled to say that the self,
the permanent element, is experienced just as directly
as the aches and pains, the colors and sounds,
which make up the transitory experience?
(Boyd Henry Bode, 1940, p. 108)

On the theory that after more than four decades of marriage my wife might possibly know more about how I work at my writing than I do, at least consciously, I asked her to help me with this essay. "When you're working," she said, "you're upstairs." Meaning upstairs in my garret study in Oswego, New York, on blue Lake Ontario's shores:

THE VIEW FROM A WINTER GARRET

Skies are gray and winter is settling down
Past my attic window as I write.
I see my neighbors' roofs adrift through town

Blown by the wind winding them in white.
The current of my mind begins to spill
Into a fault of time. I watch a flight

Of gulls come rising out of chimneys, fill
A fold of sky that falls in siftings there
Into Ontario below the hill.

I hear the wind build palaces of air
And ice along the shore of Whitman's lake.
Only silence will make a dwelling where

Music must turn to crystal to survive,
And seagulls scull like snowfall come alive.
(Turco, 1992)

I waited for further information, but none was forthcoming.

"That's it?"

She thought for a moment. She smiled. "When you come downstairs you're in a good mood." And that *is* it in a nutshell: writing makes me happy. I'm one of those people who enjoy writing, but to begin with, of course, I enjoyed reading.

In order to enjoy reading, however, one must be introduced to the practice. This is critically important, and one's early environment, I believe, is the key. Some people come to reading by accident; others are lucky to have parents who read; and often one's cultural heritage is either a help or a hindrance. In an essay titled "In Search of Italian/American Writers" (1997) Fred Gardaphé wrote:

> There were no bookshelves in my home. Reading anything beyond newspapers and the mail required escaping from my family. I soon developed a chronic reading problem that identified me as the "merican" or rebel. My reading betrayed my willingness to enter mainstream American culture, and while my family tolerated this, they did little to make that move an easy one. (p. 6)

Gardaphé came to reading circuitously:

> Once, while I was being chased by the police for disturbing local merchants so my partners could shoplift, I ran into the public library. I found myself in the juvenile section and grabbed a book to hide my face. Safe from the streets, I spent the rest of the afternoon reading, believing that nobody would ever find me there. And I was right, so whenever I was being chased, I would head straight for the library, which became my asylum. (p. 6)

Nothing could have been further from my own experience; however, thinking back on my early life, I consider it remarkable that my own parents, given their individual histories—impoverished childhoods in Sicily and Wisconsin; my mother a product of rural American penury; my father someone who wanted to be "someone," the only evident way to that goal being to join the local Mafia, a course he contemplated for a time—brought up their children as members of the middle class who had no doubt at all we were as privileged as anyone else. Thus, *attitude* is important, how one regards oneself, no matter what one's background may be.

Somehow, without what we now call a "role model," unless it was one or more of her teachers, my mother had managed to pull herself out of her parents' shack in Superior, Wisconsin, and work her way first through secretarial school and then through Boston University's School of Religious Education. Likewise, my father had extricated himself from Riesi, Sicily, and all sorts of menial jobs, to become (this is astonishing to most people) pastor of the First Italian Baptist Church of Meriden, Connecticut.

Though we had no money, our house was full of books of all sorts. My mother read to me starting while I was still in the cradle, and I soon learned to read for myself. Nor was writing an abstruse act, because every week for as long as I can remember I watched my father hunched over his typewriter, hunting and pecking to write his two weekly sermons, one in English and one in Italian.

From an early age, also, I was aware that my mother's family had a long and fascinating, if not always distinguished, history. George Puttenham, back in the sixteenth century, had been the author of *The Arte of English Poesie* (1589), a fact that was fraught with omens for me, omens of which I was not completely aware when in 1959 I began writing my own *The Book of Forms: A Handbook of Poetics* (1968). I knew, too, that Israel Putnam had been a general in Washington's colonial army and that Amelia Earhart had been married to George Palmer Putnam, the publisher. There have been many writers, librarians, and teachers among the Putnams (my daughter, Melora, is a librarian in Winthrop, Maine), but there have been lots of farmers and artisans as well (my brother is a toolmaker). From my reading I knew of the involvement of the Putnam clan in the Salem witch-hunt in colonial America—in high school I wrote an addendum chapter to Hawthorne's *The House of the Seven Gables* and a senior skit for the Fantaseers, our "science fiction reading club," about the trials of the Salem witches.

In retrospect I can see that I was subjected to anti-Italian prejudice, even on the part of at least one of my teachers, but either I did not recognize it or I ignored or disdained it, for I always felt myself to be seminally involved with English and American literature because of my family connections with the majority culture. Felix Stefanile (1975), reviewing *Pocoangelini, A Fantography and Other Poems* (1971), said, "Turco seems to have the whole of the English lyric tradition at his fingertips." That's because I have studied it closely all my life, taught it for more than three decades, and write out of it perfectly "naturally."

But it was a poet *not* in that lyric tradition who gave me the impetus to write my first ambitious poem: I read Walt Whitman's poem "Mannahatta" in "Doc" Michel's eleventh-grade English class (Turco, 1991). Michel was a wonderful French teacher with a diplôme supérieur from the Université de Rennes and a Ph.D. from Laval University in Quebec; but like many of the teachers at Meriden High School in 1950, she had to teach both in and out of her discipline, and I was glad she did. I was fortunate to have had, during two of my three years in high school, fine English teachers—in my sophomore year Mary Flynn had encouraged me in my writing, though she felt I would eventually be able to earn more money as a fiction writer than as a poet.

I had been writing both fiction and poetry; in fact, in 1949 I had begun publishing both in the local papers—the Meriden, *Morning Record* and *Journal*. For a while after Flynn's counsel my literary fate hung in the balance. Perhaps it was reading Whitman's upbeat, Pollyanna-ish effusion and participating in a subsequent trip to the Bowery that brought me down mainly on the poetic side of the fence. Or maybe not. Perhaps it was something as pragmatic as going into the navy after my graduation from high school, for in the service I followed in my mother's footsteps by becoming a typist and clerk—invaluable training for a writer. As a navy yeoman I was in a situation more conducive to writing short pieces than prose narratives.

Although I had read a bit of his work before high school, I'd not been exposed to a great deal of Whitman. It was shortly after Doc Michel's class had read "Mannahatta" that I took my first trip to Manhattan and saw for myself what Whitman's glorious city had become in the twentieth century. The vague sense of offense I'd felt when I read his poem crystallized, after the trip, into a lifelong aversion to the work of the "good gray poet." Yet, in a curious sense, my negative response to Whitman was as formative for me as a positive response has been for many another writer, for he was the motivating force behind my longest poem to that date, the most serious, and the most consciously formal, in contrast with what I perceived at the time to be the aformal splatter of Whitman's good gray prose poetry.

I don't recall the occasion of the field trip to New York City, ninety miles away from Meriden down the Merritt Parkway, but it was an excursion by bus. Not much remains in my memory of the outing. I do remember that we saw Chinatown and the Bowery. I recollect the skyscraper canyons and the dirt. But there is one image that is still vivid—it was of a derelict on the Bowery.

He was, or he seemed to be, an old man. I saw him up close. He wore a tattered T shirt and a pair of the palest blue denim dungarees, frayed around his ankles; he wore no shoes or socks and his toenails were long and filthy. An old piece of rope was knotted around his waist for a belt. The creases of skin on his face were filled with dirt, and in his ears the dirt was caked like topsoil. His hair was white; it fell down over his eyes, which were as pale blue as his jeans—washed out, empty, the eyes of a chronic alcoholic. He was panhandling. It was a dismaying and disillusioning experience, to say the least, to be brought face-to-face with this wrecked human being amid the squalid alleys of New York. I returned home considerably troubled by what I had seen of the reality behind Whitman's "prophetic" vision of America.

Not long after the trip I began to write some poems about my experiences in and impressions of Manhattan. I must have shown them to Doc Michel, but it was not until the next year, in Mark Bollman's twelfth-grade English honors class, that I conceived of the epic scheme of my adolescence, "Observations of a Resurrected Corpse," as I originally titled my English honors project (1952). I went back to the original three poems I had written earlier, then began writing connecting passages between them and adding dialogue—the habit of reworking old material became permanent thenceforth. When we students had finished our projects, we spent several days discussing them and deciding which examples were to appear in the class magazine, *The Leaky Pen*.

Our teacher, Bollman, was a graduate of Muhlenberg College in Allentown, Pennsylvania, but he had taken his M.A. from Yale University in New Haven, just a couple of towns south of Meriden. He struck me as an upright if not uptight Yankee type, but that observation did nothing to prepare me for his reaction to my poem, a response more violent than mine had been to Whitman's.

I was as apolitical as anyone might imagine a 1950s teenager could be. I recall one day when Arthur Von Au, another member of Bollman's class and co-editor with me of *The Annual* (Von Au, 1952), remarked that we would probably soon be at war with the Russians. I was incredulous. How could we go to war with our beloved ally of World War II? Of course, in 1991 the Soviet Union spontaneously self-destructed, we love the Russian people again, and it turns out that I was right after all, but who could have imagined it? I venture back along the pathway of recollection and wonder exactly when it was that we stopped worrying about the atomic bomb, and I realize that it has been something like a quarter-century since anyone actually thought that one would be dropped anywhere.

Somewhere along the line the world, at least most people in the world, if not their governments, stopped believing in the likelihood of atomic mass destruction. I never thought the Russians would "bury us," as Khrushchev said later on, but on the other hand I never thought that communism was any kind of viable system, either. In fact, in my senior year I didn't even have a handle on what the word communism meant. I was therefore unprepared when Bollman, in the middle of the class discussion of "Observations," without forewarning, smashed his fist down upon his desk and roared—and this is a nearly verbatim—"It is from such works as this that the seeds of communism spring and grow to bear evil fruit!"

In fact, the word "unprepared" is insufficient to describe not only my astonishment but that of the class as well. I remember everyone sitting bolt upright, our mouths open and eyes wide, first staring at Bollman and then turning to look at each other. I leaned forward and whispered to my friend Ray Staszewski in the seat ahead of me, "What's 'communism'?" Even when I found out later, I was baffled by Bollman's outburst. Could he possibly imagine that a senior in Meriden High School was a raving Bolshevik? However it is true that, at the time, I assumed it was the government's responsibility to take care of the sick, the poor, and the aged, and I would not be disabused of my misconception of the role of government until I entered the navy after high school and discovered that only those actually in government service were thus protected from the worst ravages of fate and nature.

Bollman's view of my work notwithstanding, I thought well enough of "Observations of a Resurrected Corpse" to enter it in that year's Scholastic Writing Awards competition, sponsored by Scholastic Magazines. My attack upon Whitman received a citation, one of several I won that year in the state competition in both fiction and poetry, and it was the only poem from Meriden that won a Key Award in the national contest.

A dozen years later I still thought well enough of my first earnest attempt to court the muse to take it out and revise it once more, this time for full publication in a little magazine, *Quartet*, in 1964. That version is sufficiently like the original to give a fair impression of the work Bollman felt was a threat to democratic society. In revising the poem I changed its title to "The City's Masque" (1991), thus emphasizing its inherently dramatic form, and this has been one of my habits all of my writing life: I seldom throw anything away, and I often rework old material. Before 1959, I was working on *The Sketches* (1962), my first sequence of poems. T.S. Eliot said it for me. Christopher Ricks, in the Preface to his edition of Eliot's *Inventions of the March Hare*, wrote: Eliot was asked in 1959, "You seem often to have written poems in sections. Did they begin as separate poems?" He replied: "That's one way in which my mind does seem to have worked throughout the years poetically—doing things separately and then seeing the possibility of fusing them together, altering them, and making a kind of whole of them" (Ricks, 1997).

But to return to this business of prejudice: it is not uncomplicated. The title of my entry that year in the school's Hicks Prize essay contest—one of the six finalists—was "A Row of Hedges," and it used an elaborate metaphor: the hedges outside the English honors classroom represented the succession of our school years; the window cut off the view of the downhill end of the hedges, which represented the future, etc., etc. Quite corny, but decently written for the work of a high school senior, evidently. I was told by other teachers that two of the three faculty judges thought my essay was the best one submitted that year, but that one judge, Mark Bollman, refused to support it for the prize. In 1993 our old music teacher, Antonio Parisi, confirmed what I had long suspected: "Bollman hated Italians," he said. "You never stood a chance." At Fenn College (now Cleveland State University) at the beginning of my second year of teaching in 1961, I was asked to address the incoming freshmen at the fall convocation. Reaching back into my not-so-distant past, I refurbished "A Row of Hedges" and turned it into an exemplary talk about the importance of writing in college. Afterward one of the freshmen approached me to say, "I hope you don't expect us to write as well as that!" I didn't, but I wished I could have written so.

Doc Michel's treatment of my work was quite different from Bollman's. She had given us, her junior English class, an assignment to write an essay on a personal experience. Having recently returned to school in October of 1950 after an emergency appendix operation, I had plenty of material, so I sat down at my father's old Underwood Standard typewriter in the sun porch behind the bookcases, and I hunted-and-pecked out a piece I titled "Appendix Excitis." My brother

Gene, who followed me through the same high school, told me that Doc Michel was still reading "Appendix Excitis" to her English classes five years later. It was, I understand, the only essay by a former student that she ever read to any of them.

One supposes that teachers ought at least to try to be evenhanded with all their students and to recognize and reward merit no matter where it arises, but there is prejudice toward Italians even among members of the Italian-American community itself. Some of my father's Italian parishioners were unhappy because they had a "Sicilian" pastor, a standard distinction, and a common bias, for Sicily is considered by northern Italians to be ethnically part of Africa. And one can perhaps also imagine what the Italian Roman Catholics thought—they called my brother and me "the priest's kids."

Most of our parishioners lived in the neighborhood of the church, like the Poles who lived on Polish Hill near St. Stanislaus church. The Irish had their section of the city, as did the Germans, but none of the "ethnic" families that I knew wanted their children to be "Italian-Americans" or whatever-"Americans." They wanted them to be "Americans." The sooner into the melting pot, the better. My view of my "Italianness" has always been much closer to John Ciardi's, than to Gardaphé's.

Vince Clemente, in an essay titled "The Writer as Hyphenated-American" (1995) wrote, "The critic Harold Bloom once came down heavily on the poet Stanley Kunitz for 'evading his Jewish heritage' in his poetry. Kunitz thought about that for a long time, and in his response articulated perfectly the plight of those American writers who carry with them, along with the burden to recreate the truth as they see it, the freight of ethnicity, this 'dual citizenship.' In a spring 1982 *Paris Review* interview Kunitz remarked:

> It's obvious that Jewish cultural aspiration and ethical doctrine entered into my bloodstream, but in practice I am an American free-thinker, a damn stubborn one, and my poetry is not hyphenated. . . . True, I have no religion, but I have strong religious feelings. Moses and Jesus and Lao-tse have all instructed me . . . and three of the poets who most strongly influenced me—Donne, Herbert, and Hopkins—happen to have been Christian churchmen. (as quoted in Clemente, n.p.)

Clemente continued, "The American poet and translator of Dante, John Ciardi, himself the son of Italian immigrant parents, wrote in an early letter to me, 'I have poured out endless poems about my Italian "roots." Yet Jefferson, Tom Paine, and even—God save the mark,

Emerson—are as much at the roots of my mind and feeling as the It[alian] of my Am[erican]. I am an American man of letters!' Like Kunitz, Ciardi insisted his 'poetry is not hyphenated.' In fact, he once told me, 'In truth, my boyhood (in Boston's Little Italy and Medford, Massachusetts) was not so much an Italian-American one as *my* boyhood.' And just two weeks later, in another letter, he recalled, 'I had a longish poem about Italy in the *Atlantic* some years back, and when Robert Lowell wrote to praise its Italo-Amer[ican] voice, I took offense. Did the S.O.B. suppose I had used an Amer[ican] Eng[lish] inferior to his, or that I inherited and made mine less Amer[ican] Eng[lish] than his?'

"About that time," Clemente wrote, "I proposed to him the prospect of an anthology of 'Italian-American Poets.' He never really warmed up to the thing and wrote to the poet-critic Lewis Turco, 'I've never thought in terms of Italian-American poetry; I don't know any Italian-American poets, as such. Lew Turco is an American poet who happened to have [an Italian father]. Theodore Roethke is a ditto with German parents' [Cifelli, 1991]. Now, all these years later," Clemente discovered, "I know just what Ciardi meant: Why isn't Archibald MacLeish a Scottish-American poet? Whitman, on his mother's side, a Dutch-American one? I like to feel the American experience is broad enough, indeed all-encompassing as Whitman's vision of it, to include all of us as simply 'Americans' without the hyphen" (Clemente, 1995, n.p.).

In 1975, in a videotaped interview that he made for the Brockport "Writers' Forum" series—a tape I played about once a year for two decades in my course on contemporary American poetry, Robert Hayden was asked about "black poetry." His response was that such a term, which had the approval of many militant black poets, was useful primarily to white academics who wish to ignore poetry written by blacks. The inference to be drawn therefrom, Hayden said, is that somehow poetry written by black Americans is not good enough, or not universal enough, to be included in the Anglo-Saxon literary canon (Hayden, 1975).

In a letter dated February 24, 1976, Radcliffe Squires, in his capacity as editor of *Michigan Quarterly Review*, published by the University of Michigan, where Hayden was teaching at the time, wrote to one of his regular reviewers, who happened to be a white academic—myself, in fact, "to ask you if you could review Robert Hayden's *Angle of Ascent*. . . . He feels bad that every place seems to feel it must have him reviewed by another black. I agree that is both silly and intolerable. Anyway, I hope you will be willing to undertake this" I was, and I did.

Hayden always wanted to be judged merely as a poet among poets, not one to whom special rules of criticism had to be applied in order to make his work acceptable in more than a sociological sense. His stance, reiterated in the Brockport interview, was well known for a long time both to militant blacks and to "liberal" whites. Thus, if the latter relegated Hayden to the literary ghetto along with other black poets, the former have seen him, if not as an "Uncle Tom," at least as a reluctant resident. Perhaps this situation best explains why Hayden was virtually ignored during his lifetime. Yet Hayden, like Ciardi, wrote as much out of his ethnicity as anyone else. He was a paradigmatic poet of the English language who was also true to his roots and history, though not circumscribed by what is merely racial, ethnic, or personal.

Just as Stanley Kunitz, John Ciardi, and Robert Hayden did, I sometimes write out of my ethnic "heritage." In *La Storia: Five Centuries of the Italian American Experience*, Jerre Mangione and Ben Morreale wrote, "Not all of the immigrants' offspring who became poets were as much at ease in America as Ciardi. But the most gifted of them were able to transcend the specifics of the Italian American experience through the more subjective and symbolic language of their craft. For poets deeply imbued with the experience of trying to straddle two cultures, such as Lewis Turco and Frank Polite, poetry became the vehicle by which they could transmit the loneliness of their alienation with impunity, without denying or betraying their Italian connection" (1992, p. 432).

But I don't remember being alienated as an *Italian*-American, though I certainly was alienated as a *Protestant* Italian-American. Mangione and Morreale continued: "Lewis Turco, one of the most prolific of the Italian American poets, gradually distanced himself from his past as he journeyed toward the mainstream. By the time he was in his thirties, in 1973, when he published *Pocoangelini: A Fantography*, Italianate poems constituted only a third of the contents. They were a group of so-called 'Sketches,' which A. R. Ammons characterized as 'an autobiography of biographies'" (p. 434). Although it is true that I distanced myself from my youth, of course (everybody does), I never distanced myself from my ethnicity. I simply write poems and stories—and, of recent decades, essays—as they occur to me, and if later on I feel that older material can be mined, transformed, or linked together to form longer works or sequences, as I first did in "Observations" and *The Sketches*, so be it. Now that I think of it, that was how Walt Whitman worked, too. Hmm.

References

Cifelli, Edward M. Ed. (1991). *The Selected Letters of John Ciardi*. Fayetteville: University of Arkansas (p. 314).

Clemente, Vince (1995). "The Writer as Hyphenated-American." *Boston Book Review*, vol. 2, 7 (August).

Gardaphé, Fred (1997). "In Search of Italian/American Writers," *Italian America*, vol. 2, 1 (March).

Hayden, Robert (1975). "The Poetry of Robert Hayden," "Writers' Forum" series. State University of New York, College at Brockport (March 3).

Mangione, Jerre and Ben Morreale (1992). *La Storia, Five Centuries of the Italian American Experience*. New York: Harper (pp. 430–434).

Puttenham, George (1589). *The Arte of English Poesie*.

Ricks, Christopher (1997). Preface to T. S. Eliot, *Inventions of the March Hare, Poems 1909–1917*. New York: Harcourt.

Squires, Radcliffe (1967). Unpublished letter (February 24). Collection of Lewis P. Turco.

Stefanile, Felix (1975). *Italian Americana*, vol. I, 2 (Spring).

Turco, Lewis Putnam (1952). "Observations of a Resurrected Corpse." Excerpts published in *The Leaky Pen*, edited by members of the Honors English Class of Meriden (Conn.) High School. See "The City's Mask," op. cit.

Turco, Lewis Putnam (1962). *The Sketches and Liveuil: A Mask*. Cleveland, Ohio: American Weave.

Turco, Lewis Putnam (1968). *The Book of Forms: A Handbook of Poetics*. Dutton: New York.

Turco, Lewis Putnam (1973). *Pocoangelini, A Fantography and Other Poems*. Northampton Mass.: Despa.

Turco, Lewis Putnam (1986). *The New Book of Forms*. Hanover: N.H.: University Press of New England.

Turco, Lewis Putnam (1991). "The City's Mask." In "Whitman and I," *The Public Poet: Five Lectures in the Art and Craft of Poetry*. Ashland: Ohio: Ashland Poetry Press (pp. 1–19).

Turco, Lewis Putnam (1992). "The View from a Winter Garret." Christmas card, engraved by George O'Connell. Oswego, N.Y.: Grey Heron. Reprinted as part of an autobiography, "Lewis Putnam Turco" (1995.) In *Contemporary*

Authors Autobiography Series, vol. 22. (Ed. Joyce Nakamura.) Detroit: Gale Research.

Von Au, Arthur and Lewis Turco, Eds. (1952). *The Annual*, Meriden, Conn.: Meriden High School.

Chapter 21

Writing the Classed Body: "Is It Work Yet?"

Wendy Kohli

> Education has accordingly not only to safeguard an individual against the besetting erroneous tendencies of his own mind—its rashness, presumption, and preference of what chimes with self-interest to objective evidence—but also to undermine and destroy the accumulated and self-perpetuating prejudices of long ages.
> (John Dewey, 1910, p. 25)

> Learning . . . is a process of organizing experiences so as to give depth of meaning to new facts.
> (Boyd Henry Bode, 1940, p. 145)

Em-body-ed Writing, Sit-uated Writer

Sitting down to write this essay about writing, about *my* writing, brings me directly in touch with me, with who I am in the present moment, as well as with some emotional companions from the past. I sit. I sit in white cotton summer shorts and a T shirt, thighs strong and sweaty from an earlier bike trip to my chiropractor. A chiropractor who sees me twice a week to "adjust" my body, actually to re-adjust my body to a more "normal" alignment in futile compensation for hours, days, months, years of sitting. Sitting in front of a typwriter. Sitting in front of a computer. Sitting. Working. Writing. Reading. Sitting.

Now I sit again before a computer screen, feet curled up under a wooden chair in my temporary summer work space, back in the New York college town where I finished writing my doctoral dissertation nearly fifteen years ago.

This invitation to think about *how I work,* how I write, takes me involuntarily back to that time when I asked my then-husband, William, to *tie me to the chair* for forty-five-minute stretches. The body remembers; the body knows. That's how I worked then. It felt like torture to complete that "paper," a code word to trick me into thinking I could actually get the damn thing done and be a Ph.D.

But that was then, and this is now. It is far less agonizing for me to do this kind of work now than it was in the past. And I do my best care for my self, my body: my neck, shoulders, hands, wrists, head, and butt, remembering the lessons of my yoga teachers, my healers, my "body workers," to prevent any undue damage from this sedentary life, or lifestyle.

Yet, I am compelled to ask: "Am I sitting here of my own free will?" Honestly? The answer I give myself all too often is, "Not really." I say I would much prefer to be reading the *New Yorker* at a local coffee shop, or taking a bike ride in the country, or shopping at my favorite alternative dress shop on the Commons, or catching up with an old friend, or even cleaning my closet. Any distraction will do. In many ways, writing *still* feels like torture for me, even though I *know* better. (In fact, I have to admit that writing this particular piece is almost fun.) Almost.

So I need to ask again, What ties me to the chair these days? What desires, what discipline, what guilt, what hopes keep me sitting? Clearly, there are some powerful forces that structure the conditions of my writing, that pave the way for me to produce—or not produce—written documents.

Luckily, I am a university professor who takes home a monthly pay check; I do not literally make my living as a writer, as novelists or freelance commercial writers do. My position at a research one institute requires me to write a certain amount each year to maintain my status as a member of the graduate faculty and to be in good standing with my colleagues. And of course, my own scholarly interests and ego create a set of expectations that keep me writing. But, in many ways, I still need to be chained to my seat. Why? What am I holding on to? What has a hold on me?

Working/Writing

The past still has a firm, though loosening grip on me. It keeps me from fully embracing myself as a writer, as someone who writes for a large part of my work life. Working. Writing. Two words that were antonyms in the lexicon of my working-class family. As banal as it sounds, for my parents and neighbors working meant using your hands. Forget that I do use my hands all the time to write! What makes "typing" for a living a perfectly acceptable and honorable occupation in my family and "writing" not?

In order to make any sense about me as a writer, about my writing process, about the struggle to name myself as a writer, I must take a long look at the disabling effects of classism. Although I have no doubt that gender plays a role in how I perform my writing acts, it has become clearer to me each year that my particular class experience put walls in front of me that continue to impede.

The first wall was laid in decades ago, when the very idea of my going to college was anathema to my parents. Not the upwardly mobile kind of Americans, they intuited that a college education would take me away from them. Their (and consequently my) world was deeply bifurcated, as much from within as from without: the rich and the not-rich; the college people and the rest; the haves and the have-nots; those who "put on airs" and the "salt of the earth"; them and us. Nevertheless, I knew as early as second grade that I wanted college, a way out. I also knew, as they did, that that desire would put a wedge between us, with unpredictable and serious consequences. To survive my choice, I made an unspoken deal with them: I would pursue my interest in college-track school subjects, but I would assume a stance of self-abnegation, even invisibility. I made sure I would never be accused of "showing off." That decision shadows me to this day: I still hold back far too long with my writing; I resist sharing it with others in process; and even when it is published, I think that there must have been some mistake—that it's not good enough yet for public consumption.

And yet, I do allow other reminders to creep in, even for a few brief minutes at a time: I am a good thinker, writer, scholar, teacher; I have "proved" it on many occasions and in diverse contexts. Does my CV lie? Producing knowledge, page after page, writing, putting my ideas out for others to hear, see, read, quote. How much more evidence do I need to believe that I am entitled to call myself a scholar-writer?

Entitlement. I am in awe of my friends and colleagues who (appear to) feel entitled to put their words on paper, who take for granted their right to write, who can't wait to get to the writing table. With all the writing and editing I have done to this point, I can say with certainty that moments of eager excitement and anticipation are few and far between. Dread is more fitting and familiar. But even as I write these words, it becomes apparent that they are less than true. In this reflection I am collapsing nearly two decades of "writing time" into one statement, when the "truth" is that each writing project offers up its own unique challenges and possibilities. Some things that I write in my current life flow effortlessly from the keyboard; it's as if there is a direct link between my imagination and the computer monitor. But, other projects elude me. I have yet to test my mettle with my own book. "Book" has an overwhelming power for me. The class baggage really sucks me in here. The swirling voices in my head remind me of that early bargain with my family: *"Who do you think you are, writing a book? Getting too big for your britches, don't you think? Why don't you get a real job?"* Certainly no one in my family actually says those things to me these days, at least in so many words. Nevertheless, the sentiment remains, sedimented in me and in my relation to them. I've interpellated that sediment by denying my capacity for original thought, by doubting my ability to have anything of real import to say—especially anything important enough to require a book-length manuscript. Essays maybe. Short articles perhaps. Book reviews, Ok. But a book? No way.

Deliberate Diversions

Recently I have taken an honest look at the way I construct my work life: how I spend my time; what priorities I set; whose agenda I follow; when I put myself first or last. I am a master of diversions, especially ones that look perfectly acceptable, even honorable. When it comes to my writing, "it can wait" seems to be the MO of choice. Surely, my rationale goes, teaching and advising must come first, followed by my commitment to the development of good teacher education programs. And of course, there is my service work for professional organizations and the university. Writing? I squeeze it in. I avoid it. I dread it. I lose sleep over it. I do it under duress.

Of course there is nothing wrong with being a committed teacher, adviser, and colleague. I think even research one universities need people who are willing to give their time in these various roles. We should all take our fair turn at them. But I must admit to a pattern of refusal, refusal to claim myself as a *bona fide* scholar who deserves to take time for thinking, reading, writing.

In analyzing the psychological layers of my choices of work, it became clear that the role of "server" fits very nicely with my working-class construction of self. To compensate for my lack of entitlement as a professor-scholar, perhaps I could earn my keep as one who gives selflessly in other capacities. Flooding my psyche were images of my mother cleaning bedpans for people in hospitals, or my father digging ditches on a road crew, and myself organizing meeting after meeting after meeting. If I worked so hard at service and teaching, perhaps they would finally see that I did have a real job. It was much easier explaining what I do this way than saying that I had a deadline to meet on an article for *Educational Theory*. And it staved off my terror of writing.

Getting to Work

So, with that psychological foregrounding, I am ready to get to the question of how I work and how I write. I used to insist on having huge blocks of "free" time before even beginning a writing project—a convenient deterrent to getting into the writing chair. Now I've come to see that I really can make use of even a small chunk of time. I have a more flexible approach to the writing process and take advantage of short spurts of thinking/writing time. A positive change.

At the start of any writing task, I surround myself with dozens of related books or articles. I read, highlight, write marginalia, and type out notes to fortify my own thoughts, to justify my approach. The benign interpretation of this ritual is that it is simply good scholarship. If Judith Butler said it first, I must be on the right track. *Author, authority, authoritativeness, authorial voice.* Even for this piece on my own writing, I photocopied more than one article as a resource. And though I made a commitment to myself not to, I am itching to quote others. For instance, there's a marvelous interview with Donna Haraway peeking out at me under my papers near my computer that speaks to the issue of authority and the situatedness of the author. But I will resist citing her words. I will insist on trusting my own thinking for a change, trust that what I say is just as good as what some expert in the field would say. After all, who could be more of an expert on my writing process than me? But oooh, it is so tempting to use Haraway.

This undermining of my own "authority" has plagued me since graduate school, when I bit off more than I could chew (so to speak) with a dissertation on critical hermeneutics. No one on my committee knew anything about critical theory or contemporary hermeneutical thought. I was the "expert." Not a propitious place to be, considering how much I doubted my own knoweldge and ability. Alas! I had to rely on the words of Jurgen Habermas and Hans-Georg Gadamer to buttress my views, to enhance my arguments, to speak for me.

But in this essay I am speaking for myself. I am calling up my own experience with writing, since that was the assignment. So, given that this is not a typical academic article, I can relax a bit and let my own words flow. (Interesting that I need to make the distinction between a real academic piece and this atypical one.)

When I write, I usually situate myself at the start of the text, as I did in this article. That gets me going. It also supports my philosophical position that I don't have, as some philosophers would say, a "view from nowhere." My thoughts, my beliefs, my theoretical frame come out of my situatedness, from my particularities, from my historicized body and mind. Just as "you are what you eat," my writing very much reflects a synthesis of my interests, of who I am and whence I came.

I write. Words come out. As I write, I go through a sophisticated self-editing process. Rarely do I rely on stream of consciousness to get going. It's strange to admit, but I am even afraid to show my raw writing to myself. Before the words even hit the screen, I have policed my thoughts, my grammatical structure, my syntax, my spelling. The upside of this habit is that I often don't need much editing to get a piece into decent shape. The downside, of course, is never knowing what gems may have been lost in my premature censoring.

I write. I read. I walk. I think as I walk. Walking is central to my writing process. I like to mull over what I have written and my next steps. Preferably, I like walking alone. But if I am with the right person, I can think aloud, "writing" as I go. I am fortunate to have a wonderful writing partner in my current life, my husband Philip. He does not have to tie me to my chair. Mainly, what he needs to do is listen to me. I am thankful that he is a great listener and an ally of mine as I gain more confidence in my brilliance. Not only does he listen, but he is capable of supporting the emotional release necessary for me to free up my thinking. He understands the depth of the muck that gets in my way. I no longer suffer from huge writing blocks. By attending as much as possible to the doubt and terror that surface as I write, or in the middle of the night when I awaken from anxious dreams, I can move ahead much more quickly than I could in the past. I shake, cry, and laugh my way through the fear and sadness.

Other forms of support have been useful as well, especially writing groups with some marvelous women colleagues. These regular three-to-four person meetings contradict the isolation of writing. In particular, I've benefited from sharing my work with others and I've appreciated the discipline they require to produce something each week. Even with this, however, I need a space to do the emotional work, for what gets in the way for me is very old and continually needs chipping away.

Finishing Up

As I bring this essay to a somewhat arbitrary close, limited by editors' design, I am reminded of another familiar pattern in my writing. My endings are usually the weakest part of my work—probably a remnant of my mistaken belief that what I have to say isn't that important anyway. A similar habit finds its way into my speech patterns; sometimes my voice trails off as if it doesn't matter whether I finish my point or not. Another place to unpack, to heal.

Writing, printing, reading, thinking, revising, printing. I like to see, to read to hold my words on hard copy. I like to make even the slightest adjustments first on the paper, then on the screen. I get tremendous satisfaction from seeing the pages pile up in the printer. One by one, page by page, my work appears. I did it. I created that. I made it happen.

Next Steps

I am ready for my next challenge: the book. In fact, one incentive for finishing this piece quickly is to give my attention to my book project. I have created the time and space this summer to make some real progress on it. Having made the "poststructural turn," I see how language can constitute reality. By reciting the litany, "I am writing a book on the body," I am making it real, making it happen. Perhaps I still need to trick myself into it—thinking of the book as a series of individual doable chapters—but it will get done. Word by word, sentence by sentence, page by page, chapter by chapter. Of this I have never been more certain. At least that's the story I tell myself.

Chapter 22

Putting Coyolxauhqui Together: A Creative Process

Gloria Anzaldúa

Our intellectual progress consists, as has been said,
in a rhythm of direct understanding—technically called apprehension
—with indirect, mediated understanding—technically called comprehension.
(John Dewey, 1910, p. 120)

We are committed to the proposition that all patterns or ideals
spring from the soil of experience, that they are created by
man himself, and that they have no other purpose or
meaning than to serve as guide for the continuous
reorganization of experience.
(Boyd Henry Bode, 1940, p. 256)

Pacing your breathing to the doleful sounds of the foghorn, you walk along the coast of Monterey Bay toward the lighthouse and its beckoning light. Across the bay to the east, the yolk of the sun, swollen and lopsided, is slowly squeezed up by the mountain. Fog creeps up and swallows the gold. From the precipice you stare down at the waves crashing against the rocks, incessantly and furiously. In the middle of the rip all tides converge and churn up a white chaos. Bobbing out at sea is a small blue boat cradling its lone occupant. De la orilla del mar you mull over el cuento de tu proceso—a metastory tracking the phases of your creative process, and touching on your writing habits, rituals, and emotional upheavals; your beliefs about writing; your relationship to it; and the support you get from your writing comadres, the "godmothers" who read and encourage the work. To tell how you write is enormously appealing—like most members of the tribe of writers, you love talking about writing.

Your goal is to cultivate an acute awareness of processes at work in your own psyche, and to create symbols and patterns of its operations. The problem is that a process is arrested when you stop to watch it. Another problem is that not only do you want to make the fleeting process known; you want to create a virtual reality of the experience so that the reader goes through it as well. And you have only words to do it with.

Ultimately, with this story, as with all creative work, you, like all artists, want to alter, however slightly, the way you look at the world. You want to change the reader's sense of what the world is like. You want to make a difference, if only for one other person. A tall order. As you walk back home hueles la tempestad en el aire.

As you go about your day, the potential story calls to you. At first la llamada is just an intangible longing, a vague yearning for form. Soon it becomes a beat pulsing subliminally. It won't take no for an answer.

Symbolically, the source of the call is the dark mother, la Llorona, the ghost woman who wails for the loss of her children, whom she's murdered in crazed anger at a lover's betrayal. Aztecs know her as Cihuacóat, or Serpent woman. La Llorona is your musa bruja, la naguala that incites you to write. In her horse aspect, la Lorona will carry you from beginning of story to finish line.

As always when you first take on a call, something in you is ebullient. It expands, eager to be filled. You believe you can do anything if only you leave no stone unturned. Blessed and cursed by la llamada, you both anticipate the pleasure of using your skills and talent and quail at the toll it will take. Structuring experiences and emotions through language makes life tolerable and meaningful and allows you to escape your condition through fantasy, only to find yourself confronting the condition you're trying to escape. Mapping the different terrae incognitae with their shadowy indwellers enables you to evolve and grow, but only after putting you through a crucible. Creating theories of nearly unconscious processes va ser un jale bruto.

Having taken up the reigns of la historia, next day as you walk along West Cliff in the early morning hours a tenuous tension begins to stretch in your body. In saying yes to the call, you're taking on more than just this essay. You've been mulling over the creative process for years and know that one day a book will come out of it. El trabajo te espanta.

You come to your arboreal amada, the giant gnarled cypress you're in love with. You sit between its thick exposed roots and let them cradle you. Through the embrace of its branches you see a bit of sky looking like a blue flower. Below, waves break against the jawbones of the bluff, the water cutting itself on its canine teeth. Incessant, enduring.

You assess your situation, plan your strategy. From your pack you pull out your workbook and jot down your thoughts: how you're going to carve out the time and muster the energy to take this on and what the project means in the scheme of your life. Be realistic, you caution yourself. If you find the task too complex to finish by the deadline, you'll carry the burden of failure, of guilt over a missed opportunity. Remember the demons who always try to block you before the finish. But even more, remember that a writer must write; remember your readers awaiting your new work.

To bring into being something that does not exist in the world, a sacrifice will be required of you, sacrifice means to make holy. What will you give up in making holy the process of writing? You make a commitment, un compromiso, to create meaning, a commitment to add to the field of literature and not just duplicate what's already there. To explore untrodden caminos. Which means turning over all rocks, even the ones with worms under them—you suspect that your shadow self and its darkness have more to do with creativity than your surface self does.

Be realistic about your health—it's precarious, especially your eyes. Fluctuations of blood flow cause arteries to break and bleed. Besides struggling with diabetes and its complications, you have cross-country travel and speaking engagements, from which you make your living, the mentoring of writing interns, and being a resource. Writing is the normal condition of your life—not something you do on the side when you have time. Writing is a given—all else yields before it, except your health, and there will probably be times when you'll sacrifice even that. You'll juggle this work with your novel-in-stories and put other writing projects on hold. And, if the winter storms keep lashing the coast and the water keeps rising, you'll have to keep el niño from swamping your house.

Some things will go wrong—así es la vida. You'll need a contingency plan to deal with the cycles of stress, turmoil, and depression that you create for yourself, and for the obstacles that are part of your process. When you slam into a block or get bitten by a writing virus, remember to let it work itself through your body like water through a blowhole. You'll have to release stress by taking time out and giving yourself treats—permission to laze, your favorite comidas, escape between the covers of a thriller. You'll have to focus on the pleasure writing gives you and on what motivates you. And if your daily process doesn't allow you to finish and still have a life, you'll have to create another schedule.

You have inflated, unrealistic notions about how much you can accomplish in a day, so you double the time you think it will take. You map out the territory you want to cover, you mark deadlines and specifics for each stage. Every few days you'll reassess the work, reschedule tasks. You turn away from the rippling silk of the sea and head for home. You are now una gallina culeca sitting on your eggs. You begin to brood. You nurture the idea by ignoring it; you sit on your eggs until the tension begs to be released through writing.

When you wake up you're still between realities, in "nepantla," a Nahuatl word for the space in between, un lugar no-lugar or tierra de un medio. Via nepantla you tap el cenote, the archetypal inner stream of consciousness, a dreampool or reservoir of unconscious images and feelings stored as iconic imagery. El cenote is a mental network of subterranean rivers of information that converge and well up to the surface, like a sinkhole or an opening to the womb of the earth. The Maya in Chichén Itzá dedicated el cenote to el dios de la lluvia. Into their sacred well they threw their most precious possessions: turquoise, clay pottery, copal, virgins, and their children. Those who didn't die were supposed to bring back the rain god's promise for a good or bad year. You stand before la boca del poso sacrado, the great Pacific Ocean, and make your offering. Dreaming awake, you go deep, listen, and watch; you attend to the imaginal with the goal of translating it on paper.

Accessing the ocean of uncanny signs is one of the great mysterious acts of human imagination, for you, an act of pleasure. The creative rush of ideas, the sudden flash of an "other" reality rising out of the sea, is exhilarating. Always, it renews tu espíritu. Unlike the rest, this aspect of writing is effortless. But the deep dives scare you—there's always a monster in the cave; the deeper you go, the sharper its fangs. If you don't find a way in, it will find a way out.

The next morning you stay in bed. Eyes closed, you lie quietly. With blankets and pillows, you make a womb-cave of night, entreating the moon to keep the daylight at bay. The moon lifts the veil between inner and outer worlds, and you cross over. Protected by darkness, you descend into the warm, velvet underground cave. Rivulets of water sluice around you, swirling around, eddying. Images rise up accompanied by sensations so brief that if you're not paying attention they won't register. If they slip past you, you dream up others on the spot, one image spawning another.

A visual, aural, or olfactory memory of some trivial incident triggers a stream of images. Subliminal events in your body or sensations provoked by its organs appear and vanish like fleeting fish, leaving behind a flash of el cuerpo's knowledge. At times a drama in technicolor, complete with setting, dialogue, action, and soundtrack, unreels from el cenote.

The images spin out for hours. Soon, however, you must quit the cavernous theater of dreams to begin the work of deciphering the images, mining them for their symbolic meanings, and manifesting them in language. You put the images en la oya (cauldron) of your historia and let them cook. As soon as you wake, the familiar pressure is there: should you write or not? Yes, no, maybe. You heave your body out of bed, prick your finger, and squeeze a drop of blood onto the glucose meter. You shoot insulin into your stomach, eat, go for a walk. You concentrate on your feet touching the ground, on the blue stretch of sky, the roar of crashing waves, the pungent odor of guano. You listen to the environment as Don Juan urged Castañeda to do. Searching for analogies to your budding ideas, you scan a flock of pelicans flying low over the water, breakers shooting up the cliff walls like geysers.

You spent your childhood en ranchos in south Texas, watching cattle and horses graze, ruminate, and chew. Like them, you graze the environment, assigning ideas to images, asking what reality has to do with your creative process, what the larger focus and purpose are. Following the bay's edge, the wind gusting around you, you let nature help you create symbols for the ideas in the story, help you create ideas for its symbols, help you invent theories.

Watching for signs, you look at the emerald waves marbled with white. They remind you of the network of vessels on the whites of the eye. This morning when you looked at the mirror, you saw two bloodspots like red cactus tunas in your eyes. When capillaries bleed you see floaters and pulsating lights—everything gets blurry. Hijole, your worst nightmare: if you can't see to write and read, there goes your life.

You hurry home y te recojes en el asiento de la ventana. A blanket across your lap and predraft at the ready, you search the field of bones for una seña of the root metaphor, the umbilicus to which all elements of la historia connect, a literary equivalent to chaos theory's strange attractor. You look for an image pattern that will point to a framework which could contain the organized whole. When you find the conducting thread llegas a la historia como llegar a un templo, exaltada, temblando. You bask in the artist's high, which may be why you're moved by designs in nature—the imprint of waves on sand, the shifting shadows of wind-blown trees.

As you write, the rhythm of words and the flow of images evolve a structure and act as a catalyst for combining information in a new way. It's not always this easy. Some days you rack your brain, stretching over the surface chaos page after page before you can discern a shape. But now you're flowing. You are the watcher con ojos de águila, alerta y vigilante, scrutinizing and processing every sensory experience. You become aware of a supernatural being. It shares with you a language that speaks of what is other; a language shared with the spirits of trees, sea, wind, and birds; a language which you'll spend many of your writing hours trying to translate into words. Walking between realities—one strange, another familiar—you experience the shock of recognition, the pleasure it gives you. A deep sounding from the landscape resonates through your bodymind. And you get a hint of the ground of writing, and a few tenuous tendrils groping for a trellis. You begin working the soil.

At the edge of the foaming sea you ask: How and from what point of view am I going to tell this story? What mood do I want to evoke and sustain? What emotion does it arouse in me? What emotion do I want to arouse in the reader? How much of myself should I put into the text? Certainly, include your frustrations and elation, your fears and satisfactions, and, above all, the mystery. You take out your notebook and begin to list what this metaphysical observation of writing has taught you about yourself, about your process.

The sky darkens. Another storm is on its way. As you slosh through the field, floundering in sodden soil, you look for a container for the story, a form or frame or womb, one that will collect the scattered images, connect the symbols, and unfold layers of meaning. This idea-generating dreaming writes the narrative as you move through your day. While you are vacuuming, it pulls the story through your body. Favoring interiority, it quickens en el terreno de sueños in the silence of night.

Now it's time to start composing the predraft. Anticipation and mild dread course through your body. You walk from desk to files to shelves, looking for something, a lost note, to anchor your attention. Part of you wants to write and part of you doesn't—there's always a conflict as to which part of you is running the writing. The part that represents internalized goals and a personal standard of perfection has grandiose plans for your career, wants the story to be a work of art. Your controlling authoritarian spirit wants you to apply willpower and discipline, it wants you to produce and to be efficient about it. The rebel doesn't like to be forced and absolutely balks at any discipline. It hates ironclad schedules and routines set for specific hours; and, when left on its own, it will sabotage the clock. Your struggle to find a methodology, a way of working, is constant. Balancing these aspects of spirit isn't easy. Writing is like pulling miles of entrails through your nose.

Why resistance? Because you're scared that you won't do it justice. Because it'll take time and there's no guarantee that you'll be able to pull it off. Because it's stressful and exhausting. A veces pierdes el nervio, y Saca Vueltas tempts you to play coward and procrastinate, to do more reading or research or to work on another story. After all, writing is not only the physical act of drafting and revising. Writing is also feeding the muse books on mythology, Aztec nagualismo (shamanism), reading voraciously in all disciplines, and taking notes. Writing is also envisioning and conceptualizing the work. Writing is also dreaming the story into a virtual reality. The different stages in embodying the story are neither clearly demarcated nor sequential nor linear—they overlap, shift back and forth, take place simultaneously.

You light copal incense, hoping the smell, your ritual, will coax you into the writing. You stare at the fluttering flame of the novena candle for the Virgen de Guadalupe and invoke the memory de tus muertos, your dead, tus mamagrandes y tu papá who persevered and persisted and who walked between realities. You brew some chai tea; you find music to accompany your visionary landscape, to shift consciousness from beta toward alpha. Tex-Mex, ambient, Enigma, Lourdes Pérez? It is the cavernous cello sounds of Yo-Yo Ma playing the Bach suites.

You do a five-minute meditation, observing your mind streaming; say your writer's prayer; and begin to compose. At this time, your task is to re-member; to translate into language the images arising from your body, the sea, the theater of dreams; to allow them to surface at will; to capture them in your net of words. After a stint at the computer you walk around the house and yard limbering up a stiff back. As an aching tooth, you suck on the problem of how to embody your story. Which genre—memoir, personal essay, or a combination? Memoir is a difficult genre. It's harder to manipulate the raw material of your own life than it is the details of an invented story. The problem is how to distinguish between you, the actual writer, and you, the narrative persona. The problem is how to improvise the self you create as you compose, and how to make the self immediate and alive without falling into self-indulgence, sentimentality, or grandstanding. The problem is deciding which chunks of your inner struggle and pain to cannibalize and incorporate into the text.

What about the style—the particular way of saying things, the imprint of self you leave on the page? Style brings up the politics of utterance—who says what, how, to whom, and on whose behalf. When you use a particular language register to re-create particular realities, you include certain groups of people and exclude others. Style brings up issues of loyalty and ethics. You wonder if you are unknowingly reproducing the dominant ideology along with its literary conventions. You weigh the benefits and the detriments of using a rhetoric different from dominant practices, of mixing a discursive style with a poetic one.

At this point your concern is premature. Mostly una historia chooses its own form and style without conscious guidance from you. What you have to do is block ego's insistance that you write "better," that you use the methodology of the head. But when you try to write like a writer, the language comes out stilted and abstract. You sit on your eggs and continue brooding. For days you continue to confuse the ego and feed la musa bruja with large doses of chaos theory, the poetry of Rosario Catellanos, and reruns of *The Outer Limits.*

From your aerie high up in the loft you listen to the wind howl and the sea lions bark. Through the skylight you watch the moon, Coyolxauhqui, suspended in the sky. You favor the night, when things whisper. While the town sleeps you go through your electronic notebooks, cutting snippets and pasting them into the story file. Surfing from notebook to notebook, you gather every pertinent scrap or image you can find. You group similar ideas, order them in a semilogical sequence, shuffle the clumps of semideveloped concepts into a loose order, and divide them into sections. At the predraft stage your anxiety fixates on how to organize the information.

You take a break to squeeze a drop of blood, take your insulin shot, and grab a quick snack. Fingers back on the keyboard, you stare at the screen. You need to start drafting. Now.

Composing is a process of ossification, the formation of bone, though at times it feels like sweating blood. You conjure up el cenote, throw yourself in, and swim among images and memories of other writing times. You freewrite five to six pages at warp speed. You do not focus on form. You don't consider technical problems yet. You keep the critical, editing voice at bay. You go from tightly focused writing to brief pauses where you allow your attention to dart here and there. Keying in the words, you're the scribe, the medium channeling the story, and the conductor orchestrating the process.

Besides being pleasurable, the work of putting down words engenders its own kind of trance—the physical act of writing is another kind of dreaming. Once you get into a working rhythm, you hate to interrupt it or leave it. Sure enough—your insulin shot was due hours ago.

At the end of the day, before sleep, you program yourself—yet another type of dreaming. Concentrating on feelings of contentment, delight, and satisfaction, you put yourself through a virtual reality of the next day's activities. While waiting for sleep to kick in, you suggest to your subconscious that it dream up another part of the story and surprise you in the morning.

You listen to the falling rain, to the sump pump sucking water out of the backyard, to the humming of the computer. You stare at the framed portrait of your naguala on the wall, flash back to when your queer comadre Randy painted your portrait twenty-three years ago. Every few minutes he would tilt your head. Squinting his eyes, he looked from your face to the sketchbook. When he finished, you got up and peered over his shoulder. It looked like some sort of were-animal with fur-like feathers—exactly how you'd seen yourself in the mirror whenever you dropped angel dust. How did he know?

He made two holes in the mask for eyes and strung a piece of elastic from ear to ear. Out of bits and pieces of cloth he created a costume. That Halloween night you were both the animal in you and your animal-companion, yourself and other—naguala. You felt powerful, otherwordly, and privy to secret knowledge. For the first time you felt at home in your body. To talk about the work of embodying consciousness you appropriate the word "naguala" from your ancestors, the indigenous Mexicans, who believed that certain humans could turn into animals.

Now you stare at the sketch of la naguala, arch your back on the typing chair, and slowly exhale through your mouth. As the tension eases out, la bruja naguala takes over. La naguala is the dreaming body, a mode of consciousness that's emotionally complex, diverse, dense, deep, violent, and rich, one with a love of physicality and the ability to switch bodies and their expressive codes instantly. You invoke this sentience to help you, not to transcend the physical, but to more passionately embrace the physical. You metamorphose into something else—a fictional character, a species of alter ego, a persona, a dramatic mask. You become an internal experience, a particular emotional state or mood; you give life to tumultuous feelings, to raging anger. You become the crashing waves, the lighthouse with its beacon.

A hyperempathic perception fuses you with your surroundings; you become what you observe—a face bulging out of the wall as in a sci-fi film, a woman lurking behind the wallpaper. Shifting and fluid, the boundaries of self-identity blur. You accommodate all identities. In naguala you alternate between hyperempathy and excessive detachment, a seamless change from one form to another.

Where does the work of naguala take place? In the body. All emotions and ideas pass through it—writing is nothing if not a bodily act. An image produces a physiological reaction that is experienced in strong feelings (desire, hate, fear) and manifests itself in neuromuscular, respiratory, cardiovascular, hormonal, and other bodily changes. In other words, an image produces emotion. You can't have an emotion without having a corresponding sensory image—and vice versa. The unconscious and the physical body do not distinguish between what is really happening and what is imagined or envisioned—both are equally real. Once fed blood, once fleshed, the bones of inert and abstract ideas become embodied, become mental and emotional realities living inside your skin. Writer, then text, then reader become possessed by naguala.

After letting the predraft gestate for a few days, you pick it up again. While you eat, standing at the kitchen counter, you read the hard copy. In your study you ignore the red blinking light on the answering machine and continue flipping through it, reacquainting yourself with its overall shape, pinpointing the major sections and subsections. Identifying each part with subtitle, you integrate and merge sections and shift others. Your goal is to raise a temporary skeleton. You're aiming not for a linear, logical structure of ideas, but for an architectural body that supports and allows access to its innards.

Fresh copy in hand, you do several more flip-throughs; then you do your first complete read-through and yet another rearrangement of parts. As you're inputting the changes, you become aware that the lights are blinking. You go to the window. Rain is falling in sheets; wind is lashing the tress. You walk from room to room checking the windows, then wait for the power to come back on.

Tonight is your writing date with Irene, one of your writing comadres. You go to a local coffeehouse, get a table by a wall outlet, and plug in your laptops. You discuss your projects and encourage each other. Before leaving the coffeehouse you decide what you're going to do tomorrow, thus giving your unconscious something to work on. Next day you'll transit into the writing without having to jump-start it cold.

The moment of reckoning is at hand; it is time to write the first draft. You go over the predraft. It is an uncoordinated mass of information, a pile of bones. You start assembling los huesos in a way you hope will connect all the elements of the story, but that will add up to more than the sum of the bones.

In school you had to memorize the bones in the body, more than two hundred. A story possesses a body: its skeleton is the framework; the bones are its armature. All the bones are connected to the backbone, a single linchpin holds the story's tension and contains the crucial threads running throughout the work. The story's ideas, including the most important organ, the heart, are held, encased, and protected by the skeleton.

You use transitional devices, the ligaments, tendons, muscles, and skin of writing to join the bones and bind the nerves and organs: mood, description, plot, characterization, and dialogue. The sheer magnitude of the time and stamina required to get all los huesos in order is overwhelming. To help you organize the interaction of images and words into an 8,000-word essay and keep you from going completely crazy, you turn to a colored pen sketch you did of la Coyolxauhqui and invoke her. In Aztec mythology Coyolxauhqui is the moon goddess, a warrior woman. Making her the first human sacrifice, her brother Huitzilopochtli, the war god, decapitated her, dismembered the body, and scattered her limbs. Organizing the parts into a unified whole and drafting a full version el cuento is the act of putting Coyolxauhqui back together again.

Next day you read the first draft to find that overnight it has become a Frankenstein-like monster. The Coyolxauhqui you put together is a grotesque figure with arms sticking out of her back, her skull hanging between her legs. She has eye sockets for knees. You pull your hair and snarl at the screen. You will have to take the text apart bone by bone; go through psychic dismemberment once more; fly apart, implode, splinter once more. This stage of the writing feels violent y siempre te desmadra. This stage reminds you of helping your mother desgranar corn, scattering the hard kernels and then waiting for them to sprout. The second time you re-member the bones, Coyolxauhqui emerges less malformed. The text begins to take comely shape, begins to discover its own grace, its own organic force.

During the whole componiendo y descomponiendo drafting phase, you're in a state of extreme unease. To reduce the intolerable pressure, you tell yourself that confusion is a necessary stage of creating, that the disequilibrium brought on by disorganization and chaos forces you to use your imagination to right the balance and compose in a better order. You're trying to teach yourself, as Clarice Lispector put it, "to bear the frustrating discomfort of disorder."[1]

Maybe a walk by the ocean will help you pull yourself together. When you are halfway to Natural Bridges, a surfer crashes against the rocks; his board breaks into pieces.

You return home from your walk and continue dreaming parts of the story as you putter about in your kitchen, opening and sorting through the mail, listening to the radio and to the storm raging outside your window; you talk on the phone, monitoring what is going on inside your body. In a state of nepantla, you switch from one perception channel to another, channels reflecting the same information in different ways. The cacophony that comes from being open to multiple channels can feel like watching half a dozen TV stations at once, confusing, maddening, frustrating, until nepantla creates a wider space in your mind, allowing you to make the connections, allowing the various scenarios to merge and come into focus.

Creativity requires profound shifts of consciousness and a scattered kind of attention that goes against habits of thinking. Nepantla is your symbol for the transitional process, both conscious and unconscious, that bridges different kinds of activities by moving between and among different parts of the brain. The work of nepantla is a mysterious type of dreaming or perception which registers the workings of all states of consciousness. Shaman-like, nepantla moves from rational to visionary states, from logics to poetics, from focused to unfocused perception, from inner to outer world. Nepantla is the twilight landscape between the self and the world, between the imagery of the imagination and the harsh light of reality.

Napantla operates in the cracks between the worlds, in the liminal spaces. It navigates the razor edge of this rajadura, always teetering, about to fall either on the side of overly ordered or on the side of bacchanalian chaos, always attempting to join the two in a seamless web.

Your head is full of spiders, all weaving their glistening webs. Nepantla tries to marshal the field where images, words, feelings, and mind-sets vie for a place in the story. Nepantla averigua el conflicto. It provides associations and connective tissue. Performing mental, psychic, and spiritual gymnastics, nepantla interweaves multiple, superimposed strands of thought. Suddenly your writing is flowing smoothly as you ride with nepantla. If only you could ride this writer's high forever.

Rational consciousness sets goals and schedules. The imaginal consciousness, the dreaming naguala, seizes the booty that el cenote renders up and turns it into sentient worlds, while nepantla interlaces those worlds into a coherent whole.

You've sat on the second draft for a couple of days, and now it's time to revise it. You take a deep breath and pick it up—14,810 words, 314 paragraphs, 56 pages. You need to eliminate more than half. Then you need to redesign it. The constant destruction-reconstruction process is wearying. What if you don't get la historia to breathe, much less dance, by the deadline, less than two weeks away? Qué le hace, it doesn't matter—today's writing has to get done.

By now it's the middle of the night and the whole pueblo sleeps. Night is a fecund terrain for you—eres más hija de la Coyolxauhqui y de la noche que del sol. The mournful sounds of the foghorn and rain drumming on the roof accompany the pecking of fingers on keyboard. You reacquaint yourself with the text's overall structure, pinpoint the major renovations, examine the linchpin holding it together.

The questions you're concerned with at this stage are: Does the piece possess coordination among parts, a balanced proportion, and a varying pace that maintains interest? Will the reader find pleasure in the imagery and language and be satisfied by the form? Is spending time in your company worth the reader's time?

After re-envisioning la historia and finding out what it really is about, you draw up a rough timetable for the next revision stage; you list the sections and specifics of what you're going to do. You do the first read-through silently. You work on the large chunks, saving the detailed work for later revisions. You repeatedly cut and rearrange, shape and focus the material. You input the changes and tackle the repetitions and abstractions—your major literary vices. You throw out whole sections, paragraphs, and sentences; you expand others. You look at the tone and ask: Does it reflect your feelings about your writing process? Is this story more than just a personal record of your process—that is, have you placed it in the context of the world and some of its social, political realities?

Next day your body is wiped out, but by evening you're riding the creative high tide again. You read through the draft, merging sections, reordering, knitting the connective tissue. You help the story say what it intends to say. Todavía no baila; that requires a wide-awake energy you don't have now, an energy that's necessary if you are to be totally present and totally engaged with the work. You know that long working sessions are counterproductive, but you keep slogging away, working like an automaton. As the sun begins to rise and burn off the fog along the coast, you print out the third draft.

You pull Coyolxauhqui apart again in the fourth draft. Again naguala shape-changes, compelling a rearrangement of parts. Nepantla reassembles the fragments around a different emerging center. Months later you're on draft number ten. Just one or two more drafts and you'll be done, but you're feeling a lot of resistance. Why do you always run into a stone wall when bringing a work to completion?

Reading the tenth draft is like walking over a field of bones; you wince at the dull, heavy-handed sentences. The thing rings hollow, its heartbeat silenced by deadwood. Not a breath of poetry is to be found anywhere. Its narrative mode and your use of the first person put your ego in the text too much. Not only does the story say nothing new; it says things badly. Más claro canta el gallo. And worst of all, it doesn't engage the reader emotionally. Doubt about your ability to pull it off by the deadline gnaws your insides like a rat.

To be innovative and subversive a writer must write what readers haven't been taught to read yet—a different and unfamiliar literary form that must present an experience not yet articulated or portray a familiar one from a radically different perspective. Not only must you outdo those who have come before, but you must also outdo yourself—each successive work of art must be different from your prior work. You have failed to do all this. No has dejado huellas nuevas.

The pressure or urge to speak in new ways, to say something different, to push genre boundaries without losing the reader, is as constant as gravity. You're assailed with the angst peculiar to writers: that this piece is the worst you've ever written. After prolonged labor you have nothing to show for it. You feel that you have betrayed the piece by not writing it up to your expectations. A profound depression sweeps you under.

You don't want to work on it anymore. Maybe you've run into the endurance wall, a marathon runner finding yourself drained six miles before the finish line. Maybe you need to protect it from the weather of the harsh outer world until it's more developed. Maybe you did not allow enough time for the silence needed to attend to all the symbols in the story. When you are pressured to publish too soon, the last stage gets shortchanged. The ideas and feelings seeking expression, seeking embodiment, have not yet been worked over, have not been kneaded enough; they are only partially digested. You have ordered it too soon, you have not borne the chaos, not worked the raw materials long enough. You have forced a premature birth because you did not let the ideas grow all their fingers and toes. You did not wait long enough for the imaginative self to completely render up its treasures.

You hate having incompleteness hovering over you—the all-but-dissertation, the projects promised—but what you hate most is passing something off as finished when you feel that it isn't. Disgusted with yourself, you look around your study. Every surface is covered with folders, faxes, requests for submissions and letters of recommendation, manuscripts sent by friends and strangers who want you to write introductions or blurbs for the cover or take a couple of days out of your life to critique their 500-page masterpieces. You are angry at your own internal demand that you should be able to take on everything. You resent the pressure to produce—your own pressure, and pressure from editors, publishers, and readers.

Stuck on an edge you can't get past, toda la manãna le sacas vueltas, you pace like a caged animal, wanting only to fling yourself against the wall. Nguala transforms itself into una bestia-sombra, and like the creature from the Black Lagoon, rises up from the depths, grabs you, drags you into the deep waters of the cave. You have no immunities and few defences against the monster's unscheduled visits. Unlike others, a writer can't afford to hide from herself. You have to face the desconocimientos that you don't want to be aware. You are possessed by your inner demon, the antagonist within, the part of you whose desire is in opposition to yours. Frustrated with the deadline, you feel hurried, pressured, and harassed. You can't deny, can't hide from, the shadow side of writing.

Just as the story's success depends on a deeper integration of all the pieces and a balance between order and chaos, you know that the solution to your depression lies en esa cueva oscura and a deeper integration of your psyche. Until you admit that the interior shadow is part of you, is you, is your own irrationality, you may not survive (in your present form) to emerge with the message from the source. The problem is that you don't have time to brood in the cave. You have a deadline.

Throwing up your hands, you head for the beach. The gusting wind pushes you along West Cliff. You can't see the lighthouse beacon. Out at sea the familiar blue boat and its macintoshed figure ride the rough swells.

The more time elapses, the more resistance and dread tighten the tension. The longer the story lies untouched on your desk, the more ansia you feel. You go through some of your other antiblock strategies—deep breathing, chanting your mantra. You use whatever you can get your hands on as a battering ram against the granite block. No le hace, nothing works. Every day it gets harder to stay rooted in the reality of calendar and clock.

Hechas maldiciónes, you curse the text, barely resisting the urge to rip the misbegotten thing into little pieces and flush it down the toilet with the rest of the caca. Writing always calls your basic self-worth into question. You're a coward for not venturing far enough into yourself. You haven't gone all the way. You haven't pulled out all the stops. You haven't questioned values and beliefs deeply enough, because questioning makes you tense and vulnerable. To write is to expose yourself, to let down the protective walls—a given that comes with the territory. Today estas cansada, you're too tired to face your flawed criatura.

Face it, you've fallen out of love with it; you can't stand the sight of it. You toss the text back onto the desk, feeling a sense of relief at giving it up, of chucking the work and putting it away indefinitely. By burying it deep, you hope your unconscious will do the work of integration. In the black hole of depression, sofocando gritos como una llorona mourning her loss, you also bury yourself away from society like the unclean or dead. For days you binge-read through your depression.

When your writing comadre, Carmen, comes for your weekly session you tell her that you feel you're being tested. The beam holding up the second floor is rotting and needs to be replaced; the deck needs to be shored up; your backyard's flooded despite the sump pump going on day and night; the roof leaks in three places; and water is seeping up through the floor and warping the parquet in the living room. Sure, you've been writing, but you haven't been writing this particular piece. In fact, you're blocked. You tell her you're afraid you won't make this piece dance by the deadline.

"Sure you can do it," she says. "It takes courage and a lot of hard work to delve into your process and to expose it honestly. Don't be so hard on yourself. The kind of work you're doing is not something light."

After Carmen leaves, you hope that all you're suffering from is performance anxiety, not a creative block. Telling yourself that toiling in the muck is fun, you summon up enough energy to take up the draft once more. You transform a few abstract ideas into sensory images. You vary the sentences from simplicity to complexity; you examine their rhythmic patterns, balancing syntactical elements, repeating key words and motifs. You stop. You realize that you've fooled yourself into treating a symptom rather than tackling the huge underlying problem, fooled yourself into unraveling a single thread rather than the whole skein. But you refuse to dismember the story again.

Feet thumps on the roof. The sounds of a drill and hammer. Michele the carpenter is replacing the damaged downspouts and gutters. Three inches of rain fell yesterday and another storm system's moving in tomorrow, but today's a day of respite after months of rain.

"You're not an ice cream machine," Liliana, a comadre who's a visual artist, tells you on the phone. "Producing art is not like producing ice cream."[2]

In a burst of light a new awareness floods you. You decide that you need a respite from the stillborn corpse of the story that you've been dragging from room to room all week. Time is the only line of defense left. Time to let the piece ferment in the dark caves of the imagination until you're ready to work on it again. Time to let the scattered pieces turn over and over in the unconscious until they reformulate. But time is a commodity you've run out of. You realize that writer's block may be a condition you have manufactured yourself as a grist for the mill, the silent brooding dark intelligence of the shadow-beast sitting on its eggs. The block is the struggle that grants meaning even in failure. When you start a new project, you want to write painlessly, swiftly, to produce good work. When this doesn't happen by the deadline, you convince yourself that you're blocked. If you've invented this block, you can uninvent it. Relief courses through your body.

To dismantle your block, you need to change your behavior. To change your behavior, you have to change your attitude. To change your attitude, you've got to change some basic beliefs about yourself, your writing habits, and your ability to do the work. To do that you have to be aware of what notion about writing or what stage in particular is holding you up. That you should be able to whip out these historias faster? That is your monster—the myth that real writing comes out perfect in a couple of drafts.

You know that to get unblocked something has to give, something has to die, your ambition, your obsession with perfection. What you have to let go of is the illusion that the writer exerts full conscious control over the writing process.

After honoring the dark cave with time, three and a half months later you pick up the story, go over the marks on the cave walls. You empty yourself so your serpent spirit can dream it again. Nepantla, as a syncretistic faculty, watches the unconscious struggle between several possible readings. It finds and recognizes what belongs together and facilitates interaction between ambiguity and control, between undifferentiated confusion and defined clarity. A scene attracts a fragment which in turn attracts another that matches its resonance. You rework the material until alignment and balance occur. Then you try to get each section to lock into sync with every other section, lock and pulse together with the undercurrent rhythm of the whole piece. When it becomes an animated, live thing, comiensa a bailar—it starts to dance. Something alive is more than the configuration of components in a whole—live things continue to develop and evolve.

What you've learned from your body and chronic illness that you can apply to the creative process is that change in one part of organ triggers adjustments in all the other parts. A minor change in the text causes reverberations throughout. You've become aware that being out of control (of your blood sugars) and in being in extreme disequilibrium prompt self-organization and a return to balance. You've learned that writing about writing is more about life than it is about writing, that writing mirrors the struggle in your own life, from denial to recognition and change; that writing illumines your fears and dreams. All these insights are precious because you wrestled them out of the granite walls of your creative block.

You put your faith on this: that some mysterious ordering faculty ultimately refines the piece; that the components of the piece, the symbols, attract the necessary parts and the whole rearranges itself; the writing is an alchemical process demanding dissolution in order that the transmutation of images and emotions into words may occur. If you've done your job, the reader will also undergo an alchemical process.

The lighthouse draws you toward the horizon. When you get there you watch water sluicing over the rough edges of a round rock, slowly paring it down and sculpting it. You wonder if the water is smoothing it or making pits on its glistening surface. Maybe it's time to stop diddling with the text.

According to Kenneth Atchity, "the concept of 'finishing your work' is a contradiction in terms so blatant and so dangerous that it can lead to nervous breakdowns—because it puts the pressure on the wrong places in your mind and habits."[3] To get past this last wall you have to change your assumption of what finishing means. When you read any of your published work, you always think it needs more revision. There is never a final "fin," just a lot of small ones. You have to accept the imperfections of your work, accept its partial incoherence, accept the fact that it will never attain the surface of a water-smoothed stone. Like a person's life, all art is a work in progress.

Your faith y tu larga espera have finally paid off; your tenacity has been rewarded. Head hanging low, a runner at the end of the race, you watch each page emerge from the printer crisp and clean and almost perfectly composed, almost like a water-smoothed stone. Something tangible has emerged out of the chaos and raw material of your life. You hope that one day, after many more revisions, this Coyolxauhqui will finally emerge from the cave's cauldron and maybe, just maybe, gain artistic immortality through the elixir of the "Art." But for now you put the "unfinished" story in an envelope, stick it in your mailbox and offer it to the world.

As you walk along the cliff you stare down into the waves washing over rocks, incessantly, persistently, until the end of time. You watch the sun, looking like a perfect golden stone, being slowly swallowed up by the ocean. You watch the small blue boat in the bay return to the mainland. Dreaming another story, comiensas a empollar otro huevo. You head back home. Largo camino te queda.

Acknowledgment

I dedicate this essay to my comadres Randy Conner, Carmen Morones, and Irene.

Notes

1. Clarice Lispector. "Since One Feels Obliged to Write," *Lives on the Line: The Testimony of Contemporary Latin American Authors*. (Ed. Doris Meyer; trans. Giovanni Pontiero); Berkeley: University of California Press, 1988, (p. 36).
2. Liliana Wilson Grez. Latina visual artist, telephone conversation (April 1998).
3. Kenneth Atchity. *A Writer's Time*. (New York: Norton, 1986), p. 13.

Chapter 23

Should We Be Working?

Marshall Parks

For the great majority of men under ordinary circumstances,
the practical exigencies of life are almost, if not quite, coercive.
Their main business is the proper conduct of their affairs.
Whatever is of significance only as affording scope for thinking
is pallid and remote—almost artificial. Hence the contempt
felt by the practical and successful executive for the "mere theorist."
(John Dewey, 1910, p. 138)

All this has a specific bearing on the question
of what may reasonably be expected of the schools
in a democratic social order. . . . The central task of these schools
is to make their pupils intelligent with reference
to the issue of what constitutes a good life.
(Boyd Henry Bode, 1940, pp. 271–272)

No one knows who will live in this cage in the future, or whether at the end of this tremendous development entirely new prophets will arise, or there will be a great rebirth of old ideas and ideals, or, if neither, mechanized petrification, embellished with a sort of convulsive self-importance. For of the last stage of this cultural development, it might truly be said: "Specialists without spirit, sensualists without heart; this nullity imagines that it has attained a level of civilization never before achieved."[1]

Perhaps the single thread which unites many social critics of the late nineteenth and early twentieth centuries is an intuition—an intuition which is the by-product of an unquantifiable native region bridging our knowledge of the world and the frontier of the human heart. Whether from Weber's sense of social ignominy or from James's urgent quest to protect the "vague," it is an intuition reflected in the unwillingness of these critics to surrender their instinct for personal deliverance in the face of the juggernaut of mediocrity that is the twentieth century—an intuition that itself is revealed in the disquieting notion that we have somehow *already* failed as a civilization. John Dewey would never have tolerated such an idea, intuitive or other, although it can be argued that in his later life he must certainly have felt the weight of both his and the world's failures.

On the eve of the twentieth century, William James published two brief essays—more like mental sketches—one of which is entitled *What Makes a Life Significant*. In this particular essay he was remembering a visit to the Chautauqua Society: "I went in out of curiosity for a day. . . . I stayed for a week, spell-bound by the charm and ease of everything, by the middle-class paradise, without a sin, without a victim, without a blot, without a tear."[2] For James, Chautauqua seemed an enigmatic world without profound sentiments of any kind—whether good or bad. The year was 1899 and America, along with the rest of the European world, was in the midst of one of the greatest social transformations in western history—the rise of modernism and the new social paradigm of industrial efficiency.

James, not unlike Weber and other essayists of his time, was both bewildered at the pace of change and uncertain of what those changes would portend for the future of human insight. The occasion that stirred his essay occurred while James was on a train returning home from his visit to Chautauqua. While en route he pondered what would become of creativity and boldness if, like the placid community of Chautauqua, humanity became—in a world prepackaged for consumption—devoid of challenge or authenticity.

Likewise for Dewey, efficiency models based upon industrial management techniques were a consistent threat to his ambitions for educational transformation in America. In *How We Think*, Dewey suggests: "To pry into the familiar, the usual, the automatic, simply for the sake of making it conscious, simply for the sake of formulating it, is both an impertinent interference and a source of boredom. To be forced to dwell consciously upon the accustomed is the essence of ennui."[3]

For the social and intellectual critics who lived and wrote during the early decades of this century there was a persistent, almost nagging, question underlying their concerns about the developing industrialized world: What knowledge of value from the past was being lost on the one hand, and on the other what might be gained from sacrificing the past in favor of the great changes the future promised? The curious feature of Jamesian pragmatism and the specialness of James himself lay in his unusual capacity to retain a position both predisposed and indisposed to both the past and the future. This paper is a consideration of that talent.

Regarding the attainment of knowledge, Emerson placed a special emphasis on the *mood* of persons who are searching for knowledge and the manner in which mood influences decisions about what they will accept as knowledge of the world. If for Emerson it "depends on the mood of the man whether he shall see the sunset or the fine poem," for James it is "the re-instatement of the vague to its proper place in our mental life which I am so anxious to press on the attention."[4]

William Gavin suggests, "It is important to note that the term 'vague' is being used . . . not simply in a literal sense, but in more of a symbolic one, as an interpretative disclosure of James's overall outlook."[5] Moreover, James does not use "the vague" as a descriptive tool intended to ellicit an encounter with the unknown. Jacques Barzun notes:

> In *The Principles* James struck a death blow at Realism. The then prevailing views of the mind were that it copied reality like a photographic plate, that it received and assembled the elements of experience like a machine, that it combined ideas like a chemist. For this "scientist" mind, James substituted one that was a born artist—a wayward, creative mind, impelled by inner wants, fringed with mystery, and capable of infinitely subtle, unrecordable nuances.[6]

I would agree with Barzun that James fully intended to end the vicelike grip of mechanization, to attain freedom and artistry in discourse, whether the discussion was of truth, value, or knowledge. However, I think it is incorrect to attribute to James, through his use of the word "vague," any faith or hope in mystery. James's depressive nature, like Rorty's, is one which is quite beyond faith or hope—at least in the way we most commonly use these words. Barzun seems to suggest, just as Derrida would with "the ineffable," that mystery forever lies beyond the frontiers of the grasping mind and is the final and unconquerable enemy of reason—ultimately saving us from ourselves. James, to my way of thinking, is far more afraid that he does see behind the mask of god. There, a dark and sordid place is made all the more unpalatable by our unwillingness to extend the values we covet for ourselves when we look out toward one another's greater social needs.

Rather, I would suggest that James would be just as happy to use "the vague" as a means of sequestering mystery as he does to use it to forfeit scientific integrity or methodological purity. James is first and last a straddler of fences, and this is not because he fears being labeled with a particular opinion so much as he fears the loss of his potential to change his opinions—and this as an attitude of living in the modern world. It is very important to understand that when James refers to "vicious intellectualism," he is referring to the tendency of intellectual "authorities" whether scientific, religious, or other to limit the possible scope of discourse by limiting what is considered *reasonable* as a subject of discourse. For James these authoritarian appeals to limit conversation do not represent any genuine discovery or truth; rather, they are merely rhetorical tricks designed to limit alternative discourse.

It is to James's credit that his close understanding of the relation between intuition and the very idea of freedom are alive in his recognition that our choices and our own personal biases are intimately intertwined and as such can never provide grounds for excluding different opinions in any society that claims to be free. To this end, James concluded that what is missing from the professionalized discourse of contemporary society is the very richness and intensity of life in the living. Consequently, James intends to use "the vague" to defend human sentiment and intuition against those who would marshal an army of doctrinaire principles against it—as it is often human intuition that is called to account by those who demand rational accountability in society and discourse.

For James, it is the sense of unpracticed thought and creativity that lends richness to living and learning in the world. It is this richness that James most desires to preserve and encourage when he uses the word "vague" to dismantle absolutism in discourse. It is not mystery for the sake of mystery that James wants to defend, but rather the idea that what living holds in the less articulate sentiments of thought is precious particularly because it is always sensitive to redescription. The mature intensity that James brings to the concept of sentiment lends a different hue to our intellectual perspective and relieves us of social requirements for incessant replication. Likewise, what James most abhors is the routinization indicative of the administrative outlook, with its emphasis on efficiency models, standardized techniques, and methodological purity. James attacks the notion behind radical efficiency, which implies that standardization is inherently correct by undermining the idea that nature provides a key by which we might unlock and correctly reorder the priorities of human activity and thought: "A permanently existing 'idea' or 'Vorstellung' [introduction], which makes its appearance before the footlights of consciousness at periodical intervals, is as mythological an entity as the jack of spades."[7]

James is willing to compromise between extremes such as religion and science, not merely because he can see how small doses of each can be therapeutic, but also because he is unwilling to allow either to get a stranglehold on his right to be done with both. James amicably ignores the authority of the past as well as the weight of the pressing future. Further, he uses his own peculiar relativism as a median position to distance himself from being inundated by the sacrifices that either the past or the future would impose were he willing to accept only one idea of the truth while turning his back on the other. James's willingness to accommodate both traditional "religious" truism and progressive scientific truth means ultimately that he dismisses both the importance of tradition and the scientistic dream of progress.

Dewey emotionally abandoned Jamesian pragmatism because of this relativistic position regarding our role in history. Education was dominated throughout Dewey's later career by schools of thought more interested in business models than in creativity. The demand for efficiency in education in the first half of this century dealt a crushing blow to the social and political hopes of progressive reformers. The sterility of administrative methodologies purged learning of its self-informed creativity and abolished the richness and intensity of life and living that James admired and Dewey struggled to defend.

For James, this richness of life was found in the intensity of learning itself. Further, James found that in ideas like "the vague" (or Whitman's "peace that is beyond argument," or Emerson's "moods," or Dewey's "organically expanding democratic frontier"), he could defend those aspects of learning which are creative and intimate. He realized that these ideas—whether one sees them as spiritual, purely psychological, or simply emotional—when subjected to the goals of rationality and efficiency, are sequestered and sterilized.

In one sense the demand for extreme accountability finds its history in the enlightenment tradition suggesting that we must reveal the foundation of individual human value on the one hand while revealing the correct path for social progress on the other. However, history suggests that this illusory foundation leading to the path of enlightenment has been unable to provide any ahistorical or universal impact either on the role of individual rights or on the political and social progress of the modern world. In fact, liberal society has always routinely utilized *rhetorical* devices, rather than universal principles, to reify its own ends in creating a common agenda for society. No more historically useful example of this process can be found than in the massive American project for public education.

All pragmatisms are not equal. James and Dewey, in many respects, are a most unlikely duo. James sees the relative nature of all things as beneficial to breaking away from any consistent opinion except tolerance, whereas Dewey uses different perspectives as an opportunity to build a consensus for unified democratic action in society. For James, psychology means therapy; for Dewey, it is one key to unifying the natural conditions for a democratized method. In background, temperament, and vision, James and Rorty are also quite different. Rorty, although he might be a Jamesian at heart, is torn between his own progressivism which seeks a stronger grasp of social matters, and his strong desire to see the effort to attain social democracy, like the phoenix, rise again from its own ashes.

It is useful to cling to James's concept of truth in differentiating the point of departure between Dewey's pragmatism and Rorty's neopragmatism. For James, truth is merely "that property of a belief by virtue of which it 'agrees with' the mind that holds it."[8] Equally, "'The true,' to put it very briefly, is only the expedient in the way of our thinking, just as 'the right' is only the expedient in our way of behaving."[9] James uses the expression "in our way" for quite the same reason that Rorty enjoys emphasizing it. The whole point of the James/Rorty critique of *the true* and *the right* is how to get around the rhetoric of these words in order to get what you want. Rorty emphasizes the Jamesian desire to get around truth when he suggests, "To say that truth is not out there is simply to say that where there are no sentences there is no truth, that sentences are elements of human languages, and that human languages are human creations."[10]

In differentiating between Dewey's pragmatism and Rorty's neopragmatism, it is also helpful to note a distinction between James and Dewey with regard to experience. For James, the experience of presence or that which is given in experience is rough and uneven—James would call it "vague." Further, it is in the vagueness of experience that we uncover what is, for James, most endearing about the concept of experience—the perceived, yet still unseen, ground of possibility. It is in the unformed potentiality of experience that James finds worth in experiencing life. In this regard, James's notion of the vague in experience is a precursor of Heidegger's later notion of *aletheia* or the primordial lighting of *being*.

Conversely, when Dewey speaks of experience, whether or not he understands his concept of experience to be rooted in the way he uses the word, he expresses concepts which are determinate and have a specific purpose: "Concrete experiences, not logical conceptions by themselves warrant statements about matters of existence."[11] Dewey does not seem content with giving up on the possibility for getting things right—at least to the extent that he wants some assurance for the role of experience in nature as well as the primacy of democratic culture.

Dewey once said, "When truth is defined as utility, it is often thought to mean utility for some purely personal end, some profit upon which a particular individual has set his heart. So repulsive is a conception of truth which makes it a mere tool of private ambition and aggrandizement, that the wonder is that critics have attributed such a notion to sane men."[12] It strikes me that James, rather than Rorty, would have responded: "What else could you possibly want from truth than personal utility?" For Rorty there must also be social utility. Consequently, there is a difference in the social expectations of Dewey and Rorty on the one hand and James on the other.

James, unlike Dewey, was no progressive. James was a modernist, as surely as Rorty is consonant with several themes of post-modernism. James embraced relativism warmly as a means of escaping from the stranglehold of metaphysics, whether in the form of religion or science. Rorty notes, "By taking a true belief as a successful rule for action, [James] hoped to rub out the purported difference between scientific beliefs as 'evidenced' and religious beliefs as adopted without evidence."[13] Rorty himself seeks to escape from the analytic tradition and its logical rules and boundaries for discourse, using precisely the same technique. The distinction between Rorty and James lies in the similarity between Rorty and Dewey. James never intended to reform society, so much as he desired to show others how he coped with it. James is not a romantic. Rorty, like Dewey before him, is engaged by the romance of pressing for a more progressive, democratic world. However, where the various methods for attaining social progress begin, the similarity between Rorty and Dewey ends.

Rorty considers philosophy as intellectual history with supplementary commentary—importing the tradition of *Geistesgeschichte* stories, or intellectual histories with a moral twist. For Jamesian pragmatists, as well as neopragmatists, theirs is a journey more like an odyssey of the self—a quest for personal freedom and autonomy with a polite insistence on public hope and well-being. This is clearly not enough for Dewey, who not only is emphatic about the relation between scientific method and democratic society but is constantly nagged by a desire to see a Hegelian synthesis between the two.

Dewey's chief point of social departure from James and Rorty lies in his insistence that "government, business, art, religion, all social institutions have a meaning, a purpose," and that social purpose in a democracy was and should be intractably related to social ends. Dewey suggests that "if democracy has a moral and ideal meaning, it is that a social return be demanded from all and that opportunity for development of distinctive capacities be afforded to all."[14]

Although much of Dewey's pragmatism developed outward from James, it is nonetheless true that Dewey demanded far more of pragmatism than did James, whose chief desire was to protect the private or personal sphere from encroachment by modern pressures. Rorty goes one step further than James in expressing his desire to shape social ends to foster the liberal sentiments that he admires.

The first and most obvious criticism of Rorty's brand of pragmatism, when it is given as the inheritor of the social duties of Dewey's pragmatism, is its Jamesian acquiescence. People rarely fault James for this quality because James tended to shy away from any pretension that his philosophy might have common social, rather than merely personal, utility. Although this criticism may be misapplied to Rorty, as we have perhaps inadequately reflected on what society is or should be from a post-foundational context, it is nonetheless true that Dewey himself is as close to failure in his social expectations and beliefs as any human in history.

For as prophets go, and though he had no such intention, it is William James (alongside Henry Adams, Friedrich Nietzsche, and Max Weber), rather than John Dewey, who has best guessed our fate. We are not a shining social democracy where human beings are brought to their fullest capacities and in turn use those capacities for the increased well-being of society. On the contrary, it is the rich who jealously reserve and dominate the lion's share of the world's resources and pleasures, while the rest are left in a struggle, often bitter, for survival and dignity. Corporationalism, rather than social democracy, has won the game that we began in the Enlightenment, while the academic community arguably plays an even more diminished role in social affairs than it did a century ago. Further, it is James, rather than his critical contemporaries, who saw that learning is the best escape.

I am stating that we have most assuredly been consumed by our own greed and failed miserably to save even among ourselves the dream that the greater part of humanity is worth saving. Most of us in the middle classes today would, whether openly or privately, prefer that others poorer and more destitute than we should work harder to make life easier for us. This is not the sort of failure we can turn around. It is a failure of our own ability to establish a sense of justice within ourselves *as* a social conscience to guide our activities. There can be little wonder at this, given that a central part of our understanding of equity and justice is based upon a system operating primarily, as Dewey rightly understood, for private industry and aggrandizement. Jamesian therapy would seem to be all the more appropriate for us than for James himself—there is little left.

The question regarding education's decades-old fear of being unaccountable to the public—that is, the fear that we will not be able to *appear* worthy of the task of educating the people—seems somehow dimmed when one considers the world that people are being educated *for* these days. That Dewey himself would have been profoundly disappointed goes without saying. However, there is little need for fear—we, as educators today, can hardly do worse to society than has already been done. Further, we may still have some small opportunity to alter our society for the better. The manner, however, may be very different indeed from that envisioned by the progressives nearly a century ago—and in the end it might be the manner that matters.

Critics of Rorty like Richard Bernstein have faulted Rorty for scuttling the most important aspects of Dewey's political legacy while importing James's own brand of political impotence. Unfortunately, these critics seem unconcerned that Dewey's political agenda, irrespective of its sincerity, was extraordinarily unsuccessful. It is not simply a question of bad timing or poor information—Dewey's dream for transforming America during this century could not have been more socially misaimed, given the minds of the people, the intellectual community and social critics of his time, and the real political base of power in this country—the American corporation.

The lesson for us is not merely historical; it is also providential. We have lost Dewey's battle. As educators we were supposed to change the world in a big way. He wanted us to, and we failed—but so did he. It can be of no surprise to anyone anymore that Dewey was quite correct in his assessment of public education as a tool for the powerful. The game that we have been playing in this century has been prearranged to benefit the business community, with its increasing designs for a more competitive role in the world economy, rather than to address the more complex issues regarding the quality of life for people in general. Dewey's comments about public education being used to create "industrial fodder" are as applicable today as they were when he proclaimed them at the beginning of this century. For if any age has stood intimately as an exultation or indictment of any one person's thinking, the twentieth century has stood as malefic to the ideals of human worth and selflessness modeled in the writings of John Dewey. There could be no more striking exemplar of this miserable truth than the state of American public education today.

The neopragmatic testament to this saga is that we should take stock of our situation at the close of this disastrous century and regroup for Jamesian therapy. Although this may seem an evasion of the political and social issues at first glance, a second glance is something we all have plenty of time, under the present circumstances, to consider. The best question to ask is the kind of question that William James knew how to ask. For example: What sorts of things would you want to learn for yourself, for no other purpose than to increase your own "strong sense" of what Rorty calls self-poetry, where self-poetry suggests a keen sense of intellectual different-mindedness?

For James the idea that there might be a superior method for looking at society, literature, art, or politics is inappropriate to the space these occupy—a space where the whole point of unencumbered expression is not to be methodologically burdened. Equally for the neopragmatist, Dewey's idea of the absolute importance of method here seems both unattractive to those usefully engaged in these activities and ineffectual in the furtherance of democratic and liberal principles in general.

Education could learn a lesson from the failure of method. It would be a lesson that each of us would immediately recognize as the gratification we receive simply by engaging in a myriad of social, intellectual, and artistic activities. We might learn to revere the sense of strong identity in the heart of anyone who has come through suffering to the realization that there is an extraordinary difference between the brutish knowing which has come to symbolize scientistic learning in our age and understanding in the luxuriant sense.

As teachers we might steal the best of Dewey's sense of the naturalness of learning while attaining what has been in any age the highest of goals—the richness of experience that marks a life well-lived. For Dewey, the place most likely to initiate this process was the public school—a place that today, ironically, remains among those most marred by rigidity and the hopelessly misguided cult of efficiency. Should we be working? This is not a witless question about the virtues of "play" rather than work. The question should be taken to mean: Why should we be working for the benefit of those who seek to harm the world—those who ultimately benefit from the sacrifice of others? Many would say that my question is inappropriate for public education in the twenty-first or any other century—that public education must be accountable to the many churlish activities that society and industry demand. I would counter that those who genuinely wish to learn gain nothing from externally imposed ambitions from which genuine learning will never prevail. So what should one do?

Do not take your work seriously. When your students come to you, dissuade them from cooperation or gratitude. When they ask you to consider their educational goals, ask them to consider what their life is worth and why. When you are asked to cooperate with the system, do so for the sake of spreading dissent through the silent, preoccupied academic mob. Even though our actions may not save the world, we may save our own souls.

Notes

1. Max Weber, *The Protestant Ethic and the Spirit of Capitalism* (Trans. Talcott Parons). New York: Scribner, 1958, p. 182.

2. William James, *On Some of Life's Ideals* (New York: Holt, 1912), p. 37.

3. John Dewey, *How We Think* (Boston: Heath, 1933), p. 282.

4. William James, *Principles of Psychology* (New York: Holt, 1890), p. 254.

5. William Gavin, *William James and the Reinstatement of the Vague* (Philadelphia: Temple University Press, 1992), p. 2.

6. Jacques Barzun, *The Energies of Art* (New York: Random House/Vintage, 1962), p. 320.

7. *Principles of Psychology*, p. 236.

8. William James, *Essays in Pragmatism* (New York: Hafner, 1948), from the introduction by Alburey Castell, p. xiv.

9. *Essays in Pragmatism*, p. 170.

10. Richard Rorty, *Contingency, Irony and Solidarity* (Cambridge University Press, 1989), p. 5.

11. John Dewey, *Characters and Events* (Ed. Joseph Ratner). New York: Holt, 1929), vol. 1, p. 64.

12. John Dewey, *Reconstruction in Philosophy* (New York: Holt, 1920), p. 157.

13. Richard Rorty, *Pragmatism without Method* (unpublished manuscript), p. 63.

14. John Dewey, *Democracy and Education* (New York: Macmillan, 1966), p. 122.

Contributors

Peter Alson graduated from Harvard with a degree in English. At various times he has earned his living as a repo man, an ambulance driver, and a poker player. His novel *Confessions of an Ivy League Bookie: A True Tale of Love and the Vig* was published in 1996, New York: Crown Publishers.

Gloria E. Anzaldúa is a Chicana tejana (Texan) patlache (Nahuatl word for dyke) feminist writer. She is the author of *Friends from the Other Side (Amigos del otro lado*, 1993, Boston MA: Horn Book, and *Prietita and the Ghost Woman (Prietita y la Llorona* (1996), Boston MA: Horn Book, a Smithsonian Notable Book as well as a winner of the Americas Honor Award. She has received an NEA Fiction Award, the Lesbian Rights Award, the Sappho Award of Distinction, the Before Columbus Foundation American Book Award, and the Lamda Lesbian Small Book Press Award. The *Library Journal* chose her *Borderlands (La frontera): The New Mestiza*, San Francisco, CA: Aunt Lute Books as a Best Book of 1987. She was profiled in *MS. Magazine* and presented in UTNE as one of its visionaries of 1996.

Alan A. Block is associate professor of education at the University of Wisconsin Stout. He has published widely in the area of curriculum theory and practice, including three books *Anonymous Toil: A reevaluation of the American Radical Novel in the Twentieth Century* (1992), Lanham, Md.: University Press of America, *Occupied Reading: Critical Foundations for an Ecological Theory* (1995), New York: Garland, and *I'm Only Bleeding: Education as the Practice of Social Violence Against Children* (1997), New York: Peter Lang.

Bill Davis has been playing guitar and singing with Dash Rip Rock for 14 years. He graduated with a masters degree in journalism from Louisiana State University in 1984. Currently, he writes on the internet through Yall.com and Dashriprock.com. His band has just released its eighth CD, entitled *Pay Dirt*.

Brent Davis is assistant professor of education at York University, Toronto, Canada. His principal interests—cognitive theory and cultural studies—are focused in the areas of mathematics education and curriculum theory. He is the author of *Teaching Mathematics: Toward a Sound Alternative* (1996), New York: Garland.

Toby Daspit is assistant professor of curriculum theory and cultural studies at Western Michigan University. He is co-editor with John Weaver of *Critical Pedagogy and Popular Culture: Reading, Constructing, Connecting* (1998), New York: Garland.

Mary Aswell Doll is professor and chair of the English Department at Holy Cross College in New Orleans. She publishes and lectures on myth, feminism, and literature. Her books include *Beckett and Myth: An Archetypal Approach* (1988), Syracuse, NY: Syracuse University Press. *In the Shadow of the Giant: Thomas Wolfe* (coedited) (1988) Athens, Ohio: Ohio University Press, and *To the Lighthouse and Back: Writings on Teaching and Living* (1995), New York: Peter Lang. She is writing a book on the mythopoetics of curriculum.

Susan Edgerton teaches curriculum theory and cultural studies at Western Michigan University. She is the author of *Translating the Curriculum* (1996), New York: Routledge.

Skip Fox is a poet and professor at the University of Southwestern Louisiana. He has published three small books of poetry as well as poems in little magazines devoted to experimental poetry (e.g., *Hambone, Talisman, Croton Bug*). He has also published articles on poetry and poetics as well as *Robert Creeley: Edward Dorn, and Robert Duncan: A Reference Guide* (Boston: Hall, 1989).

Jane Futcher is the author of *Promise Not to Tell* (1991), New York: Avon; *Afterglow* (1993), Los Angeles, CA: Alyson Publications; *Crush* (1995), Los Angeles, CA: Alyson Publications; and *Dream Lover*

(1997), Los Angeles, CA: Alyson Publications. Her short fiction and essays have appeared in many anthologies, including *Hot Ticket* (1993), Los Angeles, CA: Alyson Publications; *The Next Step* (1994), Los Angeles, CA: Alyson Publications, *A Loving Testimony* (1995), Chicago Il: American Library Association; and *Dyke Life* (1996), New York: Basic Books. She lives in Novato, California and works at the *Marin Independent Journal.*

Jamake Highwater has taught and lectured throughout the United States and has served on the panels and boards of several arts councils. He has written more than twenty-five award-winning novels on such far-ranging topics as myth, Mick Jaggar, vision, sexuality, and dance, including *The Primal Mind: Vision and Reality in Indian America* (1981), New York: New American Library, and recently *The Mythology of Transgression: Homosexuality as Metaphor* (1997), New York: Oxford University Press. He established the San Francisco Contemporary Theater and the Native Land Foundation.

David W. Jardine teaches in the faculty of education at the University of Calgary. His most recent work concerns ecology and pedagogy. A collection of his essays is entitled *"To Dwell with a Boundless Heart": On Curriculum Theory, Hermeneutics and the Ecological Imagination* (1998), New York: Peter Lang.

Rebecca Luce-Kapler is assistant professor of language and literacy in the faculty of education, Queen's University, Kingston, Ontario, Canada. Her current research examines the relationships among computer technologies, writing processes, and identity formation. She recently completed her doctoral dissertation, *As If Women Writing,* which explores women's relationship to the subjective spaces of writing. She is also a poet and fiction writer. Her most recent poetry collection (unpublished) *The Grey Moon Points Back*, focuses on Canadian artist and writer, Emily Carr.

Wendy Kohli teaches at the New School for Social Research. She is the editor of *Critical Conversations in Philosophy of Education* (Routledge, 1995).

Marla Morris is a Ph.D. candidate in curriculum theory at Louisiana State University. She has published in the *Journal of Theta Alpha*

Kappa/National Honor Society for Religious Studies/Theology, JCT: The Journal of Curriculum Theorizing, Taboo: The Journal of Culture and Education, Educational Theory, and *Teaching Education*. She has most recently been appointed assistant editor of *JCT: The Journal of Curriculum Theorizing*. Her dissertation will examine the Holocaust, representation, and curriculum as memory text.

Petra Munro is associate professor of education and women's and gender studies at Louisiana State University. She is the author (with Janice Jipson, et al.) of *Repositioning Feminism and Education* (1995), Westport, CT.: Bergin and Garvey, and *Subject to Fiction* (1998), Philadelphia: Open University Press. She is currently at work on *Engendering Curriculum History*.

Marshall Parks teaches philosophy of education at Western Illinois University. He took his doctorate with Richard Rorty at the University of Virginia.

William F. Pinar teaches curriculum theory at Louisiana State University, where he is the St. Bernard Parish Alumni Endowed Professor. He has also been the Frank Talbott Professor at the University of Virginia and A. Lindsay O'Connor Professor of American Institutions at Colgate University; he taught at the University of Rochester from 1972 until 1985. He is the author of *Autobiography, Politics and Sexuality* (1994), New York: Peter Lang, and the editor of *Queer Theory in Education* (1998), Mahwah, N.J.: Lawrence Erlbaum, *The Passionate Mind of Maxine Greene* (1998), London, UK: Falmer, and *Contemporary Curriculum Discourses* (1999), New York: Peter Lang.

Mike Siddoway is associate professor and chair of the department of mathematics at Colorado College. His research interests include commutative algebra, module theory, and the history of mathematics. He spent the first weeks of his last sabbatical leave playing Steve Earle songs in the Paris metro.

Dennis J. Sumara is associate professor of education at York University, Toronto, Canada. He has published numerous articles in curriculum theory, action research, teacher education, and language arts education. He is the author of *Private Readings in Pubic: Schooling the Literary Imagination* (1996), New York: Peter Lang.

Denise Taliaferro teaches curriculum theory and black cultural studies at Colgate University.

Lance Ternasky teaches at Western Illinois University, in the department of educational and interdisciplinary studies. His research interests include applied ethics, civic discourse, moral education, and school reform.

Lewis Putnam Turco is professor emeritus of English and poet-in-residence at the State University of New York, College of Arts and Sciences, at Oswego. The most recent of his numerous awards was the Bordighera Bilingual Poetry Prize for his *Book of Fears* (1998), West Lafayette, IN: Bordighera, Inc. The author of more than three dozen books, he now lives part time in Dresden, Maine, where he runs the Mathom Book Shop.

Delese Wear is associate professor of behavioral science and associate director of two programs at Northeastern Ohio Universities College of Medicine: Human Values in Medicine and Women and Medicine. Her most recent books include *Literary Anatomies: Women's Bodies and Health in Literature* (co-written) (1994), Albany: State University of New York Press, and *Privilege in the Medical Academy: A Feminist Examines Race, Gender, and Power* (1997), New York: Teachers College Press.

COUNTERPOINTS

Studies in the Postmodern Theory of Education

General Editors
Joe L. Kincheloe & Shirley R. Steinberg

Counterpoints publishes the most compelling and imaginative books being written in education today. Grounded on the theoretical advances in criticalism, feminism, and postmodernism in the last two decades of the twentieth century, Counterpoints engages the meaning of these innovations in various forms of educational expression. Committed to the proposition that theoretical literature should be accessible to a variety of audiences, the series insists that its authors avoid esoteric and jargonistic languages that transform educational scholarship into an elite discourse for the initiated. Scholarly work matters only to the degree it affects consciousness and practice at multiple sites. Counterpoints' editorial policy is based on these principles and the ability of scholars to break new ground, to open new conversations, to go where educators have never gone before.

For additional information about this series or for the submission of manuscripts, please contact:

Joe L. Kincheloe & Shirley R. Steinberg
637 West Foster Avenue
State College, PA 16801

To order other books in this series, please contact our Customer Service Department at:

(800) 770-LANG (within the U.S.)
(212) 647-7706 (outside the U.S.)
(212) 647-7707 FAX

or browse online by series at:

www.peterlang.com